PAUL KOZELKA has for years been literally immersed in the theatre. Since 1947 he has been at Teachers College, Columbia University, producing and teaching. He holds an extraordinary number of positions in organizations, among them: he is a member of the Board of Directors of The American National Theatre and Academy and of the American Educational Theatre Association; he is chairman of the Committee on Creative Dramatics in the Elementary Schools for AETA and secretary-treasurer of the American Society for Theatre Research. He has produced nearly sixty dramatic presentations, prepared study guides and film strips, served as an editor and article writer. Readers interested in the drama are fortunate that Paul Kozelka has chosen to prepare this anthology of 15 AMERICAN ONE-ACT PLAYS.

Fifteen American One-Act Plays

Edited and with Introductions by Paul Kozelka

THE ANTA SERIES OF DISTINGUISHED PLAYS

WASHINGTON SQUARE PRESS
PUBLISHED BY POCKET BOOKS NEW YORK

A Washington Square Press/Pocket Books Publication
POCKET BOOKS, a Simon & Schuster division of
GULF & WESTERN CORPORATION
1230 Avenue of the Americas, New York, N.Y. 10020

Copyright © 1961 by Simon & Schuster, a division of
Gulf & Western Corporation

ISBN: 0-671-47036-1

First Pocket Books printing February, 1961

30   29   28   27   26

WASHINGTON SQUARE PRESS, WSP and colophon are
trademarks of Simon & Schuster.

Printed in the U.S.A.

PREFACE

The plays in this anthology were selected for several reasons. The authors are among the finest established American writers of one-act plays. Millay, Benét, Kaufman, and Goodman are represented here by plays that have become classics in the American theatre.

The plays are outstanding examples of marvelous storytelling in play form. Some are tragic, some comic, some melodramatic, and some fantasy. For example, *Red Carnations, Feathertop,* and *The Undercurrent* all deal with parent-child relationships but the authors' points of view, their attitudes toward life, and their intentions made the first play a comedy, the second a satiric fantasy, and the third a serious drama.

The plays also represent a wide variety of locale. *The Lottery, The Neighbors, Dust of the Road, The Man Who Died at Twelve O'Clock, Trifles,* and *The Devil and Daniel Webster* tell as much about rural communities in the United States as they do about the characters in the plays. *Thursday Evening, Red Carnations, The Undercurrent, The Trysting Place, The Still Alarm,* and *Sorry, Wrong Number* are concerned with city life and city people. *Aria da Capo* contrasts, in its own distinctive way, pseudosophistication and pastoral simplicity.

Where do playwrights get ideas for their plots? Usually a writer has an experience or idea that starts his imagination going and he develops characters and situations around the idea until he is satisfied that the play says what he wants it to say. *The Devil and Daniel Webster* and *Feathertop* are good illustrations of how gifted writers can transform American folklore into effective theatrical statements.

There is no printed cast of characters at the beginning of each play because I believe that readers should meet characters as the author introduces them. Stage directions have been simplified or omitted in order to make the reading of a play as smooth as possible. In their present form, the plays will be a stimulating, enriching introduction to American culture whether they are read privately or by an informal group or class.

If a group decides to produce one of these plays, it must obtain permission from the proper source and it should use the acting edition of the play, which includes a floor plan and other helpful guides to successful performance.

—PAUL KOZELKA
Teachers College
Columbia University

CONTENTS

Amateur groups who wish to produce any of these plays will find production information for each play on pages 307-308.

THURSDAY EVENING

CHRISTOPHER MORLEY (1890–1957), born in Haverford, Pennsylvania, received unusual recognition early in his career. After three years in England as a Rhodes scholar, he joined the staff of a Philadelphia and later of a New York newspaper. For a long period he was a contributing editor of *The Saturday Review of Literature*, and he served as an editor for two revisions of Bartlett's *Familiar Quotations*. Among his widely known novels are *Kitty Foyle* and *The Trojan Horse*.

In his popular short play *Thursday Evening*, Mr. Morley opposes the common mother-in-law stereotype with two very likable and charming women. Even more, he makes the young married couple equally responsible in maintaining a happy home. It may seem difficult for the reader to accept a housewife who can afford a cook but who has to keep house with an old-fashioned icebox and an oil stove. When this play was written, however, such conditions were the rule, not the exception. In any case, oil stoves give way to electric ranges and iceboxes are replaced by colorful refrigerators, but young couples still have babies and in-laws and dirty dishes and arguments and reconciliations.

THURSDAY EVENING

Christopher Morley

The scene is a small suburban kitchen in the modest home of MR. and MRS. GORDON JOHNS. A meal has recently been cooked, as is shown by a general confusion of pots and pans and dishcloths. Along the back wall we see an icebox standing in the corner, an oil range, and two shelved cabinets, one containing groceries and household sundries, the other dishes and glassware. Some baby linen and very small shirts (such as would be suitable for a child of about ten months) are hanging on a clotheshorse near the stove. A door in the right wall leads out to the back porch; there are two windows in this wall, one each side of door. A door in the left wall leads to dining room. Near the icebox is a door opening on back stairs, which ascend to upper parts of the house. Below the dining-room door is a sink and oilcloth-covered drainboard or shelf beside it. In the center of stage a small table covered with oilcloth. A kitchen chair in corner, near porch door.

When the scene opens, GORDON and LAURA are carrying in soiled dishes through dining-room door. They come in and out several times, making methodical arrangements for cleaning up. They pile the dishes on the shelf by the sink. GORDON takes dishpan from a hook under the sink, and fills it with hot water from the kettle on the stove. LAURA, who is an at-

Copyright, 1922, by Christopher Morley; copyright renewed, 1950, by Christopher Morley. All inquiries should be addressed to David McKay Company, Inc., 750 Third Avenue, New York, N.Y. 10017.

tractive little person, aged about twenty-three, is in that slightly tense condition of a young hostess who has had a long and trying day with house and baby, and has also cooked and served a dinner for four.

GORDON: All right, Creature, just wait till I light my pipe and we'll polish this up. (*Lights pipe and rolls up shirt sleeves.*)

LAURA (*taking an apron from chair in corner*): Put this on first. That's the only decent pair of trousers you've got. (*Enter MRS. SHEFFIELD, carrying dishes.*)

MRS. SHEFFIELD: Now you children run along and take it easy. I'll do all this.

LAURA: No, no, Mother. You go and talk to Mrs. Johns. (*Pointedly*) Don't let her come in here.

MRS. SHEFFIELD (*ultramaternally*): Poor baby, she's tired. You've been on your feet all day. Now let Mother wash up for you. That was a big dinner to cook.

LAURA: No tireder than you are, Mother, darling. You cooked lunch.

GORDON: Both of you clear out; I can get this done in no time.

MRS. SHEFFIELD (*patting LAURA's cheek*): Busy with the baby all afternoon, and then cooking such a delicious dinner— Dearie, won't you let Mother do this for you?

LAURA: There isn't room in this kitchen for everybody— (*Enter MRS. JOHNS, carrying dishes.*)

MRS. JOHNS: Gordon, you and Laura go and rest. Let the two grandmothers—

GORDON: Now listen, little people, this is my job. I always wash up on Thursday evenings—

MRS. JOHNS: You go and read your newspaper. I can see you're all fagged out after that long day in the office—

MRS. SHEFFIELD (*to LAURA*): *Please* go and lie down, baby. You're *so* tired.

LAURA (*with waning patience*): You two go and amuse yourselves; Gordon and I'll attend to this. (*They gently eject the two mothers-in-law.*)

GORDON: Come on, now, the good old system! (*He takes the small table from center of stage, and puts it carefully midway between sink and dish cabinet. Takes chair from corner and sets it beside table. LAURA sits down on chair and wipes silverware and dishes as he hands them to her after washing.*)

LAURA: The silver first, while the water's clean.

GORDON: Right. We make a pretty good team at this, don't we?

LAURA (*holds up a small silver jug*): That darling old cream jug. Mother used that when she was a little girl.

GORDON: I love our little Thursday-evening suppers. I think they're more fun than any other night.

LAURA: I'm glad, Gordie.

GORDON: We get better grub on Thursdays, when Ethel goes out, than we ever do when she's in.

LAURA: I tried to have everything specially nice tonight. Some visitors are very critical.

GORDON: It was lovely. I'm afraid it was hard for you, Creature, to have Mother come just now. (*A short pause.*) Especially when *your* mother was here.

LAURA: Didn't she know Mother was here?

GORDON: No. I hadn't told her. You see, your mother is here so much more often. I didn't know your mother would still be here. I was afraid Mother might be a little hurt—

LAURA: Mother helps me a great deal. I think it's a queer thing if a wife can't have her mother stay with her once in a while—

GORDON (*aware of danger, changes the subject*): Ye Gods, Ethel has cracked the Copenhagen platter. (LAURA *is silent.*) That's one of the set Mother gave us when we were married.

LAURA: It's a stock pattern. You can get another at any department store.

GORDON: I'll bet Ethel didn't empty the icebox pan before she went. I never saw a cook yet who could remember to do that—

LAURA: If you had to go out and hunt for them, you wouldn't be so particular. She's better than no one.

GORDON (*goes to icebox and removes a large, brimming pan from under it*): What did I tell you! (*The water slops over from pan as he carries it gingerly to sink and empties it. He replaces the pan under icebox.*)

LAURA: You'd better heat some more water. You've poured that ice water into the dishpan.

GORDON (*getting a little peevish; refills kettle and puts it on stove*): It's perfectly absurd not having any pantry to keep the icebox in. In here, the heat of the stove melts the ice right away. (*Goes back to icebox and slams its doors shut.*) Of course, she never keeps the doors properly closed. (*He returns to sink and resumes dishwashing.*) It's a funny thing.

LAURA: What is?

GORDON: Why, that a presumably intelligent person can't understand the doors of an icebox are meant to be kept tight shut, to save ice. What does she suppose those little clamps are for? (LAURA *is silent. There is a pause, while* GORDON *scrapes portions of food off the soiled plates. He examines some of these plates rather carefully, and picks out several large pieces of meat, lettuce, butter, etc., which he puts on one plate at one side. Then he seems to resume his good humor and relights his pipe.*) Well, it's jolly to have both the grandmothers here together, isn't it?

LAURA: Gordon, dear, put the silver away in the sideboard before it gets wet again. (*He gathers up silver from the table in front of her and exits into dining room.* LAURA *steps out on the porch, and returns, bringing garbage can, which she puts down by the sink. She begins to wash dishes, and sees the plate of odds and ends which* GORDON *has carefully put to one side. She scrapes its contents into the garbage pail. While she is washing,* GORDON *enters.*)

GORDON: Now, Creature, let me do that. You don't want to spoil those pretty hands. (*Takes them, with an attempt to be affectionate.*)

LAURA: I guess it isn't any worse for them than washing the baby's things.

GORDON: Come on, old man, let *me*. (*Gently removes her from sink, and pushes her to the chair by the table. She sits down and wipes dishes as he hands them to her.*) It doesn't take long when there are two of us.

LAURA: Gordie, these dishes aren't properly clean. You can't get that grease off without hot water.

GORDON: I guess that kettle's hot by now. (*To stove, feels water in kettle.*) Give it a minute longer. (*Stands by stove and puffs at his pipe. In a moment of false security, he foolishly reopens a dangerous topic.*) You know, I'm a little worried about Mother.

LAURA (*putting away dishes*): Why?

GORDON: I don't think she's as well as usual. She hardly ate any of her salad.

LAURA (*turns as though about to say something, but checks herself and pauses a moment. This time it is she who tries honorably to avert the gathering storm*): Oh, Gordie, I forgot to tell you! Junior drank out of a cup today—the first time!

GORDON: He did! The little rascal!

LAURA: Look, here's the cup. (*Shows a small silver cup.*)

GORDON (*affectionately, putting his arm around her*): Well, well. (*Looks at cup.*) What cup is that? I don't seem to remember it—

LAURA: Why—Mother brought it with her. She used it when she was a baby.

GORDON: Where's that nice old christening mug of mine? I think Junior would like to use that once in a while, too.

LAURA: I put it away, dear. I was afraid Ethel might dent it.

GORDON (*takes kettle from stove, goes back to sink*): I hope Mother isn't feeling poorly. I noticed at supper—

LAURA: When hot meat is served, refined people usually call it *dinner*—

GORDON (*looks at her cautiously, and suddenly seems to realize that they are on the edge of an abyss*): Now, honey, you're tired. You go and rest; I'll finish up here.

LAURA: No, thank you. I like to see that everything gets cleaned up properly. Someone might come snooping out here, and then there'd be hints about my housekeeping. Of course, I'll admit I wasn't brought up to be a cook—

GORDON (*seeks inspiration by relighting his pipe, and takes up a handsome silver coffeepot*): One thing I never can make out is how to prevent coffee grounds from going down the sink. (*He talks desperately, trying to tide over the mutually realized danger point.*) Perhaps if I could invent some kind of a little coffee-ground strainer I'd make our fortune. That coffee was delicious, Creature.

LAURA: Take care of that urn; it's one of the few handsome things we have.

GORDON: It *is* a beauty.

LAURA: Jack Davis gave it to me—

GORDON (*puts it down with distaste*): I guess I'd better attend to the garbage.

LAURA (*nervously*): It's all fixed.

GORDON: I always like Thursdays because that's the one evening Ethel doesn't get a chance to throw away about five dollars' worth of good food.

LAURA: I fixed the garbage. You can put the pail outside.

GORDON (*hunting among plates on the shelf beside sink*): Where's that plate I put here? There was a lot of perfectly good stuff I saved—

LAURA (*blows up at last*): Well, if you think I'm going to keep a lot of half-eaten salad your mother picked over—

GORDON (*seizes garbage pail, lifts it up to the sink and begins to explore its contents. His fuse also is rapidly shortening*): My Lord, it's no wonder we never have any money to spend if we chuck half of it away in waste. (*Picking out various selections.*) Waste! Look at that piece of cheese, and those potatoes. You could take those things, and some of this meat, and make a nice economical hash for lunch—

LAURA: It's a wonder you wouldn't get a job as a scavenger. I never *heard* of a husband like you, rummaging through the garbage pail.

GORDON (*blows up*): Do you know what the one unforgivable sin is? The sin against the Holy Ghost? It's *waste!* It makes me wild to think of working and working like a dog, and half of what I earn just thrown away by an ignorant cook. Look at this, just look at it! (*Displays a grisly object.*) There's enough meat on that bone to make soup. And ye gods, here's that jar of anchovy pastel (*Holds it up.*) I thought you got that for me as a little treat. I wondered where it had gone to. Why, I hadn't eaten more than just the top of it.

LAURA: Well, you left it, and left it, and it got mildewed.

GORDON: Scrape it off. A little mildew won't hurt anybody. There'll be mildew on my bank account if this kind of thing goes on. (*Still examining garbage pail.*) Look here, about half a dozen slices of bread. What's the matter with *them*, I'd like to know.

LAURA: I think it's the most disgusting thing I ever heard of. To go picking over the garbage pail like that. You attend to your affairs and I'll attend to mine.

GORDON: I guess throwing away good, hard-earned money is my affair, isn't it?

LAURA: You're always quick enough to find fault. I know Ethel's careless, but she's the best I can get out here in this godforsaken suburb. Maybe you'll be good enough to find me a better servant. A well-trained girl wouldn't work in this old dump, where there isn't even gas. You don't seem to know when you're lucky. You come back at night and find your home well cared for and me slaving over a hot dinner, and do you ever say a word of thanks? No, all you can think of is finding fault. I can't imagine how you were brought up. Your mother—

GORDON: Just leave my mother out of it. I guess she didn't spoil me the way yours did you. Of course, I wasn't an only daughter—

LAURA: I wish you had been. Then I wouldn't have married you.

GORDON: I suppose you think that if you'd married Jack Davis or some other of those jokers you'd never have had to see the inside of a kitchen—

LAURA: If Junior grows up with your disposition, all I can say is I hope he'll never get married.

GORDON: If he gets married, I hope it'll be to some girl who understands something about economy—

LAURA: If he gets married, I hope he'll be man enough not to be always finding fault—

GORDON: Well, he *won't* get married! I'll put him wise to what marriage means, fussing like this all the time—

LAURA: Yes, he *will* get married. He *shall* get married!

GORDON: Oh, this is too absurd—

LAURA: He *shall* get married, just to be a humiliating example to his father. I'll bring him up the way a husband *ought* to be.

GORDON: In handcuffs, I suppose—

LAURA: And his wife won't have to sit and listen to perpetual criticism from his mother—

GORDON: If you're so down on mothers-in-law, it's queer you're anxious to be one yourself. The expectant mother-in-law!

LAURA: All right, be vulgar. I dare say you can't help it.

GORDON: Great Scott, what did you think marriage was like, anyway? Did you expect to go through life having everything done for you, without a little hard work to make it interesting?

LAURA: Is it necessary to shout?

GORDON: Now let me tell you something. Let's see if you can ratify it from your extensive observation of life. Is there anything in the world so cruel as bringing up a girl in absolute ignorance of housework, believing that all her days she's going to be waited on hand and foot, and that marriage is one long swoon of endearments—

LAURA: There's not much swooning while you're around.

GORDON: Why, I believe you actually think your life is wrecked if you aren't being petted and praised every minute. You pretend to think marriage is so sacred and yet you're buffaloed by a few greasy dishes. I like my kind of sacredness better than yours, and that's the sacredness of common sense. Marriage ought not to be performed before an altar, but before a kitchen sink.

LAURA (*furiously*): I ought to have known that oil and water won't mix. I ought to have known that a vulgar, selfish, conceited man couldn't make a girl happy who was brought up in a refined family. I was a Sheffield, and why I ever became a Johns is more than I can imagine. Johns—I suppose that's camouflage for Jones. You're too common, too ordinary, to know when you're lucky. You get a charming, aristocratic wife and expect her to grub along like a washerwoman. You try to crush all the life and spirit out of her. You ought to have married an icebox—that's the only thing in this house you're really attentive to.

GORDON: Now listen—

LAURA (*will not be checked*): Talk about being spoiled—why, your mother babies you so, you think you're the only man on earth. (*Sarcastically.*) Her poor, overworked boy, who tries so hard and gets all fagged out in the office and struggles so nobly to support his family! I wonder how you'd like to run this house and bear a child and take care of it and shuffle along with an ignoramus for a maid and then cook a big dinner and be sneered at and never a word of praise. All you can think of is picking over the garbage pail and finding fault—

GORDON (*like a fool*): I didn't find fault. I found some good food being wasted.

LAURA: All right, if you love the garbage pail better than you do your wife, you can live with it. (*Flings her dish towel on the floor and exits into dining room.*)

(GORDON *stands irresolutely at the sink, and makes a few gloomy motions among the unfinished dishes. He glares at the garbage can. Then he carefully gathers those portions of food that he had chosen as being still usable, contemplates them grimly, then puts them on a plate and, after some hesitation, puts the plate in the icebox. He takes the garbage can and puts it outside the porch door. He returns into the kitchen, but then a sudden fit of anger seizes him.*)

GORDON: It's always the way! (*Tears off apron, throws it on the floor, and goes out on porch, slamming door.*)

(*After a brief pause, the door at the rear, opening onto the back stairs, is cautiously opened, and MRS. SHEFFIELD enters quietly. She takes one swift look around the disordered kitchen, picks up dish towel and apron from the floor, and sets to work rapidly to clean up. Then the back-stairs door is again opened in the same stealthy way, and MRS. JOHNS enters. The two ladies seem to take each other's measure with instinctive shrewdness, and fall into a silent, businesslike team play in putting things to rights. MRS. JOHNS takes charge at the sink, and the remaining dishes spin under her capable hands. MRS. SHEFFIELD takes them from her, rapidly polishes them, and puts them away on the shelves. There is unconscious comedy in the trained precision and labor-saving method of their actions, which are synchronized so that every time MRS. JOHNS holds out a washed dish, MRS. SHEFFIELD is moving back from the cabinet, ready to receive it. They work like automatons. For perhaps two minutes not a word is said, and the two seem, by searching side glances, to be probing each other's mood.*)

MRS. JOHNS: If it wasn't so tragic I'd laugh. (*A pause, during which they work busily.*)

MRS. SHEFFIELD: If it wasn't so comic I'd cry. (*Another pause.*) I guess it's my fault. Poor Laura, I'm afraid I *have* spoiled her.

MRS. JOHNS: *My* fault, I think. Two mothers-in-law at once is too much for any young couple. I didn't know you were here, or I wouldn't have come.

MRS. SHEFFIELD: Laura is so dreadfully sensitive, poor child—

MRS. JOHNS: Gordon works so hard at the office. You know he's trying to get promoted to the sales department, and I suppose it tells on his nerves—

MRS. SHEFFIELD: If Laura could afford to have a nurse to help her with the baby, she wouldn't get so exhausted—

Mrs. Johns: Gordon says he wants to take out some more insurance, that's why he worries so about economy. It isn't for himself; he's really very unselfish—

Mrs. Sheffield (*a little tartly*): Still, I do think that sometimes— (*They pause and look at each other quickly.*) My gracious, we'll be at it ourselves if we don't look out!

(*She goes to the clotheshorse and rearranges the garments on it. She holds up a Lilliputian shirt, and they both smile.*)

Mrs. Johns: That darling baby! I hope he won't have poor Gordon's quick temper. It runs in the Johns family, I'm afraid. I was an Armstrong before I married Gordon's father. I didn't know what temper was until I married— either my own or his.

Mrs. Sheffield: I was a Thomson—Thomson without the *p*, you know, from Rhode Island. All families are hot tempered. All husbands' families, anyway.

Mrs. Johns: Gordon's father used to say that Adam and Eve didn't know when they were well off. He said that was why they called it the Garden of Eden.

Mrs. Sheffield: Why?

Mrs. Johns: Because there was no mother-in-law there.

Mrs. Sheffield: Poor children, they have such a lot to learn! I really feel ashamed, Mrs. Johns, because Laura is an undisciplined little thing, and I'm afraid I've always petted her too much. She had such a lot of attention before she met Gordon, and was made so much of, it gave her wrong ideas.

Mrs. Johns: I wish Gordon was a little younger; I'd like to turn him up and spank him. He's dreadfully stubborn and tactless—

Mrs. Sheffield: But I'm afraid I *did* make a mistake. Laura was having such a good time as a girl, I was always afraid she'd have a hard awakening when she married. But Mr. Sheffield had a good deal of money at that time, and he used to say, "She's only young once. Let her enjoy herself."

Mrs. Johns: My husband was shortsighted, too. He had had

to skimp so that he brought up Gordon to have a terror of wasting a nickel.

MRS. SHEFFIELD: Very sensible. I wish Mr. Sheffield had had a little more of that terror. I shall have to tell him what his policy has resulted in. But really, you know, when I heard them at it, I could hardly help admiring them. (*With a sigh.*) It brings back old times!

MRS. JOHNS: So it does! (*A pause.*) But we can't let them go on like this. A little vigorous quarreling is good for everybody. It's a kind of spiritual laxative. But they carry it too far.

MRS. SHEFFIELD: They're awfully ingenious. They were even bickering about Junior's future mother-in-law. I suppose she's still in school, whoever she may be!

MRS. JOHNS: Being a mother-in-law is almost as painful as being a mother.

MRS. SHEFFIELD: I think every marriage ought to be preceded by a treaty of peace between the two mothers. If they understand each other, everything will work out all right.

MRS. JOHNS: You're right. When each one takes sides with her own child, it's fatal.

MRS. SHEFFIELD (*lowering her voice*): Look here, I think I know how we can make them ashamed of themselves. Where are they now?

MRS. JOHNS (*goes cautiously to dining-room door, and peeps through*): Laura is lying on the couch in the living room. I think she's crying—her face is buried in the cushions.

MRS. SHEFFIELD: Splendid. That means she's listening with all her ears. (*Tiptoes to window.*) I can't see Gordon, but I think he's walking around the garden—

MRS. JOHNS (*quietly*): If we were to talk a little louder he'd sit on the back steps to hear it—

MRS. SHEFFIELD: Exactly. Now listen! (*They put their heads together and whisper; the audience does not hear what is said.*)

MRS. JOHNS: Fine! Oh, that's fine! (MRS. SHEFFIELD *whispers again, inaudibly.*) But wait a moment. Don't you think it would be better if *I* praise Laura and *you* praise Gordon? They won't expect that, and it might shame them—

MRS. SHEFFIELD: No, no! Don't you see— (*Whispers again, inaudibly.*)

MRS. JOHNS: You're right. Cunning as serpents and harmless as doves— (*They carefully set both doors ajar.*)

MRS. SHEFFIELD: I only hope we won't wake the baby— (*They return to the task of cleaning up, and talk very loudly, in pretended quarrel.*)

MRS. JOHNS: Where do these dessert plates go?

MRS. SHEFFIELD: On this shelf.

MRS. JOHNS: You're here so much more often than I, naturally you know Laura's arrangements better.

MRS. SHEFFIELD: It's a lucky thing I *am* here. I don't know what poor Laura would do without me at such a dreadful time—

MRS. JOHNS: *Poor* Laura! I should say she's very fortunate, such a good husband—

MRS. SHEFFIELD: I think it's rather sad for a girl who has had as much as she has to come down to this—

MRS. JOHNS: It's perfectly wonderful how Gordon has got on in business—

MRS. SHEFFIELD: He ought to, with such a lovely home, run like a clock—

MRS. JOHNS: Yes—an alarm clock.

MRS. SHEFFIELD: Well, I'm not going to see my daughter's happiness ruined—

MRS. JOHNS: I always knew he'd make some girl a fine husband—

MRS. SHEFFIELD: Perhaps. But he seems to have picked the wrong girl. Laura has too much spirit to be bullied—

MRS. JOHNS: Well, perhaps it was all a mistake. Poor Gordon, he works so hard. I believe his hair is going white over his ears already.

MRS. SHEFFIELD: Stuff! That's lather from where he shaved this morning. He's too slovenly to wash it off.

MRS. JOHNS: It isn't right that a young man should have to slave the way he does—

MRS. SHEFFIELD (*apparently in a passion*): Do you think that business slavery can compare to household slavery? I think it's heart-rending to see an attractive girl like Laura shut up in a poky little house doing drudgery and tending a baby. Think of it, having to take care of her own baby! Why, it's an outrage. If Gordon was half a man, he'd get her a trained baby nurse so she wouldn't have to *look* at the poor little thing—

MRS. JOHNS (*scathingly*): Yes, how sad that Gordon should have to entrust his son to amateur care when it needs scientific attention.

MRS. SHEFFIELD: Poor darling Laura—she never ought to have had a baby.

MRS. JOHNS: Gordon is too intellectual to be bothered with these domestic details. He ought to be able to concentrate on his work.

MRS. SHEFFIELD (*coming close to* MRS. JOHNS, *feigning great rage, but grimacing to show it is merely acting*): Well, if you don't think my daughter is good enough for your son, I can always take her home with *me*. I guess I can find room for her and we can put the child in an institution. (*Both nearly laugh, but recover themselves.*)

MRS. JOHNS: Don't worry. *I'll* take the child. He's a Johns anyway, not a Sheffield. And you just watch Gordon, when he's relieved of all this family worry and quarreling. He'll make his mark in the world. He's too fine to be tied down by a wife that doesn't understand him.

MRS. SHEFFIELD: Oh, how happy Laura will be to hear this. My sweet, clever, attractive, economical, sensible little girl, free at last. Her married life has been a nightmare. That great, hulking, selfish man has tried to trample all the joy out of her. He shan't do it.

MRS. JOHNS: I never heard of a young husband as self-sacrificing as Gordon. I don't believe he *ever* goes out for an evening with other men, and he *never* spends anything on himself—

MRS. SHEFFIELD: I think the way Laura runs her little home is just wonderful. See how she struggles to keep her kitchen in order—this miserable, inconvenient little kitchen—no gas, no pantry, no decent help. I think it's *terrible* she has had to put up with so much— (*They pause, and listen at the dining-room door. The kitchen is now spick and span.* MRS. JOHNS *makes a gesture to indicate that* LAURA *is taking it all in, off stage.*)

MRS. JOHNS: Well, then, it's all settled.

MRS. SHEFFIELD: Yes. As Laura's mother, I can't let her go on like this. A husband, a home, and a baby—it's enough to ruin any woman.

MRS. JOHNS: It's only fair to both sides to end it all. I never heard of such brutal hardships. Gordon can't fight against these things any longer. Throwing away a soupbone and three slices of bread! I wonder he doesn't go mad.

MRS. SHEFFIELD: We've saved them just in time. (*They look at each other knowingly, with the air of those who have done a sound bit of work. Then they stealthily open the door at the rear, and exeunt up the back stairs.*)

(*There is a brief pause; then the dining-room door opens like an explosion, and* LAURA *bursts in. She stands for a moment, wild-eyed, stamps her foot in a passion. Then she seizes one of the baby shirts from the rack, and drops into the chair by the table, crying. She buries her head in her arms, concealing the shirt. Enter* GORDON, *from porch. He stands uncertainly, evidently feeling like a fool.*)

GORDON: I'm sorry, I—I left my pipe in here. (*Finds it by the sink.*)

LAURA (*her face still hidden*): Oh, Gordie, *was* it all a mistake?

GORDON (*troubled, pats her shoulder tentatively*): Now listen, Creature, don't. You'll make yourself sick.

LAURA: I never thought I'd hear such things—from my own mother.

GORDON: I never heard such rot. They must be mad, both of them.

LAURA: Then you were listening, too—

GORDON: Yes. Why, they're deliberately trying to set us against each other.

LAURA: They wouldn't have *dared* speak like that if they had known we could hear. Gordon, I don't think it's *legal*—

GORDON: I'm afraid the law doesn't give one much protection against one's mothers.

LAURA (*miserably*): I guess she's right. I *am* spoiled, and I *am* silly, and I *am* extravagant—

GORDON: Don't be silly, darling. That's crazy stuff. I'm *not* overworked, and even if I were I'd love it, for *you*—

LAURA: I don't *want* a nurse for Junior. I wouldn't have one in the house. (*Sits up, disheveled, and displays the small shirt she has been clutching.*) Gordon, I'm *not* an amateur! I love that baby and I *am* scientific. I keep a chart of his weight every week.

GORDON: Yes, I know, ducky, Gordon understands. Soon we'll be able to buy that scale you want, and we won't have to weigh him on the meat balance.

LAURA: *Nobody* can take away my darling baby—

GORDON: It was my fault, dear. I *am* obstinate and disagreeable—

LAURA: I'll speak to Ethel about the garbage—

GORDON: Ethel's all right. We're lucky to have her.

LAURA: Gordon, you mustn't work too hard. You know you're all I have (*a sob*) since Mother's gone back on me.

GORDON (*patting her*): I think it's frightful, the things they said. What are they trying to do, break up a happy home?

LAURA: We *are* happy, aren't we?

GORDON: Well, I should say so. Did you ever hear me complain? (*Takes her in his arms.*)

LAURA: No, Gordie. It was cruel of them to try to make trouble between us; but, perhaps, some of the things they said—

GORDON: Were true?

LAURA: Well, not exactly true, dear, but—interesting! Your mother is right, you *do* have a hard time, and I'll try—

GORDON (*stops her*): No, *your* mother is right. I've been a brute—

LAURA: I'm lucky to have such a husband— (*They are silent a moment.*)

GORDON: I suppose you'll think it an awful anticlimax—

LAURA: What, dear?

GORDON: Suppose we have something to eat?

LAURA (*happily*): Good idea. Quarreling always makes me hungry. (*They go to the icebox.*) I didn't really get any supper to speak of; I was worrying about everything so—

GORDON (*opening icebox*): You mean *dinner*, honey—among refined people!

LAURA: Don't be a tease. Come on, we'll have a snack— (*She discovers* GORDON's *plate of leftovers.*)

GORDON: Throw out that junk—I was idiotic to save it.

LAURA: No, Gordie, you were quite right. We must save everything we can. Four or five heads of lettuce would make a new shirt for Junior.

GORDON (*bewildered*): Lettuce?

LAURA: I mean, if we saved that much, it would make enough money to buy him a new little vest. He's getting so *enormous*— (*She puts plate of leftovers on the table, with some other cold food.*)

GORDON: There, now, this is better. (*They sit down at table.*)

LAURA (*thoughtfully*): You know, Gordie, we mustn't let them know we heard them.

GORDON: No, I suppose not. But it's hard to forgive that sort of talk.

LAURA: Even if they did say atrocious things, I think they really love us—

GORDON: We'll be a bit cold and standoffish until things blow over.

LAURA (*complacently*): If I'm ever a mother-in-law, I shall try to be *very* understanding—

GORDON: Yes, Creature. Do you remember why I call you Creature?

LAURA: Do I not?

GORDON: There was an adjective omitted, you remember.

LAURA: Oh, Gordie, that's one of the troubles of married life. So many of the nice adjectives seem to get omitted.

GORDON: Motto for married men: Don't run short of adjectives! You remember what the adjective was?

LAURA: Tell me.

GORDON: *Adorable*. It was an abbreviation for Adorable Creature. (*Holds her. They are both perfectly happy.*) I love our little Thursday evenings.

LAURA (*partly breaks from his embrace*): Sssh! (*Listens.*) Was that the baby?

DUST OF THE ROAD

KENNETH SAWYER GOODMAN (1883–1918) made the Little Theatre movement a success in Chicago by his support as a playwright and as a worker behind the scenes. He learned his craft as a playwright from B. Iden Payne and Thomas Wood Stevens, two versatile and talented director-producers. Mr. Goodman was the author of many one-act plays; in addition, he wrote five plays in collaboration with Ben Hecht and six with Thomas Wood Stevens. The Goodman Theatre of the Chicago Art Institute, one of the most beautiful theatres in America, was erected in his memory by his parents Mr. and Mrs. William O. Goodman. Over the entrance to the theatre are inscribed these words from a masque written by Mr. Goodman: "To Restore the Old Visions and to Win the New." This could be the motto of every producing group in this country.

Dust of the Road, like another play in this anthology, *The Neighbors*, was first produced by the Wisconsin Dramatic Society. It is popular with many kinds of audiences because it is so direct and uncomplicated in its story line, because the supernatural element is introduced so disarmingly, and because it makes everyone who listens to it take stock of himself. Many writers have tried to imitate this play, but none has reached the level of powerful theatre that Kenneth Sawyer Goodman did in *Dust of the Road*.

DUST OF THE ROAD

Kenneth Sawyer Goodman

The scene is the living room of a comfortable and fairly prosperous Middle Western farmhouse. At the right of the stage is a fireplace with a glowing fire in it. Beside the fire is a large armchair in which PRUDENCE is sitting. At her elbow is a small table with a lighted lamp, having a shade of green tin. At the left is a door going into other parts of the house; at the back a door going outside. There is a larger table at the center of the room. There is also a lighted lamp on this table, but the back of the stage is in semidarkness. Near the outside door is a window, the curtains of which are drawn. The time is about one o'clock of a Christmas morning in the early seventies. As the curtain rises, an OLD MAN has just shut and bolted the outside door as if shutting someone out. He is partly dressed and carries a lighted candle in his hand.

PRUDENCE: Well, what did he say?

OLD MAN: Nothing. He's gone, if that's any comfort to you.

PRUDENCE: It is a comfort to me. I don't like folks coming to the door at this time of night.

OLD MAN: You might have stirred yourself to take a look at him. He was that cold I could hear his teeth chatter.

PRUDENCE: What was he like?

OLD MAN: Youngish, I'd say, with thin cheeks and a yellow beard. But I never seen such old-looking eyes as he had.

PRUDENCE: Go to bed, Uncle.

Copyright, by Marjorie R. Hopkins, Marjorie S. G. Dewey and Kay S. Goodman (d.b.a. The Stage Guild), Chicago, Illinois. Published, 1913: Copyright renewed, 1939. All rights to reproduction, publication or performance reserved.

OLD MAN: Both his hands were bandaged. I could see the blood on 'em.

PRUDENCE: Well, what of it? We can't be feeding every beggar that comes to the house.

OLD MAN (*at the window*): He ain't turned the willows at the bend of the road. I could holler to him yet.

PRUDENCE: Go back to bed, I tell you, and let me read my Bible till Peter comes in.

OLD MAN (*going toward the inside door*): You've set me thinking, Prudence Steele. You've set me thinking again.

PRUDENCE: Hush your mouth, and go to bed.

OLD MAN: Aye, aye, that's it! "To them that hath shall be given, and from him that hath not shall be taken away even that which he hath." If folks only knows enough to keep their mouths shut.

PRUDENCE: Now you're blaspheming again.

OLD MAN: Maybe I am. But if I was to open my mouth now and tell what I can remember clear as day, wouldn't I be serving the Lord? Answer me that.

PRUDENCE: Nobody'd believe you.

OLD MAN: I ain't asking 'em to. If you and Peter can disremember what happened in this room, it ain't for me to turn against my own kin.

PRUDENCE: Nothing happened in this room.

OLD MAN: Maybe I never seen thirty one-hundred-dollar bills counted out on this table.

PRUDENCE: Go to bed.

OLD MAN: I'm going, I'm going, but it would do me good to see them that's proud pulled down and her that wouldn't spare a crust for a lame beggar on Christmas Eve losing a piece of money like that as a judgment. It would be as fine a judgment as ever I see in that there book of yours.

(*The* OLD MAN *goes out chuckling.* PRUDENCE *follows him to the door, closes it, listens a moment, then blows out the lamp on the larger table and returns to the chair by the fire. She turns the pages of the book and then lays it face down on her knee and puts her hand over her eyes. The whole stage is now nearly dark, the only light coming from the lamp on the small table and from the fire in the grate. THE TRAMP opens the outside door and steps into the room. PRUDENCE stirs a little and the book drops from her lap, rousing her. She sits up and listens. THE TRAMP closes the door and shoots the bolt.)*

PRUDENCE: You're powerful late getting in.

TRAMP: Aye, maybe I am. (*He rattles the door to see if it is fast.*)

PRUDENCE: Hush your noise with the bolt, can't you! You'll be having Uncle down here again.

TRAMP: I'll take my chance of that!

PRUDENCE: What's the matter with your voice?

TRAMP: It's the river fog sticking in my throat.

PRUDENCE (*rising*): Come here and let me look at you. I never heard you speak with that voice before.

TRAMP (*stepping into the light*): I dare say you never did!

PRUDENCE: God save us! I thought you were my husband!

TRAMP: I gathered as much from your friendly greeting. (*He comes a step nearer.*)

PRUDENCE: Stand off or I'll scream! What do you want? Who are you?

TRAMP: What's the need of your knowing?

PRUDENCE: Tell me what you want and get out of my house. You needn't grin at me. I'm not afraid of you!

TRAMP: You're a bold woman!

PRUDENCE: I have cause to be, with a husband leaving me lonesome half the nights of the year, and beggars prowling the dark like rats.

TRAMP: You've a brave tongue in your head, and a kind voice, like a chilly wind on a tin church steeple. You'll ask me to sit by your fire next and offer me a sup of something hot.

PRUDENCE: I'll point you the door you came in by, and set the dog to your coattails.

TRAMP: Fine hospitality for the beginning of Christmas Day.

PRUDENCE: Who are you?

TRAMP: Dust of the road, my dear, like any other man. Dust with a spark of fire in it.

PRUDENCE: You're a tramp, by the looks of you—or worse.

TRAMP: A tramp is it? That's what you'd call a gay fellow tramping the hills for the clean joy of sun and air; keen snow in winter and the voice of the birds in the warm season. It's what you'd call the lifeless wretches, skulking from doorstep to doorstep for the leavings of other folks' tables. I'm neither the one sort nor the other, but the name fits me well enough.

PRUDENCE: Whatever you call yourself, you've got no business in a decent person's house at the middle of the night.

TRAMP (*taking a pipe from his pocket and filling it*): Is your husband like to be home soon?

PRUDENCE: You'll hear him at the door any minute now. If you're thinking of robbery you'd better be quick about it. There's little enough to take.

TRAMP (*lighting his pipe and seating himself on the edge of the large table*): You can keep your hand off that trinket at your neck and make your mind easy about the spoons. I'm a disreputable character, a prowler in the night, a betrayer of friendship. I've none of what you'd call common decency. I'd as leave eat your bread and kiss your hand and do you a dirty turn afterward as not, but—well—I've a different whim. I'm not here to make you trouble.

PRUDENCE: Fine ideas you've got! What'll my husband say when he smells the smoke of your pipe?

TRAMP: I'm waiting to see him myself when he comes in.

PRUDENCE: Like as not he'll break your head for your pains.

TRAMP: Aye, like as not.

PRUDENCE: You've got gall to be sitting there swinging your feet.

TRAMP: I'm thinking what I'll say to you in the meantime.

PRUDENCE: You won't be doing much thinking when he's pounded you till the teeth ache in your jaws.

TRAMP (*in a cold, sharp voice and speaking very slowly*): Why did you send that other beggar away just now, Prudence Steele?

PRUDENCE: So you know my name, do you?

TRAMP: Yes! It's a cruel-sounding name, Prudence Steele, and you've a cruel way of speaking and of looking at a poor man, my dear!

PRUDENCE: You're a fine hand at a compliment, Mr. Tramp.

TRAMP: Why did you send him away?

PRUDENCE: Send who away?

TRAMP: The lame man with the bandages on his hands and feet.

PRUDENCE: What's that to you?

TRAMP: I was standing in the road. I saw him knock at your door. I saw it open a little. I saw it close again. I saw him go away—just as I've seen him go from thousands of other doors.

PRUDENCE: He must be a friend of yours.

TRAMP: No. He was one once. Now he's a creditor.

PRUDENCE: By the looks of it, he'll have a hard time getting his money.

TRAMP: Money's easy to find—sometimes too easy. Now if you'd care to feel in my pockets— (*He jingles coins in his pockets.*)

PRUDENCE: Well, pay him then, and keep him from pestering other folks.

TRAMP: One isn't always minded to pay one's debts. And sometimes it's not so easy as you'd think. Only one day of the year I walk the same road with him. I follow him with the money in my hand. I met him at your gate just now and offered it. He turned aside his face. Would you like to see the coins? (*Holding out his hand with coins.*) You must. Thirty pieces of silver coined in the Roman mint at Jerusalem.

(*Faint blue light now illumines the face of* THE TRAMP *and becomes brighter as the scene goes on.*)

PRUDENCE (*fascinated, looking at the money*): You frighten me. What are those stains?

TRAMP: Blood, my dear! It's blood money.

PRUDENCE: Whose blood?

TRAMP: The man's who knocked at your door.

PRUDENCE: What did he want?

TRAMP: He came to give—not to ask.

PRUDENCE: What beggar would be going about the country giving something away?

TRAMP: Yes, Prudence Steele, what beggar would be doing that? It's a riddle for you to read.

PRUDENCE: And I suppose now you've got something to give me!

TRAMP: Yes, something you won't be likely to take.

PRUDENCE: Huh! Advice, I suppose. That's the cheapest thing I know.

TRAMP: Sit down. (PRUDENCE *sits down.*) Where the man with the wounded hands knocks once, he knocks again. Wherever he's turned away, I find the door unlatched. But open the door to him, and I stand in the road outside—I'm glad! Oh, I'm a person of strange contradictions—like any other man. You don't understand me.

PRUDENCE: No.

TRAMP: No matter! When he knocks again, let him come in.

PRUDENCE: What do you mean?

TRAMP: Let him come in, I tell you, and save the joy of life in your heart.

(*There is a stamping outside and the door is shaken.*)

PETER (*outside*): Hi! Open the door! Prudence, I say! Wake up and open the door!

PRUDENCE (*starting and passing her hands across her eyes*): It's Peter. It's my husband.

TRAMP: Open the door for him!

(PRUDENCE *runs to the door and opens it.* PETER *enters and she clings to him, half hysterical.* THE TRAMP *remains seated on the larger table, but the light fades from his face.*)

PRUDENCE: Peter—oh, Peter, Peter!

PETER: What's biting you? Let go my arm, woman! Are you trying to claw the coat off me?

PRUDENCE: Send him away! Send him away! Send him away!

PETER: Take your hands off me.

PRUDENCE: Send him away!

PETER: Send who away?

PRUDENCE: That man! That man over there! I'm afraid of him!

PETER: What man?

PRUDENCE: He came in without knocking. I thought it was you! He's terrible—he's crazy! Look at his eyes! Send him away!

PETER: Go on! Don't be a fool. There's nobody here!

PRUDENCE: Over there! He was standing by the table. The table over there— He's gone!

(*They both move across the room, but* THE TRAMP *has disappeared in the darkness.*)

PETER: You've been asleep! You've had a nightmare. You've been worrying again. You'd no call to sit up waiting for me. There's been nobody here.

PRUDENCE: I could have taken my solemn oath!

PETER (*roughly*): You'll take no oaths except them I tell you to. Go to bed!

PRUDENCE: Where've you been?

PETER: Up to the church. I stayed to a vestry meeting. I walked home slow.

PRUDENCE: You've decided what we're going to do?

PETER: Go to bed and let me think. I'll tell you in the morning.

(PRUDENCE *moves toward the inside door.* PETER *calls her back.*)

PETER: Look here! You'll keep your mouth shut? You'll stick to that?

PRUDENCE: Yes. (*She makes a move as if she were coming back to say something.*)

PETER: Get out of here and let me alone. (*He sits down in the chair by the fire and puts his face in his hands.* PRUDENCE *goes out.* THE TRAMP *reappears.*)

TRAMP: Well, Peter Steele, is it easy to think of perjury and theft on Christmas morning?

PETER: God! Who's talking to me!

TRAMP: A greater rogue than yourself.

PETER (*rising*): I see you now, confound you! Where were you hiding when I came in?

TRAMP: No matter!

PETER: So, my wife wasn't dreaming, eh!

TRAMP: No more than you are.

PETER: You frightened her, eh! I'll make short work of you. (*He begins rolling up his sleeves.*)

TRAMP: I only gave her a little advice.

PETER: I'll give you something else! (*He moves toward* THE TRAMP.)

TRAMP (*coolly*): Sit down!

PETER: Get out of here with your advice! Get out, I tell you, before I kick you out.

TRAMP (*more harshly but without moving*): Sit down.

PETER: You can't frighten me with your talk. I'm an honest man, I tell you.

TRAMP: So was I once.

PETER: What have you got to do with me, damn you?

TRAMP: "For there is nothing covered that shall not be revealed, neither hid that shall not be known."

PETER (*with a sigh of relief*): Oh, I see now. You're only a traveling preacher.

TRAMP: No, but I've traveled much and worn the cloth in my time.

PETER: I'm dashed if I see what you're driving at!

TRAMP: You will presently.

PETER: I won't listen to you.

TRAMP: You know what's coming.

PETER: How should I know what's coming? I'll—I'll—

TRAMP: You'll listen, Peter Steele, because I'm going to tell you something about yourself and you'll know it for the truth.

PETER: If—if someone sent you here to pump me, you'd better be off, or I'll have the law on you both.

TRAMP: You had a friend, Peter Steele, and you loved him. He'd often left his affairs in your hands. You'd served him honestly and he trusted you.

PETER: And why wouldn't anybody trust me? I've been an honest man, I tell you.

TRAMP: He came to you in this room. It was the spring the

war began. He had enlisted in a company. Before he left you he brought you money, money to keep for his boy.

PETER: It's a lie! I tell you, it's a damned lie! What right's the boy got to think his father gave me money to keep for him? He ain't got a receipt, has he? It ain't shown in the accounts, is it?

TRAMP: No, Peter Steele, the boy can't show a receipt and the entry's not to be found in the accounts.

PETER: By what token do you think a man would be fool enough to leave money lying around loose like that?

TRAMP: By the token that he trusted you.

PETER: I never had it! I tell you I never had it! What do you know about it?

TRAMP: The drums were beating in the road. Your friend was in his captain's uniform. His sword lay on the table by the door; his cloak over the back of that chair. You sat here. He stood across the table from you. Your wife sat where you're sitting now; her uncle over there by the window.

PETER: Who told you all that? What tricks are you trying to play on me?

TRAMP: Your friend laid the money on this table; thirty one-hundred-dollar bills. He said to you, "Peter, I want to leave this money with you. In case I don't come back, I'd rather my boy didn't count on anything at all when he makes his start. I've fixed things safe for him till he can earn his keep. This is something extra, a nest egg for him, when he's twenty-one." Then he shook you by the hand. As he went down the path, the drums stopped beating, and when the room was still again you heard the voice of the money!

PETER: God, how did you know that?

TRAMP: Oh, you meant to keep faith, Peter Steele, but you never entered the three thousand dollars in your accounts. Well, he never came back. You read his name in the lists. It set you thinking about the boy and his money. Years went by. The boy began to work and earn his keep. You watched him grow up and wondered if he guessed. Last week, you remembered that your debt fell due on the day after Christmas. Then you sat down to figure interest. You'd used the money well and you tried a just rate. The total startled you. Then you tried three per cent; still too much! Then you sat quiet and the money whispered to you, "Why give me up at all? No one can prove you ever had me."

PETER: And they can't prove it! My wife and her uncle can swear they never saw it paid.

TRAMP: Certainly.

PETER: The boy can't show a receipt.

TRAMP: None.

PETER: No. I don't know who told you all this, but if you're trying to blackmail me, there's the door, and be damned!

TRAMP: I'll not trouble you again, whatever decision you come to.

PETER: Then what in hell did you come here for? Answer me that!

TRAMP: To advise you to give the boy his money of your own free will.

PETER: Ha, ha! Anything else?

TRAMP: No.

PETER: Who in the devil are you, stranger?

TRAMP: Come closer!

PETER: I can see you well enough from here.

TRAMP: Come here and look at me. Have you ever seen me before?

PETER: No, thank heaven! I never have.

TRAMP: Look in my eyes.

  (PETER *moves toward him as if dazed.*)

PETER: They're like the eyes of a cat! There's fire in 'em.

TRAMP: Flame from a sunset under Calvary. Look at my throat!

PETER (*shrinking away*): I've seen marks like that on a man—

TRAMP: I hanged myself to a dead tree on a stony hillside. Listen! (*He jingles the money in his pocket.*)

PETER: It's the sound of money!

TRAMP: Thirty pieces of silver, coined in the Roman mint at Jerusalem; the price of my soul, that's walked the evil edge of the world for nineteen centuries.

PETER: In God's name, tell me who you are!

TRAMP: The one being that knows best the priceless value of the thing you're so ready to sell—Judas of Kerioth. (*He advances toward* PETER, *who sinks into the chair by the fire, cowering away from him.*)

PETER: Let me alone, I say! Let me alone!

TRAMP: You'd been an honest man, Peter Steele, and the sun had warmed you and the birds piped to you when you plowed the fields. You'd looked against the faces of red hills when dawn was new, and strained your eyes across blue valleys at the close of day. And men spoke you fair in the roads and children turned to you as you passed, till a little while ago. What came over you that you'd put the joy of living in pawn for thirty pieces of money?

PETER: Let me be! I've become a hard man; and money's a big thing in the world. What's the piping of birds to me? Leave me alone and let me sell my soul if I like! It's mine to sell!

TRAMP: Aye! It's yours to sell. To sell over and over, if you like. There's money to be got for it, more than the first price you take, and pride, and ease of body, and fear of men! But it isn't only your soul you sell, Peter Steele, and nothing you get will compare with that which goes out of you when the first payment clinks in your hand.

PETER: Let me be! Let me be!

TRAMP: You'll miss the joy of small things crying in the grass, and the pleasant sadness that comes of watching the fall of yellow leaves. You'll take no comfort in the sound of a woman's singing, or the laughing of a child, or the crackling of a fire in the grate.

PETER: I was never a hand at noticing such things.

TRAMP: No, but an honest man shares all the common gifts of God. He feels and is grateful without knowing how or why. He seldom knows the joy of it all, till he's lost the power of feeling.

PETER: Let me be.

TRAMP: You'll walk the sunshiny roads and have only the dust of them in your throat. You'll see little lakes lying in the bosom of the hills, like purple wine in cups of green jade, and have only the pain of daylight in your eyes. You'll lie down to sleep with the crystal stars blinking at you, and have only the empty blackness of night in your heart. I know how it will be with you, Peter Steele.

PETER: What do you want me to do?

TRAMP: Give up the money of your own free will.

PETER: What interest have you got in seeing me go straight? Whose work are you doing?

TRAMP (slowly): It's one thing to die in a splendid agony and save the world. It's another to drag the weight of a name like mine from century to century; to live on and on, and suffer every pain of death; to save a man here and a man there only to balance my own long account; to die, to be forgotten.

PETER: To balance your long account?

TRAMP: Turn you from the thing you're about to do, and I toss a grain of dust into the scales. There's a heavy weight to be balanced, Peter Steele, and it's only one day of the year I'm free to search.

PETER: Let me be.

TRAMP: Would you rob me, too?

PETER (putting his hand to his head): Let me think, I tell you! Let me think!

(The inside door opens, and PRUDENCE enters, dressed in a wrapper and carrying a small lamp. As the light illuminates that side of the room, the glow fades on THE TRAMP's face and he disappears. PETER sits with his head in his hands, just as PRUDENCE had left him.)

PRUDENCE: Peter, Peter, are you asleep?

PETER (starting): Eh? No.

PRUDENCE: Why haven't you come to bed? It's near daylight.

PETER: I've been thinking, Prudence—I've been thinking.

PRUDENCE: About—about?

PETER: Say it. I've been thinking of perjury and theft on Christmas morning. I've been thinking of selling my soul for thirty pieces of money. (He rises.) But, thank God, I haven't sold it yet.

PRUDENCE (going to him): Oh, Peter! Peter!

PETER: The boy will get his money on the nail. I'm an honest man, Prudence. I'm an honest man, I tell you!

PRUDENCE: Oh, Peter, I'm glad, I'm glad!

PETER: Every penny he'll get and interest. Fair interest!

PRUDENCE: It's a great deal of money, but I'm glad!

PETER: Little enough to give for keeping the joy of living in your heart on Christmas Day.

PRUDENCE: I want to tell you something. I couldn't sleep, either. Oh, Peter, I couldn't sleep.

PETER: You've been thinking of it, too.

PRUDENCE: Not about the money. There was a lame man here just before you came in. I sent him away. It worries me, Peter. I'm sorry I didn't let him in. Uncle saw him. He'd been hurt. His feet and hands were bandaged. I thought— I thought perhaps— I feel as if he'd stopped somewhere near the house.

PETER: Which way did he go?

PRUDENCE: Toward the willows at the bend of the road.

PETER (*reaching for his hat and coat*): Like as not he'd try to shelter himself there. (*He moves toward the outside door.*)

PRUDENCE: Where are you going?

PETER: To find him and fetch him back. We can't let him freeze.

(*They go together to the outside door and open it. It is morning outside.*)

PETER: It's morning already.

PRUDENCE: Did you ever see such a dawn on the snow?

PETER: Never in my life. (*He kisses her and goes out.*)

PRUDENCE (*calling after him*): I'll have the coffee on the stove.

THE UNDERCURRENT

FAY EHLERT (1886–   ) has many interests. She is the wife of the Chilean consul in Chicago. As a social worker, she visited many homes like the one in *The Undercurrent*. At the Morals Court, the Domestic Relations Court, and the Psychopathic Laboratory, she often observed what happened to children brought up by selfish, ignorant parents. She saw how some immigrants to this country brought with them outworn patterns of behavior so rigid that children did desperate things to break away from their homes. Mrs. Ehlert realized that such children did not consciously break laws but that some force or undercurrent swept them along, freeing them from the rigid, unreasonable, and unloving discipline of the home but at the same time dragging them unprepared and untrained into a realistic world. Mrs. Ehlert saw that she could tell her story best in a one-act play and *The Undercurrent* is the result.

The Undercurrent won first prize in a Little Theatre Tournament in Chicago and became a popular attraction in vaudeville theatres all over the United States and Canada. It is a powerful play, relentless in its exposure of certain truths. Because it is so spare and concentrated, it must be read carefully. Only when the reader sees the characters as three-dimensional people caught in an ugly trap will the play make its full impact.

THE UNDERCURRENT

Fay Ehlert

The scene is a basement kitchen which also does duty as living and dining room in an old-fashioned New York apartment building. An air of orderliness pervades the room, which is furnished with the meager belongings of the FISHYER family. Shabby, faded curtains hang limply on each side of the small, iron-barred window in the left wall. The galvanized sink is in the back, flanked on the right by the kitchen range and on the left by an old cupboard. A coat rack has been nailed to the side of this cupboard. Over the sink is a shelf, holding an alarm clock, comb and brush, and shaving mug. The kitchen table, covered with a red tablecloth, occupies almost the exact center of the room. Upon the table are four plates, knives, forks, cups and saucers, half a loaf of rye bread, a glass jar filled with teaspoons, and a partly filled bottle of milk. There are four chairs around the table. To the left of this table and near the front of the room stands a dilapidated horsehair sofa. Directly across from this sofa on the right side of the room is a Morris

Copyright, 1938, by The Drama Magazine; copyright, 1929 (revised and rewritten), by Fay Ehlert; copyright, 1956 (in renewal), by Fay Ehlert. All rights reserved. CAUTION: Professionals and amateurs are hereby warned that *The Undercurrent*, being fully protected under the copyright laws of the United States of America, the British Empire, including the Dominion of Canada, and all other countries of the Copyright Union, is subject to a royalty. All rights, including professional, amateur, motion pictures, recitation, public reading, radio and television broadcasting and the rights of translation into foreign languages are strictly reserved. Amateurs may give stage production of this play upon payment of a royalty of Five Dollars for each performance, one week before the play is to be given, to Samuel French, Inc., at 25 West 45th St., New York 36, N.Y., or 7623 Sunset Blvd., Hollywood 46, Cal., or if in Canada to Samuel French (Canada) Ltd., at 27 Grenville St., Toronto, Ont.

chair which through long usage has sagged and re-molded itself to PA FISHYER'S two hundred odd pounds. The door in the right wall leads into a short corridor through which the FISHYERS must pass in order to reach the bedrooms, boiler room, storeroom, back stairs, etc. A small table, laden with pipes, tobacco jar, and the Bible is on one side of this door, and the wall phone on the other. A clothesline with its motley array of rags has been fastened to a hook above the phone and then stretched diagonally across the stove to the shelf above the sink. As this room is below street level, it is necessary to mount a short flight of stairs in the left wall in order to reach the areaway door.

It is evening, about five minutes of six, and a light snow is falling. The feet of the passers-by can be seen through the dimly frosted windowpanes.

MA FISHYER is peering through the window. Her whole attitude is one of terrible anxiety and she turns with a half sob of relief as she hears the areaway door open stealthily.

MA FISHYER (*under her breath*): A-annie?

MRS. FLOYD (*stalking down the stairs*): Hello, there!

MA FISHYER (*swallowing her disappointment*): Ach, it's yuh, Mis' Floyd! I—I thought yuh vas (*she turns back to the window again*) s-somebody else!

MRS. FLOYD (*maliciously*): Didya now! (*Eyes* ANNIE'S *place at table.*) Who, fer instance?

MA FISHYER: Ach, eferybody alvays comes to de jeniter for something—maybe Mis' Richards about de g-garbage pails—

MRS. FLOYD: . . . or mebbe even Annie, huh?

MA FISHYER (*unaware of the other's curt smile*): Shure, it's Thursday today, and she alvays comes—

MRS. FLOYD: Is that so? Well, ya never kin tell! (*Shakes fist at door to corridor.*) Huh, I got some news to spill in yer ear! (*Seats herself in* PA FISHYER'S *chair, at the table.*)

MA FISHYER: Ach, not—not now! (*Still peering out of win-*

dow.) Pa'll be here right avay and by six he vants to eat. Not a minute efter six vill he vait— (*She looks at the clock*.)

MRS. FLOYD (*leaning over*): It's about someone ya know!

MA FISHYER: ... and ef Annie ain't here on time— (*She turns, startled, as* MRS. FLOYD's *last words reach her*.) A-about somevun vat I know—vat I kn-know?

MRS. FLOYD (*venting her spite*): I'll tell de world ya do!

MA FISHYER: It ain't nothin' bad?

MRS. FLOYD: Bad? Well! (*She glares at the door to corridor*.) I imagine some people what thinks *my* son ain't good company fer their daughter—certainly are going to have a fit tonight! (*With compressed lips*.) I'll say he is! Yes, siree!

MA FISHYER (*coming slowly towards her*): It ain't 'bout Annie?

MRS. FLOYD: Nuthin' else but!

MA FISHYER (*moans*): Ach! (*Goes fearfully toward door to corridor and, half opening it, listens intently*.)

MRS. FLOYD: My son may be a little wild, but he ain't never been *arrested* yet.

MA FISHYER: Arrest—(*She darts forward and puts her hand over* MRS. FLOYD's *mouth*.) Shhhh!

MRS. FLOYD (*sputtering*): Say—

MA FISHYER (*she glances terror-stricken to door*): Pleese to go now—he-he's comin', h-he's c-comin'!

MRS. FLOYD: What of it? I ain't skeered of him.

MA FISHYER: P-pleese, not now! (*Desperately*.) Not now—come efter vile—pleese— (*Tugs at her dress*.)

MRS. FLOYD (*rising*): All right! I'll go! (*Shakes her off*.) But stop pushing! I'm going! (*Hobbles up the stairs and slams door. Before* MA FISHYER *can breathe her relief, she opens the door again*.) But I'll be back later!

MA FISHYER: Yess, yess, l-later—
    (*Scarcely has the door closed after* MRS. FLOYD *when* PA FISHYER *enters wearily from corridor*.)

FISHYER (*throwing his denim jacket over Morris chair*): Huh! (*He strides over to the sink and begins washing himself*.) Huh! Supper ready?

MA FISHYER (*at the table*): A-almost—

FISHYER (*he growls*): Almost? Don'tcha know yess or no? (*He pushes up his spectacles and glares at the clock.*) Vere's Annie? It's nearly six already!

MA FISHYER: De c-clock iss a l-little f-fest— (*Walks nervously to window.*)

FISHYER: Fest? Dat clock iss *alvays* right, you hear me? Alvays right!

MA FISHYER: Yess, P-pa!

FISHYER (*his wrath increasing*): Vell, vere iss she?

MA FISHYER (*busies herself at stove*): Na, Pa, she'll be h-here eny minute soon! Yuh know h-how de l-lady k-keeps her! (*She glances at the door through which* MRS. FLOYD *has left.*) And m-maybe—in dis b-bed veather, she kent come at all!

FISHYER: Vat! (*Drying his hands.*)

MA FISHYER: I—I mean—efen in *good* veather, only vunce a veek does she haff a day off.

FISHYER: Dat'll do! (*Throws towel on sink*). Ve vait till six (*takes Bible from table and seats himself in Morris chair*) and den ve eat! (*Groans as he rubs his rheumatic left arm.* EMIL *enters.*) Na, Dummy, vat did she vant? (*Points upward.*)

EMIL (*timidly*): She fergot her key and—

FISHYER: . . . and yuh hed to open de door for her! (*He growls.*) Vy don't yuh say dat right avay? (*He begins reading the Bible, following each word with his finger.*)

MA FISHYER: Come, Emil (*she nods warningly in* FISHYER'S *direction*) and vash yerself.

FISHYER (*he reads laboriously*): "Train op a child in de vay he should go" (*glares at* EMIL *and then repeats*) "de vay he *should* go!" (*Reads.*) ". . . and ven he iss old" (*repeats to himself*) "old—he vill not depart from it—"

   (*There is a knock at the outer door and* MA FISHYER *stands transfixed, her face ashen.* EMIL, *his hands half-washed, looks inquiringly at his father.*)

FISHYER: Na, open de door!

EMIL (*hurriedly wiping his hands on his trousers, he mounts the steps and opens the door*): Whatcha want?

MISS PAGE: Good evening! Does Annie Fishyer live here?

EMIL: Yeh—(*he shuffles back to the sink*)—come on in!

MISS PAGE (*descending the stairs*): Thank you. I wasn't quite sure. (*Kindly to* MA FISHYER.) You must be Annie's mother and—

FISHYER: I em Karl Fishyer!

MISS PAGE: Ah, yes, Annie's father. (*She smiles her quick, warm smile.*) I don't think you know me. I am Miss Page, a special investigator from the Morals Court!

MA FISHYER (*tremulously to* FISHYER): De lady, Pa, de l-lady vat Annie v-vorks f-for—

FISHYER: So?

MISS PAGE (*surprised*): Works for me?

MA FISHYER (*hurriedly*): Pleese to come and sit down, mis', here on de sofa! (*She deftly dusts the sofa with a swish of her apron and then steps back and looks at* MISS PAGE *apprehensively.*)

MISS PAGE: I think you are mistaking me— (*She stops as she sees* MA FISHYER'S *drawn face.*)

MA FISHYER (*indicating the sofa*): P-pleese, mis'—
(PA FISHYER *meanwhile replaces the Bible on the table.* MISS PAGE *sits down without another word.*)

MA FISHYER (*quickly*): Annie a-ain't home yet, b-but—

MISS PAGE (*puzzled*): Isn't home yet? Are you expecting her?

FISHYER: Huh? (*He turns towards them.*) Shure, I expect her to come!

MA FISHYER: Y-yess, she always c-c-comes here on her day off—Pa means!

MISS PAGE (*probing gently*): Her day off?

MA FISHYER: Maybe she n-nefer tells yuh, b-but she alvays c-c-comes here Thursdays. (*She wets her lips.*) D-don't she, Pa?

FISHYER (*grudgingly*): Huh! (*To* MISS PAGE.) Since she's vid yuh, mis', yess!

MA FISHYER (*she talks to* MISS PAGE, *but her eyes are anxiously on* FISHYER): And efery cent vat she earns by yuh, she brings to her pa!

MISS PAGE: She—does what? (*Drawing off her gloves.*)

MA FISHYER: E-efery cent she brings to her pa! She iss a fine girl—

FISHYER (*cutting her short*): Vat's dot to brag ofer?

MISS PAGE (*soothingly*): Well, I'm sure Annie is—

MA FISHYER (*eagerly*): Yuh hear, Pa? Efen Mis' Page sez vat a fine Annie ve got.

FISHYER: Huh, she's purty goot *now!* But before she vent mit yuh, mis' (*he clenches his fist in wrath*) I—her fadder—didn't know vhere she vas for three month efen— (MISS PAGE *suppresses a start.*)

MA FISHYER (*imploringly*): But, Pa, yuh know *now* vere she vas! (*To* MISS PAGE.) H-he m-means de time ven she v-vas by yuh in (*she swallows hard*) de *country.*

(MISS PAGE *conceals her astonishment.*)

FISHYER: Efen ef she vas—

MA FISHYER: . . . and how vell she looked ven—

FISHYER: . . . she come home agen! (*He paces angrily back and forth.*) I hear dot a million times already, too!

MA FISHYER: But, P-pa—

FISHYER: All I say iss—dot's no vay to treat yur fadder! And efter de strict bringing op I giff de children, dey must remember—alvays—dat I em dere fadder! *I em de boss here!* (*To* EMIL, *crouching against the wall.*) Yuh hear me?

MA FISHYER (*imploringly*): Pa, pleese, Pa.

FISHYER (*glaring at the clock*): It's six; ve eat now! (*He seats himself at table and begins slicing bread, motions* EMIL *to his seat.* EMIL *sits facing the audience.*)

MISS PAGE (*she has been watching them attentively*): Yes, don't let me interrupt you!

FISHYER: I alvays eat at six! (*Turns towards stove.*) Vere iss dot girl? (MA *comes to table with platter of stew, which she places quickly before him.*) Vat time yuh let her come today, mis'—?

(*Before she can answer, steps are heard and* ANNIE *enters hurriedly from the areaway door.*)

FISHYER: Dere she iss! (*Points at her with knife.*)

ANNIE (*breathlessly*): Oh, Pa, I couldn't—I couldn't help it, I wuz—(*She sees* EMIL's *finger surreptitiously signaling* MISS

PAGE's *presence. She gives* MISS PAGE *a terror-stricken look, then shrinks back against the wall for support.*)

ANNIE (*gasps*): Oh!

MA FISHYER (*she goes toward her quickly, and holding her tight against her breast, speaks so as to give her time to recover*): Ach, no vunder she iss surprised to see her lady here!

ANNIE (*clinging to her*): Ma!

MISS PAGE (*slowly, with great significance*): I had an errand to do in this neighborhood, Annie, and as I passed this house, I stopped in (*sees* MA FISHYER's *pleading look*) to—to get acquainted with your parents!

FISHYER: And ve are gled to know yuh also. (*He motions to the table.*) Yuh eat mit us?

(EMIL *pushes out* ANNIE's *chair for her.*)

MISS PAGE: No, thank you. If you don't mind, I'll just sit here.

FISHYER: Shure! Make yurself to home. (*He bangs on the table with his knife.*) Ma, ve eat now!

(ANNIE *hangs her coat and hat on coat rack.*)

FISHYER (*motioning to* ANNIE): Sit down!

(ANNIE *slips into her chair, facing her father.* MA FISHYER *brings coffeepot to table.*)

MISS PAGE (*observing* EMIL *with interest*): I didn't know Annie had a brother.

MA FISHYER (*hurriedly, before* FISHYER *can answer*): Ach, yess, and sotch a good boy! He helps his pa take care off de house.

FISHYER (*grudgingly*): Huh!

MA FISHYER (*dishing out the food to* EMIL *and* ANNIE): And someday he'll be a jeniter, too! And like our coffee man sez: "Jeniter vork iss nuthin' to sneeze at!" So vat vid Pa's rheumatism, ve are gled to haff Emil help so nice!

FISHYER: Emil—bahhh! (EMIL *crouches behind his mother's arm.*)

MA FISHYER: And yuh haff no idea, mis', how mutch vork dere iss here to do! (*Pours coffee.*) So vid our Emil—

(FISHYER *laughs derisively.*)

MISS PAGE (*soothingly*): Yes, you must be kept very busy, Mr. Fishyer!

FISHYER: Bizzy? Yuh don't know it, mis', how crazy (*he points upward with his knife*) dose vomens get me! First, vun comes and sez de vater iss too hot—dat efery time she turns it on, she a Turkish bath gets! Den— (*The phone rings.*) Yuh see, not efen peace on a meal I got— (*Pushes back his chair.*)

MA FISHYER: Vait, Pa, I go! (*She hurries to phone.*) Hollo! Yess, Mis' Richards, yess, he *iss* by de boiler (PA FISHYER *motions for* EMIL *to go out*) puttin' more coal on! Yess, mam! (*She turns from phone just in time to see* EMIL's *scowling gesture at his father's back.*) Emil! (EMIL *grabs his cap in frantic haste.*) Yur cap— (*Pushes him toward door.*) Quick!

    (PA FISHYER, *unaware of what is passing in back of his chair, pounds the table emphatically with his fist. With a terrified look,* EMIL *rushes out, letting* MA FISHYER *close the door behind him.*)

FISHYER (*he raises his head stubbornly*): I tell yuh, dat voman could by de devil sit and yet be cold!

MA FISHYER: Yess, yess, Pa! But ve are gled to haff dis job! And vat—mit our Emil and Annie helpin' so nice—

FISHYER: Helpin'! Bahhhh!

MA FISHYER: Ach, Mis' Page, efery night I thank de good Gott for my Annie—

ANNIE (*turns quickly and gives her mother a beseeching glance*): Ma—oh, M-ma— (*Her coffee cup falls from her nerveless hand, spilling its contents on her dress.*)

FISHYER: Huh!

ANNIE: Pa—P-pa—it slipped! I—I'll change my dress! (*She rushes out door to bedroom.*)

FISHYER (*looks after her*): Huh! (*Accuses* MA FISHYER *while he dips his bread in his coffee.*) Fine manners she got!
    (*Phone rings again.*)

MA FISHYER (*running to phone*): Yess, yess, Mis' Richards! (*Into receiver.*) Hollo— Yess, Mis' Richards, he *iss*—

FISHYER (*exasperated*): Oh, vat a dummy of a son I got! (*To* MA FISHYER.) Maybe he fell in de coal bin again! (*Exits, rubbing his rheumatic left arm.*)

(MA FISHYER *turns from the phone, listens a moment at the door through which* PA FISHYER *has gone, then quickly crosses the room to* MISS PAGE. *Her whole manner has changed; she seems to have shrunk suddenly.*)

MA FISHYER: I em gled to know yuh, mis'! (*She clasps and unclasps her hands.*) And my Annie—my Annie—

MISS PAGE (*gently*): Sit down, Mrs. Fishyer!

MA FISHYER (*she sinks down in* ANNIE's *chair at the table*): She—she iss mit y-yuh?

MISS PAGE (*compassionately*): In a way—yes.

MA FISHYER: In a vay?

MISS PAGE: Yes, I am interested in her welfare and am looking after her.

MA FISHYER (*scarcely audible*): S-she don't live m-mit yuh?

MISS PAGE: Not exactly—

MA FISHYER: Ach, don't tell dis to Pa! (*In despair.*) Pleese, pleese, don't tell him enyding vat iss agenst her!

MISS PAGE (*leaning forward*): I don't understand.

MA FISHYER: If—if he knows eferyding (*swallowing with difficulty*) h-he kills her!

MISS PAGE (*gently*): Do *you* know everything about her?

MA FISHYER (*terrified*): No, no, don't tell me! Pleese not to tell me! I don't vant to know!

MISS PAGE: Not even when you may be able to help her?

MA FISHYER (*shaking her head*): All I kin do (*motioning to the boiler room*) iss to keep *him* from findin' out d-dings about her! (*She looks her full in the face.*) I don't vant to know enyding agenst my Annie!

MISS PAGE (*puzzled*): But if you remain in ignorance, how can you be of assistance?

MA FISHYER (*tremulously*): I kin help her only by—knowin' nodding.

MISS PAGE: What do you mean? You as her mother should be anxious to know.

MA FISHYER: Yess, yuh haff right! But yuh don't know Pa! (*She whispers.*) He alvays suspicions eferybody! Me—Emil—Annie! He dinks I hide from him someding about de children! (*She pauses.*) And den—it best iss I don't know dings. (*Slowly.*) Ven yuh don't know dings, he kent be scoldin' yuh all de time!

MISS PAGE (*aghast*): But—why should he?

MA FISHYER (*bitterly*): Ach, vy! Vy should he? (*She passes her hand across her eyes.*) Vat kin yuh do mit a man vat hass in his head only *vun idea!*

MISS PAGE: One idea?

MA FISHYER: Vun idea! (*Brokenly.*) Dot all children should be brought op *strict*—mit mutch scoldin' and vhippin'.

MISS PAGE (*indignantly*): But can't you convince him that such harsh methods—

MA FISHYER (*sobs*): I k-kin do nodding mit him—no vun kin! (*She beats her clenched fist against her forehead.*) He hass dot vun idea in his head and (*she stares frantically at the door through which* MRS. FLOYD *has gone*) h-he must n-nefer find out!

MISS PAGE: Find out what? (*As* MA FISHYER *rocks back and forth, weeping.*) Don't be afraid. Tell me.

MA FISHYER (*tearfully*): Pleese, Mis' Page, don't let him find out dings a-agenst A-Annie! (*Weeps.*) P-p-pleese, pleese, see I go on m-my knees t-to yuh! (*Sinks down at* MISS PAGE'S *knees.*) Pleese—p-p-pleese!

MISS PAGE (*her eyes filled with tears*): Don't cry, don't! (*She places her arm around* MA FISHYER'S *shaking shoulders.*) Why didn't you come to see me?

MA FISHYER (*weeping as she grasps* MISS PAGE'S *hands in agony*): Ach, I vanted to c-come so m-meny t-times and esk yuh—take c-care off Annie! L-look efter her—b-but I vas afraid!

MISS PAGE: Afraid?

MA FISHYER: Yess, because—m-maybe—

MISS PAGE (*she looks with sudden understanding toward* ANNIE'S *chair*): . . . there *was* no Miss Page?

MA FISHYER: Yess! But n-now I seen yuh! (*She grasps* MISS PAGE's *arms convulsively.*) Yuh *vill* l-look out for her, von't yuh? (*She wails.*) It iss all I haff in de vorld—my two c-children—all I haff. (*Sinks, weeping bitterly, against* MISS PAGE.)

    (EMIL's *whimpering cry is heard from the boiler room.*)

EMIL: M-ma! Oh, Ma!

MA FISHYER (*she starts up*): It's Emil! Yuh vill oxcuse me? (*Wearily.*) I gotta go—he forgot agen to open de valve maybe! (*She grabs her shawl from the coat rack.*) And Pa mit hiss rheumatism kent reach op—

    (MISS PAGE *rises.*)

FISHYER (*angrily from the boiler room*): Ma! Yuh hear me?

MA FISHYER: Yess, Pa! (*To* MISS PAGE.) Yuh *vill* take care off her?

FISHYER: Ma! Come here!

MA FISHYER (*she chokes back the tears as she opens the door to the boiler room*): Yess, Pa, I em c-comin'! (*She whispers back to* MISS PAGE.) And pleese, alvays to remember—Pa should know nodding agenst her. (*She backs out, murmuring.*) No-nodding—n-n-odding.

    (MISS PAGE *dries her own tears and looks about the room with distaste. Then she goes resolutely to the door and opens it.*)

MISS PAGE (*calling softly*): Annie! Annie! (*Motions.*) Come out here! (MISS PAGE *walks to table.*)

    (ANNIE *enters and closes door softly. She listens attentively, her face pressed against the door.*)

MISS PAGE (*back of* EMIL's *chair*): What have you been telling them?

ANNIE (*on the defensive*): Nuthin' much—only that I worked for ya as a hired girl!

MISS PAGE: Why did you do that?

ANNIE (*back of armchair*): So's to get away from here! If he thought I wuz a dishwasher in a restaurant I'd hafta live here! (*She shudders.*) Nuthin' doin'! I had seventeen years of it!

MISS PAGE: Yes, but still this is your home.

ANNIE: Yeh! (*Tremulously.*) And I know what it's like!

MISS PAGE: Didn't you tell anyone? (ANNIE *shakes her head.*) Not even your mother?

ANNIE (*goes quickly toward* MISS PAGE; *aghast*): And have him beat it outta her? Whadda ya think I am?

MISS PAGE (*puzzled*): Why did you tell them you worked for me?

ANNIE: Well, I—I hadda give somebody's name and yuh wuz de only one I could think of! (*Glances quickly toward closed door, then pleads.*) B-before that happened last year, Miss Page, I n-nearly w-went crazy, and when I fell over *that time* and ya sent m-me to de home until e-everything wuz over—I—j-jest sorta never forgotcha!

MISS PAGE (*severely*): Yes, but what has that to do with all this?

ANNIE: W-well, I n-needed some sorta alibi fer stayin' away from here (*moves slowly away*) s-so I—I told 'em I *worked* for ya and that ya wuz goin' out to de *c-country* and I hadda go 'long!

MISS PAGE (*insistent*): And what else?

ANNIE: W-well, when I got outta de *hospital*, I stuck to my story and only came here Thursdays.

MISS PAGE (*with a helpless gesture*): Oh, Annie, why can't you behave yourself?

ANNIE (*vehemently*): I *do*, Miss Page, honest I do! (*Moves away to escape* MISS PAGE's *searching eyes.*) B-but I can't help it if there's a-always somebody s-snitchin' on ya!

MISS PAGE (*reproachfully*): Snitching! But Annie—

ANNIE (*nervously, twisting and untwisting her belt*): I d-don't care *what* they say! I—I didn't pick up with that feller on de s-street! He—h-he wuz in de room when I g-got in last night!

MISS PAGE (*coming toward her, slowly*): And *how* did he get there?

ANNIE (*feebly*): Oh—er—one of de girls musta let'm have de key!

MISS PAGE (*sadly*): Those girls! (ANNIE *shrinks farther away.*) Why do you live with them? You promised me the last time you wouldn't have anything more to do with Mame and Lottie!

ANNIE (*haltingly*): But they'se so good to me, Mis' Page! I gotta live someplace—it might as well be with dem—

MISS PAGE: . . . and get yourself constantly into trouble?

ANNIE (*protesting*): Oh, Miss Page! Ya don't want me to live *here*, do ya? (*Tremulously.*) Gee, if it wuzn't fer Ma I'd n-never come h-here! B-but Ma (*her whole heart is in her voice*) she's m-my M-ma (*sobs*) s-she's m-my M-m-ma!

MISS PAGE (*walks up and puts her arm around* ANNIE'S *shaking shoulders, holds her tight*): What's going to become of you, Annie?

ANNIE (*with hopeless shrug*): I dunno—and I don't care! (*Moves away.*) Just so long (*nods to door*) as *he* don't ketch on!

MISS PAGE (*walks thoughtfully back a few steps toward door before turning*): Do you know why I came here tonight?

ANNIE: N-no.

MISS PAGE: I came here to find out the kind of home you have, so when I see the judge (ANNIE *looks up, startled*) tomorrow morning, I can tell him a little more about you!

ANNIE (*whispers*): A-about me?

MISS PAGE: Yes! (*Earnestly.*) I've always been on the square with you, haven't I, Annie? (ANNIE *nods.*) And I want to help you all I can. *But* you've been picked up four times during the last five months for loitering on the streets late at night! (*As* ANNIE *starts to appeal.*) And *last* night the *police* raided the flat you were in!

ANNIE (*protesting*): But honest, Mis' Page, I couldn't help it! (*She looks about her like a hunted animal.*) Ya see, I wuz—wuz—shhh!

　　(*The areaway door has opened and* MRS. FLOYD *appears on top stair.*)

MRS. FLOYD (*her beady eyes glisten in anticipation as she surveys* ANNIE): Hello, there! (*She stumps down the stairs.*)

ANNIE (*instinctively on the defensive*): H-hello! (*Moves forward to head her off.*) Ma's helping Pa!

　　(MISS PAGE *crosses to sofa.*)

MRS. FLOYD (*shaking off* ANNIE's *restraining hand*): Oh, is she now! (*Pulls out* EMIL's *chair.*) Then I'll wait fer her!

ANNIE (*in desperate fear, jerks* MRS. FLOYD *around*): I toldja, she's helpin' Pa!

MRS. FLOYD (*flinging* ANNIE *against the cupboard*): Lissen, girlie, I gotcha de *first* time!
    (MA FISHYER *enters hastily.*)

ANNIE (*almost hysterical in her fright*): Then beat it!

MA FISHYER: Ach, Mis' Floyd, I heard yuh close yur door! Ve—ve heff company now—maybe it be better ve go on to yer flet—

MRS. FLOYD: Oh, this suits me, I ain't pertic'ler! (*Seats herself in* EMIL's *chair. Watching* ANNIE *signaling to* MISS PAGE.) Who's her friend?

MA FISHYER (*nervously*): Oxcuse me, but dis iss Annie's Mis' Page—

MRS. FLOYD (*in response to* MISS PAGE's *nod*): Pleased to meetcha! (ANNIE *crosses over to her mother and whispers distractedly in her ear.*)

MA FISHYER: Ve ain't finished our supper yet! Maybe it's better I come ofer and see yuh efter vile.

MRS. FLOYD (*not to be budged*): After while nuthin'! What did she say?
    (PA FISHYER *enters unnoticed, wiping his hands.*)

MA FISHYER (*piteously*): Pleese, Mis' Floyd, eny minute now —Pa—Pa comes—

MRS. FLOYD (*she thumbs toward* ANNIE): Did she say she wuz arrested?

FISHYER: Arrested! (*All look up in surprise.* ANNIE *cowers against the sink.*) Who vas arrested?

MA FISHYER (*at bay*): Ach, Mis' Floyd hass just been talkin' —er—no vitch vay to me, h'aintcha, Mis' Floyd?

FISHYER: Na—all right! (*He thunders at his wife.*) But who vas arrested?

MRS. FLOYD: Who? (*Spitefully.*) Well, Mr. Fishyer, a'course it ain't none of *my* business, *but* seeing what good neighbors we been and how *pertic'ler* ya wuz to let me know that my son is a good-fer-nuthin' loafer—I take great pleasure ta letcha know that one of *yer* swell family is, wuz, or will be arrested!

FISHYER: Vat? My family vat I bring up so strict?

MRS. FLOYD (*she cackles derisively*): Uhuh! Ain't it the limit?

FISHYER (*purpling with rage*): Who iss it?

MA FISHYER (*clinging to his arm*): Pa, pleese—P-Pa—

FISHYER (*he shakes her off*): Na, are yuh deef? Na—*who*, I say?

MRS. FLOYD (*vindictively*): Who else but yer Annie!
(ANNIE *becomes deathly pale and shrinks against the wall.*)

FISHYER (*turns furiously*): Vat?

MA FISHYER (*thrusts herself between* FISHYER *and* ANNIE, *frantically*): Mis' Page, Mis' Page—

ANNIE (*clasping her mother convulsively, whimpers*): M-ma!

MISS PAGE (*quickly*): There—there must be some mistake! Where did you hear this, Mrs. Floyd?

MRS. FLOYD: Well—a friend of mine went ta the Domestic Relations Court taday ta see about that husband of her'n—a perfect brute—

FISHYER (*impatiently*): Yeh, nefer mind about de brute!

MRS. FLOYD: And so I went along, because I been readin' a dandy story about the Morals Court—yeh know (*she winks to* MISS PAGE *as she thumbs in* ANNIE'S *direction*) where them girls are taken—and so I sez ta myself, sez I—

FISHYER (*exasperated*): Vat?

MRS. FLOYD: That's what I'm comin' ta. So I sez ta myself, I'll visit the Morals Court and see if them fellas from the papers tells the truth! (FISHYER *almost beside himself with frenzy.*) But I stayed so long with my friend that the judge wuz jest closin' fer the day. *But* who should I see there—but Annie!

FISHYER (*choking with wrath, turns wildly with uplifted fist toward* ANNIE): Annie, come here!

MA FISHYER (*holding him back*): Don't, Pa, pleese, don't—

FISHYER (*trying to loosen her hold*): Keep quiet!

MISS PAGE (*resolutely*): That isn't anything at all, Mr. Fishyer!

FISHYER (*bellows*): Vat *more* yuh vant, efter bringin' up a girl so strict?

MA FISHYER (*screams in terror as she feels herself overpowered*): Pa, pleese, P-pa—

FISHYER: Vill yuh keep quiet! (*Furiously to* ANNIE, *whimpering in terror.*) First, I giff yuh someding to remember me by—and den out off de *house* yuh go!

MA FISHYER (*fighting to hold him back*): N-no, Pa, don't—

FISHYER (*throwing her on the floor in front of table*): Get out off my vay, Ma! (*He shouts, enraged.*) Annie, come here! Yuh hear me! (*He grasps her left arm and jerks her toward him.*)

ANNIE (*writhing in pain as he tightens his hold*): No—no! It's —it's a lie—a lie—

MRS. FLOYD (*rising in surprise*): Huh!

ANNIE: Yes, it is! (*She glares about her with the desperation of a trapped animal.*) Yes, it is! I—I wuz—there. (*she points sobbingly to* MISS PAGE) with her!

FISHYER: Mit her? Mis' Page?

ANNIE (*trying to loosen his grip*): Yes, I wuz helpin' her carry her books (*she nods to* MRS. FLOYD) when she musta seen me!

 (MISS PAGE *is startled at* ANNIE's *lie.*)

FISHYER (*tightening his cruel hold until she falls sobbing on her knees*): Vat yuh mean?

ANNIE (*the words fairly tumble from her twitching lips*): Mis' Page works fer de judge—h-helps him— And I often go to de court with h-her, don't I, Mis' Page?

 (*An agonizing second.* MISS PAGE *gives one glance at* MA FISHYER's *prostrated form on the floor and then rises to the occasion.*)

MISS PAGE: Yes! She's *always* there with me!

ANNIE (*sobs*): And—I been there lots of times, ain't I, Mis' Page?

 (*Quickly, before* MISS PAGE *can reply,* MA FISHYER *thrusts herself between* PA FISHYER *and* ANNIE.)

MA FISHYER (*tries to separate his iron grip from* ANNIE's *arm*): Yuh see, Pa? Yuh see?

FISHYER (*to* MISS PAGE, *slightly mollified*): Ef she's vid *yuh*, Mis'—dot's all right, den! (*Flings* ANNIE *and* MA FISHYER *from him. While* MA FISHYER *tenderly kisses* ANNIE'S *arm he turns wrathfully toward* MRS. FLOYD.) But! (MRS. FLOYD, *seeing his intentions, scurries up the stairs.*) Goodby, Mis' Floyd! (*Runs up the stairs and shouts after her.*) And next time yuh *look* first before yuh jump! (*Crashes door after her.*)

(MA FISHYER *is holding* ANNIE *tightly in her arms. Both are weeping.*)

FISHYER: So! (*Comes down stairs.*) Dis should be a lesson for yuh, Annie! Yuh see now vat maybe heppens ef I don't bring yuh up so strict! (*Shakes fist after* MRS. FLOYD.) Dat cat vat just left might be in de right!

(EMIL *re-enters and moves wonderingly toward sink.*)

MA FISHYER (*her breath sobbing in her throat*): Y-yess, Pa, y-yess—

FISHYER (*sternly flinging her away from* ANNIE *so that she falls into* EMIL'S *arms*): Let her alone, Ma! Vat kind off bringin' up is dot? (*To* MISS PAGE.) I tell yuh, mis', my fadder alvays said: "Ordor rules de vorld, but *man* iss ruled vid de *vhip!*" And he vas right! (*Glares at* ANNIE.) He ruled us vid a hand off iron! (*To* MISS PAGE.) And look on me! I haf de greatest respect for my fadder! (*Gives them all a menacing look.*) And I do de same! Alvays am I strict and ven dey grow old, dey'll tank me for it!

(*He sits down at the table and motions* EMIL *to his seat again.* EMIL *sidles into his chair guardedly.* PA FISHYER *begins his meal, dipping his chunk of rye bread in the gravy.* MISS PAGE *notices the looks of hatred darted at* PA FISHYER *by both* ANNIE *and* EMIL.)

MISS PAGE (*curiously*): And—did you love your father, Mr. Fishyer?

FISHYER (*taken aback*): Lofe? (*He stops with his coffee cup halfway.*) Shure, I lofe him ven I respect him! (*Grimly.*) Huh! (*Cracking an imaginary whip.*) He'd make us dance to de muzik off de stick ef ve didn't lofe him! Shure (*he pauses*) shure, de children alvays lofe (*fixes his eye on* EMIL, *who immediately stops drinking his coffee*) de fadder!

(EMIL *draws back in consternation.*)

MISS PAGE (*seeing the futility of the situation, turns thoughtfully to the sofa for her gloves and purse*): Well, it's late and I must be going! (*She pauses a second in thought, then comes to a decision.*) By the way, Mr. Fishyer, would you mind if I take Annie with me?

FISHYER: Right avay? I vanted to giff her a good talkin' to, yet!

MISS PAGE (*pulling on her gloves*): I'm so sorry, but I'm leaving for the country early in the morning—

MA FISHYER (*staring fixedly at* MISS PAGE): De c-country?

MISS PAGE (*smiling at her, very gently*): The *real* country, Mrs. Fishyer!

FISHYER (*he grunts, between mouthfuls*): Shure, mit yuh it's all right! (*Over his shoulder to* ANNIE.) Put on yur tings, Annie!

(*For a moment, while his back is turned,* MA FISHYER *crushes* ANNIE *sobbingly to her breast, kissing her again and again.*)

ANNIE (*covering her mother's tear-stained cheeks with kisses, she whispers brokenly*): Don't, Ma, don't, I'll be good! I'll be good!

MA FISHER (*sobs, clinging to her*): Annie— (MISS PAGE, *separating the two, holds* MA FISHYER *tight in her arms.*) Little Annie!

MISS PAGE (*while* ANNIE *gets her coat and hat from the coat rack*): Good-by, Mrs. Fishyer. You needn't worry! (*Looks sternly at* PA FISHYER, *unconcernedly eating his meal.*) I'll take good care of your Annie!

(MA FISHYER, *unable to utter a word, leans over and kisses* MISS PAGE's *hand.* MISS PAGE *turns and mounts the stairs leading to the areaway. As she opens the door,* FISHYER *looks up.*)

FISHYER: Good-by, mis', and ef she don't behave herself (ANNIE *clings to* MISS PAGE; *he balls his fist*) yuh just let me know!

MISS PAGE (*her arm protectingly around* ANNIE, *she eyes him, half sadly, half ironically*): Yes, indeed! You'd be a great help!

FISHYER (*nods his self-satisfaction and takes his second cupful of coffee*): Shure!

    (MA FISHYER *leans heavily against* EMIL'S *chair, her eyes following the two disappearing through the doorway.*)

THE MAN WHO DIED AT TWELVE O'CLOCK

PAUL GREEN, born in Lillington, North Carolina, in 1894, received his college training at the University of North Carolina, where he studied with Frederick Koch, and at Cornell University. Mr. Green has usually written about Southern people and Southern problems in his numerous plays, novels, and short stories, but his writing always has a universal application. He won a Pulitzer prize for his play *In Abraham's Bosom* and earned further fame with *Johnny Johnson* and *The House of Connelly*. Mr. Green introduced symphonic drama to this country when he wrote *The Lost Colony* in 1937. This pageant of history with music and dance is performed every summer in an outdoor theatre on Roanoke Island, North Carolina. Other symphonic dramas he has written are *The Common Glory, Wilderness Road,* and *The Founders.*

The Man Who Died at Twelve O'Clock is one of the many honest short plays Mr. Green has written about the Southern Negro. It is a sympathetic treatment of an age-old problem: How can two lovers remove the obstacles to their marriage? They use desperate methods which are plausible and serious to the three characters but which, to the reader, are frantically hilarious.

THE MAN WHO DIED AT TWELVE O'CLOCK

Paul Green

The scene is a room in the farmhouse of JANUARY EVANS in eastern North Carolina. The time is near the noon hour on a spring day, a few years ago. In the back wall of the room we see a door which opens into a narrow hall. Near the door is a battered iron cot. Above the bed on a shelf nailed to the rough joists is a cheap clock. Along the right wall is a fireplace, a narrow window, and, hanging on nails in the joists, a ragged hat, a pair of dirty overalls, and a shirt or two. Along the left wall is an unpainted washstand made of a pine goods box, partly covered with newspapers, on top of which are a pail of water and a gourd. A few splint-bottom chairs are about the room.

JANUARY EVANS' granddaughter, SALLY EVANS, a plump, neatly dressed, chocolate-colored girl, is sitting in a chair near the center of the room, sewing. She sings as she sews.

Copyright, 1925, by Samuel French, in *One-Act Plays for Stage and Study,* 2nd Series; copyright, 1953 (in renewal), by Samuel French. All rights reserved. CAUTION: Professionals and amateurs are hereby warned that *The Man Who Died at Twelve O'Clock,* being fully protected under the copyright laws of the United States of America, the British Empire, including the Dominion of Canada, and all other countries of the Copyright Union, is subject to a royalty. All rights, including professional, amateur, motion pictures, recitation, public reading, radio and television broadcasting and the rights of translation into foreign languages are strictly reserved. Amateurs may give stage production of the play upon payment of a royalty of Five Dollars for each performance, one week before the play is to be given, to Samuel French, Inc., at 25 West 45th St., New York 36, N.Y., or 7623 Sunset Blvd., Hollywood 46, Cal., or if in Canada to Samuel French (Canada) Ltd., at 27 Grenville Street, Toronto, Ont.

SALLY:

> Fall o' de evening I go down de river,
> > Sailing in a boat so fine,
> A-riding on de waters, waters,
> > Talking to dat love of mine.
>
> A-weeping by de river, river,
> > Dere's where my truelove found me.
> Call to me, kiss me, hug me,
> > Bofe of his arms around me.

(*There is the sound of footsteps in the hall, and* CHARLIE MCFARLAND *stands in the doorway. He is a well-built, open-faced Negro farmhand of twenty or more.* SALLY *drops her sewing and stands up quickly, smiling at him brightly.*)

SALLY: I do declare, heah you is, Charlie boy, quicker'n I thought.

CHARLIE (*coming up to her and patting her shoulders affectionately, but with a gloomy abstraction*): Yeh, yeh, baby chile.

SALLY: Ain't you gwine kiss me?

CHARLIE: 'Scuse me, 'scuse me, sho' I is. (*He bends to kiss her and she throws her arms around him and hugs him tightly to her.*)

SALLY: Oh, me, me! Des think of it; tomorrow we gwine be married foh good!

CHARLIE (*forcing a smile*): Yeh, yeh.

SALLY: Take a seat and rest yo'se'f. (*He sits down and hangs his hat on his knee.*) You got through plowing soon, didn't you?

CHARLIE: Unh-hunh. I told Mr. Byrd 'bout you 'n' me helping out in de school-breaking tonight, and what wid de wedding and all he said I could quit at de finish of de upper piece.

SALLY: When he want you back?

CHARLIE: A-Tuesday. Dat'll give us Monday foh de picnic on

de river. (*Hesitating.*) It would have ef—ef it all had come off de way we's planning.

SALLY: Come off? Sho' it's coming off. And of a-Sundays we kin go to other places, way up to Fuquay, Summerville, no telling whah, traveling round, too.

CHARLIE: Kin? How we gwine do dat?

SALLY: Dat's my susprise foh you, but I'll tell you, dough. Listen, sugar, we gwine take part o' dat five hundred dollars and buy us'ns a little Fo'd. Den we kin burn de wind, round and about.

(*He shows little elation at the prospect.*)

CHARLIE: Ef us gits dat money, you means.

SALLY: Why you so doubtful all of a sudden? Ain't no *ifs* and *ands* in it adder dat vision two weeks ago.

CHARLIE: Mebbe so, lak as not adder all dey is.

SALLY (*anxiously*): Why you so jubious dis mawning? Grandpap ain't gwine hinder us. You been saying all de week dat he's a changed man.

CHARLIE: Yeh, yeh, I was a-thinking dat-a-way.

SALLY: And he has changed, too. He won't go agin his vision. I'm sho' o' dat now. Bofe of us thought 'twas all bluff at fust and e'en you got me into believing he was newbawn and now seems I got to 'suade you. Whut's de matter? Last night at de practice you was lak a lark, so happy, and everything setting to our hand, and Grandpap in a good humor wid you. (*With a sudden start.*) Lawd, you ain't gitting out'n de notion, is you, and Arth gwine foh de license dis evening?

CHARLIE (*vehemently*): Naw, naw, I tell you t'ain't dat.

SALLY: Well, whut is it, den? Is you gitting skeahed o' Grandpap agin? You know well's I do dat since de morning he heard de devil talking in de air and saying he's coming foh him some day at twelve o'clock, he's been lak a clean-washed lamb.

CHARLIE: Yeh, he was lak dat.

SALLY: He ain't cussed nary a word nor touched a drap o' liquor. And, Charlie, hon, yistiddy he told me sweet as pie dat he done forgive you dat telling de sheriff 'bout his making liquor.

CHARLIE (*miserably*): Dat was yistiddy, dough. He knowed long befo' dat 'twas de sheriff skeahed me into telling on him, fur as dat's concerned.

SALLY: And tomorrow foh de wedding present he's gwine turn over all dat money Muh and Pap left me. Now you hearten up if dat's whut ails you.

CHARLIE: Hey, he mought. But my mind tells me he'll keep executing on it des de way he has since dey died.

SALLY (*going back to her chair and picking up her sewing*): Cain't see why you worry. We three's gwine live on heah happy as you please. Look at dis devil's costyume you gwine wear tonight in de play. Booh! (*She whirls toward him, holding up a long, red, tight-fitting suit, horns, tail, and hoofs attached. Two terrifying eyes and a wide, grinning mouth glare out at him.*)

CHARLIE (*starting back in alarm*): Lawd, hyuh, hyuh, don't shake dat thing at me!

SALLY: Ho, ho, ho! I sho' has made a' awful critter, ain't I?

CHARLIE (*coming up and touching it gingerly*): Lawd, Lawd, dat's a turble sight. Reckon 'twon't th'ow de folkses into fits when I comes stepping crost de stage wid dat thing on?

SALLY (*sitting down with the garment in her lap and beginning to sew again*): I got to finish dis left-hand hawn; den you kin take it on wid you. I was gwine have it all done and complete foh you if you hadn't come early. Mought 'a' put it on and skeahed you wid it.

CHARLIE: Yeh, and I'd 'a' tore up de road gwine 'way from heah. Wouldn't had no devil in de dialogue tonight, been a-roosting in de swamp. (*He sits down forlornly and watches her sew.*) You's raght handy wid a needle, ain't you?

SALLY: Is dat. And, boy, I'se gwine make you mo' shirts and things dan a few. And knit! I kin knit, too. (*Jokingly.*) You better not think of th'owing me ovah heah at de last. Ain't many gals good at housekeeping lak me.

CHARLIE (*Uneasily*): Hyuh, hyuh, don't talk lak dat. It hurts me worse'n it do you to think o' putting it off.

SALLY: Putting it off? We ain't gwine put it off.

CHARLIE (*wretchedly*): Don't seem no way out'n it.

SALLY: Way out'n whut?

CHARLIE: Everything's busted to pieces, dat's how.

SALLY: Is! How come?

CHARLIE: You don't know whah Uncle Jan is, do you?

SALLY (*with satisfaction*): Hunh, dat I do. In de bottom chopping his cawn. He's off dis mawning wid his hoe by sunrise. Needn't worry 'bout him.

CHARLIE (*bitterly*): In de bottom! He's in de bottom of a drunk, de old fool!

SALLY (*incredulously*): Hyuh, don't be trying to skeah *me* now.

CHARLIE: Trying! I wisht I had to try.

SALLY: Dat's too serious to be joking 'bout. Tell me de truf.

CHARLIE: I'se telling you de truf. He mought 'a' gone off dis mawning wid a hoe, but when I come by Luke's sto' up de road few minutes ago dere he sot on a box wid a Co'-Cola bottle in his hand, beating and a-flamming and a-cussing at de wind.

SALLY (*with a wail*): O Lawd!

CHARLIE: When he seed me a-coming, he fell to lambanging and telling 'em all to let him make at me. Dey had to hold him back or I'd 'a' had to cave in his haid. Dere's yo' new-bawn lamb and follower of Jesus foh you. He's gut fed up on pizen liquor. He was so mad at me dat he 'gun to spit and spew all over de flo'. Said he's coming raght on home and shoot me full of holes if he found me heah. (*Wrathfully.*) Hurry and git dat last hawn fixed, I gut to be moving. Lawd, I won't feel lak cutting up no shines tonight.

SALLY (*her hands lying limp in her lap*): O Lawd, whut kin we do? (*A sob breaks in her voice.*) And heah we was wid everything fixed foh good.

CHARLIE: He 'bused me black and blue in de face. Said all I wanted was yo' money and dat I'd never git it. He had it hid whah nobody could find it and he's gwine let Luke have it to put in his sto'. (*Standing up from his chair and clenching his fist.*) Wisht to Gohd I had dat Luke Ligon heah in dis room; I'd frail him to deaf.

SALLY: We gut to do something, I tell you. Dat Luke git his claws on my money and dat's de end of it. (*They both sit thinking, wretched.*) When Grandpap comes, cain't you 'n' me shet him up and make him give it up to us or tell us whah it is?

CHARLIE: Yeh, and dat man'll cut you all to pieces wid a knife. He's mean and he's full o' liquor. And 'sides, you ain't twenty-one. Dey'd have de law on bofe of us. (SALLY *gets up and moves nervously around the room.*) Gimme dat costyume and lemme leave. Wisht to de good Gohd he'd a seed de devil dressed in dis suit in his vision, and I reckon he'd 'a' not been back in his weekedness so soon!

SALLY (*stopping in her walk*): Kin you see him coming? I gut a idee.

    (CHARLIE *goes to the window and looks out.*)

CHARLIE (*excitedly*): Yeh, yeh, yonder he comes down de hill and walking all over de road. Gimme dat and lemme git away.

SALLY: Wait a speck. (*She wrinkles her brow in thought.*)

CHARLIE: Why foh?

SALLY: I believe I got a way to fix him.

CHARLIE: Hurry up. How you mean?

SALLY (*picking up the suit*): Skeah him, dat's how.

CHARLIE: Wid dat?

SALLY: Yeh, I b'lieves we kin do it.

CHARLIE: He mought shoot us.

SALLY: I'll hide his gun. (*She runs to the corner, takes the gun, unloads it, and throws it under the bed.*) Now gimme de shells. (*She gets a box of shells from the washstand, opens the window at the right, and throws them far out.*)

CHARLIE: Whut you mean to do?

SALLY (*growing excited*): Listen. Look at dat dere clock, neah 'bout twelve. Well, when twelve straks, Grandpap is gwine die.

CHARLIE: Die? We—we ain't gwine kill him, is we? Naw suh, I ain't—Sally, you—

SALLY: I hopes we won't kill him, but he's gwine think his time's come.

CHARLIE (*turning quickly back to the window*): Oh—hurry up wid yo' plans den. Yonder he is now down by de branch place.

SALLY (*breathlessly*): It des flashed on me lak a streak. It's dis. He had de vision dat he's gwine die someday at twelve when de devil comes foh him. Dat's whut de devil told him. Well, when he comes in heah to lie down and sleep off his drunk, I's gwine set up a monstrous heap o' wailings and screechings sorter lak I has to do in de dialogue, 'cepting worse. You be shet up in de entry dressed in dis heah suit. I'll skeah him to deaf wid my talk 'bout signs and sich, and den when de clock straks twelve you come in to git him. Lawd, he'll git religion dis day, see 'f he don't.

CHARLIE: How you know we kin do all that? He might git something and brain me wid it, I tells you.

SALLY: Dat he won't. He's gwine be skeahed worse'n he's ever been. And he'll cough up dat money, and tell all his sins, and 'fo' he's got straight agin, we'll be all fixed. And he ain't never gwine know it wa'n't de devil adder him. Boy, we'll sho' have all de under-holt yit.

CHARLIE (*staring at her*): Lawd, Lawd, you's de sharpest gal I ever did see in dis world.

SALLY: Dis heah's de time to be sharp if we's gwine git married tomorrow. Now, hyuh. When you come in wid yo' devil's suit on, you talk to him, ax him all sorts of question. He'll tell everything. (*Bubbling over with excitement.*) Yeh, yeh, we gut him whah we want him at last. And I'll make out all de time dat I cain't see devil or nothing. (*Coming up to him and hugging him in courageous ecstasy.*) We gwine have some fun out'n him. Adder today I bet my hat he'll be a shouting Christian.

CHARLIE (*warming to the game*): All raght, honey, dis heah's de time. I'll stick to you. And talk 'bout cutting a rust at dat schoolhouse? I's gwine make a to-do wid dat old man whut is one!

SALLY: Now you slip in de entry and shet de do' and doll up. We gwine have a sober man on our hands in a few minutes. Hurry, hurry, dere he is coming by de woodpile.

> (*She pushes the costume into his hand and hurries him out at the rear, quickly picks up the loose scraps of her sewing and hides them under the mattress; after which she sits down in her chair and bows her head in her hands. Old* JANUARY *is heard singing outside, and his white head dodders by the window. In a moment he is heard grunting and stumbling in the hall. He creeps in at the rear and stands clinging to the door-facing with long, skinny hands. He is just drunk enough to be quarrelsome and fearful. He is dressed in an old shirt, open at the front, and a pair of overalls too short for him, below which stick out his enormous black, horny feet. His hat is gone, and his hair flares up in a white tangle around his shrunken ebony face. As he comes in, he looks at* SALLY *and carries on his song.*)

UNCLE JANUARY:

> I tells you onct—I—tells you—twice,
> Niggers in hell foh shooting dice—
> Pharyoh's army got drowned,
> Oh, Mary don't you weep.

(*Waving his hand gaily.*) Heah I is, drunk and r'aring to go! (SALLY *pays no attention to him. Staggering forward, he sits down on the cot and moves his head around in a circle, mouthing and letting out deep groans. He stops and stares at* SALLY.) Hyuh, you! Is dat you, Sally? Whah's dat dog of a Charlie? (*Making an effort to get to his feet.*) Unh-hunh, I knows. (*His head swaying in drowsiness.*) I—know, I's gwine shoot his lights out. Dat's whut I come foh.

SALLY (*looking at him sadly*): He ain't heah, he's gone.

UNCLE JANUARY: Anh-hah, bedder be. Dat rascal want my money. Ain't gwine git it, nunh-unh. (*He falls back on the bed and stretches himself out.*) Tell him, if he's heah when

I git over my good time, I's coming foh him wid a gun— I's a-coming foh— (*His voice trails off. He lays his head back with a great sigh and closes his eyes.*)

SALLY: Don't you lay down lak dat. Wake up, wake up!

UNCLE JANUARY (*mumbling*): Shet up dat racket, shet up and let a old man sleep—sleep—whut needs it. (*He begins puffing away and snoring.*)

SALLY (*coming up to the cot*): Grandpap, Grandpap, git up, dey's a turble time coming on you!

UNCLE JANUARY (*dreamily and slapping at her*): Git—to-o-o-ff —o—off. (*He falls to snoring regularly.*)

SALLY (*talking to herself*): Whut I gwine do? Hyuh, hyuh, I gut to rise him out'n dat liquor. (*She looks apprehensively at the clock, which lacks twenty-five minutes till twelve.*) Bedder fix dat clock 'bout right to suit me. (*She goes to the clock and moves it up ten minutes.*) Reckon dat'll give me egzactly time enough. (*UNCLE JANUARY is puffing steadily away, at every third or fourth breath making a sort of whistling sound through his lips. She stands watching him closely, thinking.*) Now I gits ready to sail on him. (*She goes over to a broom in the corner and gets a long straw, returns to the cot, and begins to tickle his nose.*)

UNCLE JANUARY (*in a faraway voice, smacking his lips*): Lemme 'lone. Uh—m—uh—m.

   (*She tickles his nose again, and he falls to sneezing, his grizzled head and calloused feet being jerked violently upward with each movement of his diaphragm. Every convulsion is followed by a combined wheeze and shout.*)

SALLY (*angrily*): Ain't he a sight on earf! I'll wake him yit. (*She bends down and begins blowing a heavy blast in his nostrils. He rears and bucks and beats the air as if fighting flies. Then as she blows a heavier blast than ever, he begins champing like a horse and suddenly spits in her face. She starts back with a smothered exclamation of wrath.*) You nasty, stinking rascal, you done spet raght kuh-dab on me! (*She wipes her face and tweaks him by the nose, calling loudly.*) Grandpap, Grandpap!

(*As he groans and crawls up to a crouching position in bed, she slumps down in her chair and begins sobbing in seemingly heartbroken grief. Presently he slides his thin legs out on the floor and sits on the edge of the bed, holding his head in his hand.*)

UNCLE JANUARY: Who dat bothering me so? Lawd, I's perished foh water. Cain't sleep, cain't rest. (*He blinks uncomprehendingly around him. Slapping his forehead with his hand, he quavers childishly.*) Oh, my haid hurt! (*He gets to his feet and makes his way across the room to the bucket. SALLY carries on her moaning and rocking, watching him out of the corner of her eye as he drinks several gourdfuls of water and gives his head a drenching.*)

SALLY (*with a sudden shriek*): O Lawd, have mercy on us!

UNCLE JANUARY (*turning and staring at her in amazement*): Who dat! Heigh! Whut de name o' Gohd ails you!

SALLY: Oh, don't go away and leave us, don't you go!

UNCLE JANUARY: Hyuh, hyuh! Whoever dat is cutting up so, you stop it. (*Shouting at her.*) Sally, you git de linimint and rub my haid. Lawd, why you r'aring so? (*He starts toward his cot, smacking his lips and stretching his toothless mouth in great gapes.*)

SALLY (*in a storm of grief*): Too late foh linimint, too late. (*Moaning.*) Nothing kin help you now to flee from de wraf to come. Gohd done sent his sign!

UNCLE JANUARY (*sitting on the edge of the cot, twisting his head, and spitting on the floor*): Whut sign? Tell me whut ails you, I says. Is somebody daid? Oh, my po' haid!

SALLY: Not yit, not yit, but when dat dere clock straks twelve, somebody's gwine be.

UNCLE JANUARY: Is? You say somebody gwine die? (*Jerking his head up.*) Gohd A'mighty, who it is, chile!

SALLY: Don't you use de Lawd's name dat-a-way, don't you do it! And you des ten minutes from gwine to the t'other world. O Lawd, have mercy on dis sinful man! (*She buries her face in her apron.*)

UNCLE JANUARY (*belching lugubriously*): Hunh, whut t'other world? What sinful man is dat?

SALLY: It's so, Grandpap, it's so. Yo' vision's gwine happen.

UNCLE JANUARY (*blinking at her*): Whut vision?

SALLY: You know whut vision. And when dat clock straks twelve, you'll be daid as a nit. I's seed signs, plenty o' signs.

UNCLE JANUARY (*sitting up straight*): Whut signs? Whut signs? Tell me dat. Hyuh, hyuh, set up and speak fo'th. (*He watches her anxiously, his drunkenness clearing.*)

SALLY (*turning in agony on him*): Pray, pray, 'fo' it's too late. Lawdy, O Master, make him to see his danger! (*She rocks back and forth.*)

UNCLE JANUARY: Shet yo' mouf, dry up, I tells you. I ain't gwine die ner nothing, oo-h—ooh!

SALLY: Oh, yeh you is, yeh you is. Lemme tell you de signs I seed and you'll pray den all raght, but I feah it'll be too late —too late.

UNCLE JANUARY (*swaying from side to side and beginning to look uneasily about the room*): Signs! Tell me whut signs, I axes you.

SALLY: Ev'y since nine o'clock dis mawning till few minutes ago dat old dominicker hen been crowing. And she ain't crowed none since dat day last spring Mis' Penny died.

UNCLE JANUARY (*fear creeping into his voice*): Air you sho' 'twas de old dominicker, Sally?

SALLY: Sho'? Dat I is sho'. And dat ain't all, dat ain't de hunderth part. All de whole o' last night de deaf bells been a-ringing in my haid, rung so I couldn't sleep.

UNCLE JANUARY (*growing more and more sober, patting his foot nervously against the floor*): Mebbe dat don't mean me—sho' it don't mean me.

SALLY (*shaking her head sadly, and wiping the tears from her eyes*): Cain't be nobody else, cain't be, and you done had a vision 'bout it. And listen to dis—listen now to de turble warning. Early in de pink o' de mawning I was out in de gyarden and heahd de hell hounds crossing de sky.

UNCLE JANUARY (*horror-stricken*): Lawd-a-muhcy, did you? (*He locks his arms around one knee and stares at her with wide eyes.*)

SALLY: I did dat. Thought den I wouldn't tell you, but now

you come home drunk I gut to do all I kin to save you.
(*Twisting her hands together and lifting up her eyes.*) O
Lawd up dere in heaben, help save him 'fo' de devil come
foh his soul.

UNCLE JANUARY (*stretching his hand toward her in suppli-
cation*): Sally, Sally, don't you squall lak dat.

SALLY: And when dem hounds passed over dis heah house
dey des swooped down and moaned and howled louder'n
ever. Den dey passed out'n heahing 'crost de creek.

    (UNCLE JANUARY *snaps his head around and looks at
the clock, which now lacks five till twelve. With a
groan he slumps down on the cot.* SALLY *continues
her moaning and praying. Presently he raises his head
and pipes feebly.*)

UNCLE JANUARY: Was dey—was dey any mo' signs, Sally?
Quick, quick, tell me all you seed.

SALLY (*shivering and crouching down in her chair*): Oh, but
I cain't tell you de last and most awfulest one of all, I cain't
(*sobbing loudly*) I cain't tell you!

UNCLE JANUARY (*putting his hand weakly to his heart and
gasping for breath*): Whut was it? Lemme know—know de
wust.

    (*She waits, without replying. He stares at the clock, his
tongue lolling in his mouth. When it clicks prepara-
tory to striking, she turns wildly upon him and
shouts.*)

SALLY: I was out dere at de pigpen feeding de pigs raght
adder you went to de bottom, and I seed a devil's hole by a
pine stump, and I bent down and listened—and whut did I
heah, oh, whut did I heah? I heahd wailing and grinding
and hosses neighing way down dere in hell. And dey was
loud screaming and wild laughing and rattling o' chains,
and I could see a great far roaring. Den de fuss stopped,
and I heahd two voices talking, and one of 'em—one of
'em— (*she suddenly stops and bursts into loud sobs again.*)

UNCLE JANUARY (*his eyes bright with terror*): Whut did dey
say? Whut did dey say?

SALLY: One of 'em said de devil was a-coming foh you today

at twelve o'clock. (*Screaming.*) And it's twelve raght dis minute. Pray! Pray! (*She springs out of her chair and rushes wildly from the room.*)

UNCLE JANUARY (*falling on his knees by the cot and crying out in a high, slobbering voice*): Gohd ha' muhcy, Gohd ha' muhcy! (*The clock begins to strike. He backs across the room from it, watching it as if hypnotized.*) Dere you go—dere you go hurrying off de pass of time! (*He wags his finger and almost chants in the extremity of his fear.*) One —two—th'ee—fo'—five—ha'f gone—ha'f gone—six—seven—and eight—and nine—now it's ten—'leven—de last one—twelve! (*He stands closing and unclosing his hands in stupefaction, shivering as if with an ague. He waits, swaying with weakness, but nothing happens. The clock goes on ticking merrily. He opens his eyes and stares around, slaps his body, listens, then cackles hysterically.*) Glory—glory to Gohd, it's all a mistake! I's safe—safe as a dollar—hooray! (*As he starts toward the door, it opens and the devil, horned, tailed, and hoofed, slides in. With a squeak UNCLE JANUARY falls like a log on the bed and lies looking at the approaching horror with piteous eyes. A moaning sound comes through his lips and he clutches blindly at his throat. A whine that gradually rises into words bursts from him.*) Ha' muhcy! Ha' muhcy! A speck o' time. Gimme one minnit—one.

(*The DEVIL comes nearer and stares down at him.*)

DEVIL (*in a hollow voice*): January Evans, two weeks ago you was give warning 'bout yo' weeked life, but you wouldn't heed it, and you went a-tempting Gohd agin today. Now it's too late—too late—yo' time's up. Yo' soul belongs to me and tonight I roasts you in hell!

UNCLE JANUARY: Ha' muhcy! Ha' muhcy! (*Great drops of perspiration cling to his brow.*)

DEVIL (*thundering*): Muhcy! Gohd A'mighty's offered you muhcy seventy long yeah and you kept a-spetting in his blessed face.

(*SALLY comes in weeping.*)

UNCLE JANUARY (*crying out as he spies her*): He'p, he'p, Sally! Come heah, come heah and git him off.

DEVIL: And dey shall call foh muhcy and dey'll be no muhcy.

SALLY (*looking down at him in great sorrow*): Ain't you gone yit, Grandpap?

UNCLE JANUARY (*pleadingly*): Git de gun and shoot him, Sally! (*He makes a feeble effort to rise, but falls back, gasping for breath, wailing.*) Shoot him, run him out'n dis room!

SALLY (*looking around*): Who? Run who out?

UNCLE JANUARY (*his jaw dropping down like a dead man's*): Cain't you see nobody heah in de room?

(*The* DEVIL *folds his arms and waits.*)

SALLY: Dey ain't nobody but you 'n' me. (*She bends quickly over him, her breath caught with fear.*) Is you seeing something, Grandpap? Is you?

UNCLE JANUARY (*pointing weakly*): Dere, dere! It's de devil! (*Screaming.*) See him dere grinning at me!

SALLY (*starting back with a sharp moan*): Oh, Lawd, he's gwine out, he's gitting to de River Jordan. Don't let his soul be lost! (*She drops in her chair and rocks back and forth.*) Ain't no hope now and de devil done come foh him.

(*The* DEVIL *takes another step toward his victim.*)

UNCLE JANUARY (*putting out his hands to ward him off*): Somebody come he'p a po' old man. Come heah, folkses! He'p! He'p! (*He begins to whimper.*)

DEVIL: Make yo'se'f ready to go. 'Fess yo' sins. Beg fohgiveness.

UNCLE JANUARY: Cain't you heah dat talking now, Sally? (*Pleading.*) Cain't you heah nothing?

SALLY: I don't heah nothing. Whut's he saying to you? Oh, he's gitting neah de gates of de other world!

UNCLE JANUARY: He tells me to—to—'fess my sins. Yeh, yeh, I 'fesses and axes fohgiveness. Oh, Lawd, wipe 'em off'n dat Book.

DEVIL: Own up, own up all yo' meanness and it'll be easier on you in dat pit.

UNCLE JANUARY (*in a small voice, speaking as if in a dream*): I been a turble man all de days of my life. I's sorry foh it all.

DEVIL: Dat makes it easier, den. Whut you been doing mean lately?

UNCLE JANUARY: Yeh, I'll tell it all. I'll tell. Me 'n' Luke's gut us a new still at de head of de pond—put it in yistiddy. Fohgive me foh dat. (*His voice grows weaker.*)

DEVIL: What else? Speak, man, yo' time is short.

UNCLE JANUARY (*in a faraway voice*): Cain't 'member—no more—dat's all—all.

DEVIL: Dat ain't all. Don't you try to fool wid de sperits of de other world. How 'bout dat money b'longs to de gal name' Sally?

UNCLE JANUARY: Yeh, yeh, dere—dere behime a brick up inside de farplace—all dere—give it to her. Dat was a sin, I knows now. (*His voice coming back stronger.*) Yeh, yeh, and Charlie—I wants her to marry Charlie, dat was a big sin. I sees it now. (*Panting.*) Lemme live to make it all right —gimme des a day.

DEVIL: You swear to turn all her money over to her and let her marry Charlie.

UNCLE JANUARY (*eagerly*): Yeh, I swears—I'll git de license —anything. (*He closes his eyes and beats on his breast for breath. He goes on in a weakening voice.*) And I'll never drink anudder drap—nary—un. Growing dark heah—whah is you, Sally? (*He feels around him on the bed.*) Sally, Sally!

DEVIL: Den if you swears— (*He stops and peers at* UNCLE JANUARY, *who lies limp and still. In alarm.*) Whut's de matter wid you, Uncle— Whut's happened, January Evans?

(UNCLE JANUARY *makes no reply.* CHARLIE'S *voice alarms* SALLY *and she hurries to the bed.*)

SALLY: Whut you done, Charlie? Whut—

CHARLIE (*bending over him, fearfully*): Dey's something bad happened.

SALLY: Oh, me! (*Calling loudly.*) Grandpap! Grandpap! (*He makes no answer and she shakes him vigorously.*) Wake up! (*She falls to rubbing his hands feverishly.*) We got to do something raght quick. Lawd, s'pose'n he dies or something. Rub his feet, quick; his hands is cold! (CHARLIE *begins rubbing his feet.* SALLY'S *voice rises high in fear as she rubs faster and faster.*) Tell me, whut kin we do? Kin we git a doctor or somebody?

CHARLIE: I don't know—rub him, roll him. (*They both roll him back and forth across the bed.*) Feel his heart.

SALLY: Cain't tell wh'ah it's beating or not. Run, git de bucket o' water and le's put some on him. (CHARLIE *brings the bucket in a rush, hesitates a moment, and then dashes the contents full in the old man's face.*)

CHARLIE: Dat'll bring him if anything will.

SALLY: You'll drown him. Why we ever want to do dat foolishness nohow? (UNCLE JANUARY *begins to sputter and cough.* SALLY *cries out joyously.*) Thank Gohd, he's coming back! Hyuh, you run git dem clothes off'n you. Th'ow him into fits he sees you. Git! (CHARLIE *runs out at the rear.*) Grandpap! Grandpap! (*He opens his eyes and gazes at her. She bends down and kisses him on the forehead, her shoulders shaking with grief. Presently she controls herself.*) You ain't daid, is you, Grandpap? Oh, you's alive! Thank de Lawd!

UNCLE JANUARY (*raising himself up with difficulty on his elbow*): Whah is I? (*His voice is humble and sweet. Suddenly he looks around, terror-stricken.*) Whah dat devil?

SALLY (*impetuously*): Grandpap, we— (*She catches herself in time and stands waiting, laughing and almost weeping at once.*) Dey ain't no devil, and you's safe in yo' own bed.

UNCLE JANUARY (*finally working himself into a sitting position*): Dey *was* a devil, and I was a praying foh help. (*He turns excitedly to* SALLY.) Think of it, chile, I been *daid;* dat's what I has—

SALLY: Daid? We thought you was and poured water on trying to save you.

UNCLE JANUARY: And I been daid. De devil come and got me—raght dere he stood plain as de pa'm o' yo' hand—in de middle o' de flo'. And when I done promised everything, he took me off in de dark, sailing, sailing, and finally we come back where it was light. Den I woke, and heah I is. (*He puts his feet out on the floor.*) Honey, I done been treating you wrong; dat devil made me own up. Yo' money's in de farplace dere. Every cent but a few dollars I borrowed, and I'se gwine go raght off and git 'nough to pay you back.

SALLY (*laughing hysterically and twisting her hands*): Dat's all raght 'bout a few dollars, and I don't keer foh nothing since you's back wid us. (*Overcome with excitement, she sits down and stares at him.*)

UNCLE JANUARY (*beating his thigh with his skinny hand and blinking before him*): Des think of it, chile, I was r'ally daid, I b'lieve—in fact I know I was. Dat vision was eve'y bit so, and all dem signs you seed. Couldn't be no mistook 'bout dat devil—he come foh me. (*Shaking his head.*) Dunno, dough, des how I gut back heah. (*He sits lost in wonder.*)

SALLY: I believes you was daid, too, foh a while—couldn't feel no heartbeat, no nothing.

UNCLE JANUARY: No *b'lieve* 'bout it—sho' I was plumb gone to de udder world. (*His voice falling into humility.*) Ol' Master been good to me, too good, Sally, and I's gwine try to serve him de rest of my days. (*He begins to whimper again.*)

SALLY: Don't cry now.

UNCLE JANUARY: He gi'n me des dis one chanct to come back —dat devil said he mought gimme anudder trile. Reckon you could git aholt of Charlie? I wants him to know I's—I's willing foh you and him—willing and happy raght down to de bottom.

SALLY: He come 'bout de time you was tuk wid yo' spell. He's outside now.

UNCLE JANUARY: Is? (*He stand up weakly.*)

SALLY: Yeh, I'll call him. (*She goes to the door.*) Charlie! Charlie! (*He comes in, buttoning up his shirt.*)

UNCLE JANUARY (*clinging to him*): I des had de greatest 'sperience to martal man a few minnits back. I died stone daid.

CHARLIE (*gently getting loose from him*): Aw, you don't mean daid?

UNCLE JANUARY (*almost defensively now*): Daid eve'y bit and grain. And I'se come back foh anudder chanct. You ain't gwine never be boddered wid me no mo'. I makes frien's wid you now to de judgment day.

CHARLIE (*somewhat remorseful*): Lawd, Uncle Jan, you's too good to us all of a suddent.

UNCLE JANUARY: Naw, suh. (*He stops suddenly and a light breaks over his face. He whispers to himself.*) Daid, daid as a do'nail, and now heah I is. (*In loud exultation.*) Dere was dem men in de Bible, and now dey's me. (*He hitches up his suspenders and throws his hands out wide.*) Git behime me, folkses, git behime! (*He scrambles out at the rear, calling joyously.*) Ay, you Luke! I's gut a mess to tell you!

(*Wondering, they watch him go, and then their eyes turn toward the fireplace.*)

ARIA DA CAPO

EDNA ST. VINCENT MILLAY (1892–1950) is best known for her sensitive and penetrating poems: *Renascence, The Buck in the Snow,* and the Pulitzer award-winning volume, *The Harp-Weaver and Other Poems.* Her plays, all in verse, include *Aria da Capo, Two Slatterns and a King,* and the libretto for an opera, *The King's Henchman.* Miss Millay had a romantic but not a sentimental view of life. She loved nature and deplored man's abuse of his resources. Recently, Miss Dorothy Stickney, who created the role of Mother in *Life with Father,* toured the United States in a production based on Miss Millay's life and poems called *A Lovely Light.* From the letters, poems, and experiences of the poet as interpreted by Miss Stickney emerged a memorable, compassionate, sensitive figure whose perception of good and evil is brilliantly evident in all her writing.

Aria da Capo is a morality play but it is not preachy. It is Miss Millay's protest against selfishness and pettiness, written in the disarming form of a harlequinade. The title is a term in music which means the song ends as it begins. Bach, Handel, Mozart, and Beethoven wrote arias, minuets, and scherzos in this three-part form: statement, departure, and return to the original statement. By using this form, Miss Millay gains unity and emphasis for her theme. With her creative imagination she has given her play unusual vividness and directness.

ARIA DA CAPO

Edna St. Vincent Millay

The scene is a stage set for a Harlequinade, a merry
black-and-white interior. Directly behind the foot-
lights, and running parallel with them, is a long table,
covered with a gay black-and-white cloth, on which is
spread a banquet. At the opposite ends of this table,
seated on delicate, thin-legged chairs with high backs,
are Pierrot and Columbine, dressed according to the
tradition, excepting that Pierrot is in lilac, and Columbine in pink. They are dining.

COLUMBINE: Pierrot, a macaroon! I cannot *live*
Without a macaroon!
PIERROT: My only love,
You are *so* intense! . . . Is it Tuesday, Columbine?
I'll kiss you if it's Tuesday.
COLUMBINE: It is Wednesday,
If you must know. . . . Is this my artichoke,
Or yours?
PIERROT: Ah, Columbine, as if it mattered!
Wednesday . . . Will it be Tuesday, then, tomorrow,
By any chance?
COLUMBINE: Tomorrow will be— Pierrot,
That isn't funny!
PIERROT: I thought it rather nice.
Well, let us drink some wine and lose our heads
And love each other.
COLUMBINE: Pierrot, don't you love
Me now?

Copyright, 1920, 1947, by Edna St. Vincent Millay, Harper & Brothers. Reprinted by permission of Norma Millay Ellis. For permission to produce *Aria
da Capo* write direct to Baker's Plays, Boston 10, Mass. No performance may be
given without permission.

PIERROT: La, what a woman! How should I know?
   Pour me some wine: I'll tell you presently.
COLUMBINE: Pierrot, do you know, I think you drink too
   much.
PIERROT: Yes, I dare say I do. . . . Or else too little.
   It's hard to tell. You see, I am always wanting
   A little more than what I have—or else
   A little less. There's something wrong. My dear,
   How many fingers have you?
COLUMBINE: La, indeed,
   How should I know? It always takes me one hand
   To count the other with. It's too confusing.
   Why?
PIERROT: Why? I am a student, Columbine;
   And search into all matters.
COLUMBINE: La, indeed?
   Count them yourself, then!
PIERROT: No. Or, rather, *nay*.
   'Tis of no consequence. . . . I am become
   A painter suddenly, and you impress me—
   Ah, yes!—six orange bull's-eyes, four green pin wheels,
   And one magenta jelly roll—the title
   As follows: *Woman Taking in Cheese from Fire Escape*.
COLUMBINE: Well, I like that! So that is all I've meant
   To you!
PIERROT: Hush! All at once I am become
   A pianist. I will image you in sound . . .
   On a new scale . . . Without tonality . . .
   Vivace senza tempo senza tutto . . .
   Title: *Uptown Express at Six O'clock*.
   Pour me a drink.
COLUMBINE: Pierrot, you work too hard.
   You need a rest. Come on out into the garden,
   And sing me something sad.
PIERROT: Don't stand so near me!
   I am become a socialist. I love
   Humanity; but I hate people. Columbine,
   Put on your mittens, child; your hands are cold.

COLUMBINE: My hands are *not* cold!

PIERROT: Oh, I am sure they are.
And you must have a shawl to wrap about you,
And sit by the fire.

COLUMBINE: Why, I'll do no such thing!
I'm hot as a spoon in a teacup!

PIERROT: Columbine,
I'm a philanthropist. I know I am,
Because I feel so restless. Do not scream,
Or it will be the worse for you!

COLUMBINE: Pierrot,
My vinaigrette! I cannot *live* without
My vinaigrette!

PIERROT: My only love, you are
So fundamental! . . . How would you like to be
An actress, Columbine?—I am become
Your manager.

COLUMBINE: Why, Pierrot, I can't act.

PIERROT: Can't act! Can't act! La, listen to the woman!
What's that to do with the price of furs? You're blond,
Are you not? You have no education, have you?
Can't act! You underrate yourself, my dear!

COLUMBINE: Yes, I suppose I do.

PIERROT: As for the rest,
I'll teach you how to cry, and how to die,
And other little tricks; and the house will love you.
You'll be a star by five o'clock . . . that is,
If you will let me pay for your apartment.

COLUMBINE: *Let* you? Well, that's a good one!
Ha! Ha! Ha!
But why?

PIERROT: But why? Well, as to that, my dear,
I cannot say. It's just a matter of form.

COLUMBINE: Pierrot, I'm getting tired of caviar
And peacocks' livers. Isn't there something else
That people eat? Some humble vegetable
That grows in the ground?

PIERROT: Well, there are mushrooms.
COLUMBINE: Mushrooms!
  That's so! I had forgotten . . . mushrooms . . . mush-
  rooms . . .
  I cannot *live* with . . . How do you like this gown?
PIERROT: Not much. I'm tired of gowns that have the waist-
  line
  About the waist, and the hem around the bottom,
  And women with their breasts in front of them!
  Zut and *ehé!* Where does one go from here!
COLUMBINE: Here's a persimmon, love. You always liked
  them.
PIERROT: I am become a critic; there is nothing
  I can enjoy. . . . However, set it aside;
  I'll eat it between meals.
COLUMBINE: Pierrot, do you know,
  Sometimes I think you're making fun of me.
PIERROT: My love, by yon black moon, you wrong us both.
COLUMBINE: There isn't a sign of a moon, Pierrot.
PIERROT: Of course not.
  There never was. Moon's just a word to swear by.
  Mutton! Now *there's* a thing you can lay the hands on,
  And set the tooth in! Listen, Columbine:
  I always lied about the moon and you.
  Food is my only lust.
COLUMBINE: Well, eat it, then,
  For heaven's sake, and stop your silly noise!
  I haven't heard the clock tick for an hour.
PIERROT: It's ticking all the same. If you were a fly,
  You would be dead by now. And if I were a parrot,
  I could be talking for a thousand years!
        (*Enter* COTHURNUS, *Masque of Tragedy.*)
PIERROT: Hello, what's this, for God's sake? What's the mat-
  ter?
  Say, whadda you mean? Get off the stage, my friend,
  And pinch yourself—you're walking in your sleep!
COTHURNUS: I never sleep.

PIERROT: Well, anyhow, clear out.
You don't belong on here. Wait for your own scene!
Whadda you think this is, a dress rehearsal?
COTHURNUS: Sir, I am tired of waiting. I will wait
No longer.
PIERROT: Well, but whadda you going to do?
The scene is set for me!
COTHURNUS: True, sir; yet I
Can play the scene.
PIERROT: Your scene is down for later!
COTHURNUS: That, too, is true, sir; but I play it now.
PIERROT: Oh, very well! Anyway, I am tired
Of black and white. At least, I think I am.
   (*Exit* COLUMBINE.)
Yes, I am sure I am. I know what I'll do!
I'll go and strum the moon, that's what I'll do. . . .
Unless, perhaps . . . you never can tell. . . . I may be,
You know, tired of the moon. Well, anyway,
I'll go find Columbine. . . . And when I find her,
I will address her thus: "*Ehé*, Pierrette!"
There's something in that. (*Exit* PIERROT.)
COTHURNUS: You, Thyrsis! Corydon!
Where are you?
THYRSIS (*off stage*): Sir, we are in our dressing room!
COTHURNUS: Come out and do the scene.
CORYDON (*off stage*): You are mocking us!
The scene is down for later.
COTHURNUS: That is true;
But we will play it now. I am the scene.
   (*Seats himself on high place in back of stage.*)
   (*Enter* CORYDON *and* THYRSIS, *two shepherds.*)
CORYDON: Sir, we are counting on this little hour.
We said, "Here is an hour—in which to think
A mighty thought, and sing a trifling song,
And look at nothing."—And, behold! the hour,
Even as we spoke, was over, and the act begun,
Under our feet!

THYRSIS: Sir, we are not in the fancy
  To play the play. We had thought to play it later.
CORYDON: Besides, this is the setting for a farce.
  Our scene requires a wall; we cannot build
  A wall of tissue paper!
THYRSIS: We cannot act
  A tragedy with comic properties!
COTHURNUS: Try it and see. I think you'll find you can.
  One wall is like another. And regarding
  The matter of your insufficient mood,
  The important thing is that you speak the lines,
  And make the gestures. Wherefore I shall remain
  Throughout, and hold the promptbook. Are you ready?
CORYDON *and* THYRSIS (*sorrowfully*): Sir, we are always
  ready.
COTHURNUS: Play the play!
    (CORYDON *and* THYRSIS *move the table and chairs to
      one side out of the way, and seat themselves in a
      half-reclining position on the floor.*)
THYRSIS: How gently in the silence, Corydon,
  Our sheep go up the bank. They crop a grass
  That's yellow where the sun is out, and black
  Where the clouds drag their shadows. Have you noticed
  How steadily, yet with what a slanting eye
  They graze?
CORYDON: As if they thought of other things.
  What say you, Thyrsis, do they only question
  Where next to pull? Or do their far minds draw them
  Thus vaguely north of west and south of east?
THYRSIS: One cannot say. . . . The black lamb wears its bur-
    docks
  As if they were a garland—have you noticed?
  Purple and white—and drinks the bitten grass
  As if it were a wine.
CORYDON: I've noticed that.
  What say you, Thyrsis—shall we make a song
  About a lamb that thought himself a shepherd?

THYRSIS: Why, yes!—that is, why, no! (I have forgotten my
   line.)
COTHURNUS (*prompting*): "I know a game worth two of that."
THYRSIS: Oh, yes. . . . I know a game worth two of that!
   Let's gather rocks, and build a wall between us;
   And say that over there belongs to me,
   And over here to you!
CORYDON: Why, very well.
   And say you may not come upon my side
   Unless I say you may!
THYRSIS: Nor you on mine!
   And if you should, 'twould be the worse for you!
      (*They weave a wall of colored crepe-paper ribbons
      from the center front to the center back of the stage,
      fastening the ends to Columbine's chair in front and
      to Pierrot's chair in the back.*)
CORYDON: Now there's a wall a man may see across,
   But not attempt to scale.
THYRSIS: An excellent wall.
CORYDON: Come, let us separate, and sit alone
   A little while, and lay a plot whereby
   We may outdo each other.
      (*They seat themselves on opposite sides of the wall.*)
PIERROT (*off stage*):   *Ehé*, Pierrette!
COLUMBINE (*off stage*): My name is Columbine! Leave me
   alone!
THYRSIS (*coming up to the wall*): Corydon, after all, and in
   spite of the fact
   I started it myself, I do not like this
   So very much. What is the sense of saying
   I do not want you on my side the wall?
   It is a silly game. I'd much prefer
   Making the little song you spoke of making,
   About the lamb, you know, that thought himself
   A shepherd! What do you say?
      (*Pause.*)
CORYDON (*at wall*): I have forgotten the line.
COTHURNUS (*prompting*): "How do I know this isn't a trick?"

CORYDON: Oh, yes. . . . How do I know this isn't a trick
  To get upon my land?
THYRSIS: Oh, Corydon,
  You *know* it's not a trick. I do not like
  The game, that's all. Come over here, or let me
  Come over there.
CORYDON: It is a clever trick
  To get upon my land. (*Seats himself as before.*)
THYRSIS: Oh, very well!
  (*Seats himself as before. To himself.*)
  I think I never knew a sillier game.
CORYDON (*coming to wall*): Oh, Thyrsis, just a minute! All
    the water
  Is on your side the wall, and the sheep are thirsty.
  I hadn't thought of that.
THYRSIS: Oh, hadn't you?
CORYDON: Why, what do you mean?
THYRSIS: What do I mean? I mean
  That I can play a game as well as you can.
  And if the pool is on my side, it's on
  My side, that's all.
CORYDON: You mean you'd let the sheep
  Go thirsty?
THYRSIS: Well, they're not my sheep. My sheep
  Have water enough.
CORYDON: *Your* sheep! You are mad, to call them
  Yours, mine—they are all one flock! Thyrsis, you can't mean
  To keep the water from them, just because
  They happened to be grazing over here
  Instead of over there, when we set the wall up?
THYRSIS: Oh, can't I? Wait and see! And if you try
  To lead them over here, you'll wish you hadn't!
CORYDON: I wonder how it happens all the water
  Is on your side. . . . I'll say you had an eye out
  For lots of little things, my innocent friend,
  When I said, "Let us make a song," and you said,
  "I know a game worth two of that!"

COLUMBINE (*off stage*): Pierrot,
  D'you know, I think you must be getting old,
  Or fat, or something—stupid, anyway!
  Can't you put on some other kind of collar?
THYRSIS: You know as well as I do, Corydon,
  I never thought anything of the kind.
  Don't you?
CORYDON: I *do* not.
THYRSIS: Don't you?
CORYDON: Oh, I suppose so.
  Thyrsis, let's drop this—what do you say? It's only
  A game, you know. . . . We seem to be forgetting
  It's only a game. . . . A pretty serious game
  It's getting to be, when one of us is willing
  To let the sheep go thirsty for the sake of it.
THYRSIS: I know it, Corydon.
       (*They reach out to each other across the wall.*)
COTHURNUS (*prompting*): "But how do I know—"
THYRSIS: Oh, yes. . . . But how do I know this isn't a trick
  To water your sheep, and get the laugh on me?
CORYDON: You can't know, that's the difficult thing about it,
  Of course—you can't be sure. You have to take
  My word for it. And I know just how you feel.
  But one of us has to take a risk, or else,
  Why—don't you see?—the game goes on forever! . . .
  It's terrible, when you stop to think of it. . . .
  Oh, Thyrsis, now for the first time I feel
  This wall is actually a wall, a thing
  Come up between us, shutting you away
  From me. . . . I do not know you any more!
THYRSIS: No, don't say that! Oh, Corydon, I'm willing
  To drop it all, if you will! Come on over
  And water your sheep! It is an ugly game.
  I hated it from the first. . . . How did it start?
CORYDON: I do not know. . . . I do not know. . . . I think
  I am afraid of you! You are a stranger!
  I never set eyes on you before! "Come over

And water my sheep," indeed! They'll be more thirsty
Than they are now before I bring them over
Into your land, and have you mixing them up
With yours, and calling them yours, and trying to keep
    them!
    (*Enter* COLUMBINE.)
COLUMBINE (*to* COTHURNUS):
    Glummy, I want my hat.
THYRSIS: Take it, and go.
COLUMBINE: Take it and go, indeed! Is it my hat,
    Or isn't it? Is this my scene, or not?
    Take it and go! Really, you know, you two
    Are awfully funny! (*Exit* COLUMBINE.)
THYRSIS: Corydon, my friend,
    I'm going to leave you now, and whittle me
    A pipe, or sing a song, or go to sleep.
    When you have come to your senses, let me know. (*Goes*
        back to where he has been sitting, lies down, and sleeps.)
      (CORYDON, *in going back to where he has been sitting,*
          stumbles over bowl of colored confetti and colored
          paper ribbons.)
CORYDON: Why, what is this? Red stones—and purple stones—
    And stones stuck full of gold! The ground is full
    Of gold and colored stones! . . . I'm glad the wall
    Was up before I found them! Otherwise
    I should have had to share them. As it is,
    They all belong to me. . . . Unless— (*He goes to wall and*
        digs up and down the length of it, to see if there are
        jewels on the other side.) None here—
    None here—none here— They all belong to me! (*Sits.*)
THYRSIS (*awakening*): How curious! I thought the little black
    lamb
    Came up and licked my hair; I saw the wool
    About its neck as plain as anything!
    It must have been a dream. The little black lamb
    Is on the other side of the wall, I'm sure. (*Goes to wall and*
        looks over. CORYDON *is seated on the ground, tossing the*
        confetti up into the air and catching it.)

Hello, what's that you've got there, Corydon?
CORYDON: Jewels.
THYRSIS: Jewels? And where did you ever get them?
CORYDON: Oh, over here.
THYRSIS: You mean to say you found them,
  By digging around in the ground for them?
CORYDON (*unpleasantly*): No, Thyrsis,
  By digging down for water for my sheep.
THYRSIS: Corydon, come to the wall a minute, will you?
  I want to talk to you.
CORYDON: I haven't time.
  I'm making me a necklace of red stones.
THYRSIS: I'll give you all the water that you want,
  For one of those red stones—if it's a good one.
CORYDON: Water? What for? What do I want of water?
THYRSIS: Why, for your sheep!
CORYDON: My sheep? I'm not a shepherd!
THYRSIS: Your sheep are dying of thirst.
CORYDON: Man, haven't I told you
  I can't be bothered with a few untidy
  Brown sheep all full of burdocks? I'm a merchant.
  That's what I am! And if I set my mind to it
  I dare say I could be an emperor!
  (*To himself.*) Wouldn't I be a fool to spend my time
  Watching a flock of sheep go up a hill,
  When I have these to play with?—when I have these
  To think about? I can't make up my mind
  Whether to buy a city, and have a thousand
  Beautiful girls to bathe me, and be happy
  Until I die, or build a bridge, and name it
  The Bridge of Corydon, and be remembered
  After I'm dead.
THYRSIS: Corydon, come to the wall,
  Won't you? I want to tell you something.
CORYDON: Hush!
  Be off! Be off! Go finish your nap, I tell you!
THYRSIS: Corydon, listen: if you don't want your sheep,
  Give them to me.

CORYDON: Be off! Go finish your nap.
A red one—and a blue one—and a red one—
And a purple one— Give you my sheep, did you say?
Come, come! What do you take me for, a fool?
I've a lot of thinking to do—and while I'm thinking,
The sheep might just as well be over here
As over there. . . . A blue one—and a red one—
THYRSIS: But they will die!
CORYDON: And a green one—and a couple
Of white ones, for a change.
THYRSIS: Maybe I have
Some jewels on my side.
CORYDON: And another green one—
Maybe, but I don't think so. You see, this rock
Isn't so very wide. It stops before
It gets to the wall. It seems to go quite deep,
However.
THYRSIS (*with hatred*):
            I see.
COLUMBINE (*off stage*):
                Look, Pierrot, there's the moon!
PIERROT (*off stage*): Nonsense!
THYRSIS: I see.
COLUMBINE (*off stage*):
Sing me an old song, Pierrot—
Something I can remember.
PIERROT (*off stage*):   Columbine,
Your mind is made of crumbs, like an escallop
Of oysters—first a layer of crumbs, and then
An oystery taste, and then a layer of crumbs.
THYRSIS (*searching*): I find no jewels. . . . But I wonder what
The root of this black weed would do to a man
If he should taste it. . . . I have seen a sheep die,
With half the stalk still drooling from its mouth.
'Twould be a speedy remedy, I should think,
For a festered pride and a feverish ambition.
It has a curious root. I think I'll hack it

In little pieces. . . . First I'll get me a drink;
And then I'll hack that root in little pieces
As small as dust, and see what the color is
Inside. (*Goes to bowl on floor.*) The pool is very clear. I see
A shepherd standing on the brink, with a red cloak
About him, and a black weed in his hand. . . .
'Tis I. (*Kneels and drinks.*)
CORYDON (*coming to wall*):
      Hello, what are you doing, Thyrsis?
THYRSIS: Digging for gold.
CORYDON: I'll give you all the gold
You want, if you'll give me a bowl of water.
If you don't want too much, that is to say.
THYRSIS: Ho, so you've changed your mind? It's different,
Isn't it, when you want a drink yourself?
CORYDON: Of course it is.
THYRSIS: Well, let me see . . . a bowl
Of water— Come back in an hour, Corydon.
I'm busy now.
CORYDON: Oh, Thyrsis, give me a bowl
Of water! And I'll fill the bowl with jewels,
And bring it back!
THYRSIS: Be off, I'm busy now.
(*He catches sight of the weed, picks it up, and looks at it,
    unseen by* CORYDON.)
Wait! Pick me out the finest stones you have. . . .
I'll bring you a drink of water presently.
CORYDON (*goes back and sits down, with the jewels before
him*): A bowl of jewels is a lot of jewels.
THYRSIS (*chopping up the weed*): I wonder if it has a bitter
taste.
CORYDON: There's sure to be a stone or two among them
I have grown fond of, pouring them from one hand
Into the other.
THYRSIS: I hope it doesn't taste
Too bitter, just at first.
CORYDON: A bowl of jewels

Is far too many jewels to give away
And not get back again.

THYRSIS: I don't believe
He'll notice. He's too thirsty. He'll gulp it down
And never notice.

CORYDON: There ought to be some way
To get them back again. . . . I could give him a necklace
And snatch it back after I'd drunk the water,
I suppose. . . . Why, as for that, of course, a *necklace* . . .

> (*He puts two or three of the colored tapes together and
> tries their strength by pulling them, after which he
> puts them around his neck and pulls them, gently,
> nodding to himself. He gets up and goes to the wall,
> with the colored tapes in his hands.*)

> (THYRSIS *in the meantime has poured the powdered
> root—black confetti—into the pot which contained
> the flower and filled it up with wine from the punch
> bowl on the floor. He comes to the wall at the same
> time, holding the bowl of poison.*)

THYRSIS: Come, get your bowl of water, Corydon.

CORYDON: Ah, very good! And for such a gift as that
I'll give you more than a bowl of unset stones.
I'll give you three long necklaces, my friend.
Come closer. Here they are. (*Puts the ribbons about
THYRSIS' neck.*)

THYRSIS (*putting bowl to* CORYDON's *mouth*):
                              I'll hold the bowl
Until you've drunk it all.

CORYDON: Then hold it steady.
For every drop you spill I'll have a stone back
Out of this chain.

THYRSIS: I shall not spill a drop.

> (CORYDON *drinks, meanwhile beginning to strangle*
> THYRSIS.)

THYRSIS: Don't pull the string so tight.

CORYDON: You're spilling the water.

THYRSIS: You've had enough—you've had enough—stop pulling
The string so tight!

CORYDON: Why, that's not tight at all. . . .
How's this?
THYRSIS (*drops bowl*):
You're strangling me! Oh, Corydon!
It's only a game!—and you are strangling me!
CORYDON: It's only a game, is it? Yet I believe
You've poisoned me in earnest! (*Writhes and pulls the
strings tighter, winding them about* THYRSIS' *neck.*)
THYRSIS: Corydon! (*Dies.*)
CORYDON: You've poisoned me in earnest. . . . I feel so
cold. . . .
So cold . . . This is a very silly game. . . .
Why do we play it? Let's not play this game
A minute more. . . . Let's make a little song
About a lamb. . . . I'm coming over the wall,
No matter what you say—I want to be near you. . . . (*Grop-
ing his way, with arms wide before him, he strides
through the frail papers of the wall without knowing it,
and continues seeking for the wall straight across the
stage.*)
Where is the wall? (*Gropes his way back, and stands very
near* THYRSIS *without seeing him. He speaks slowly.*)
There isn't any wall,
I think. (*Takes a step forward, his foot touches* THYRSIS'
body, and he falls down beside him.)
Thyrsis, where is your cloak? Just give me
A little bit of your cloak! . . . (*Draws corner of* THYRSIS'
cloak over his shoulders, falls across THYRSIS' *body, and
dies.*)
(COTHURNUS *closes the promptbook with a bang, arises
matter-of-factly, comes downstage, and places the
table over the two bodies, drawing down the cover so
that they are hidden from any actors on the stage,
but visible to the audience, pushing in their feet and
hands with his boot. He then turns his back to the
audience, and claps his hands twice.*)
COTHURNUS: Strike the scene! (*Exit* COTHURNUS.)
(*Enter* PIERROT *and* COLUMBINE.)

PIERROT: Don't puff so, Columbine!

COLUMBINE: Lord, what a mess
  This set is in! If there's one thing I hate
  Above everything else—even more than getting my feet
    wet—
  It's clutter! He might at least have left the scene
  The way he found it . . . don't you say so, Pierrot? (*She
    picks up punch bowl. They arrange chairs as before at
    ends of table.*)

PIERROT: Well, I don't know. I think it rather diverting
  The way it is. (*Yawns, picks up confetti bowl.*)
                          Shall we begin?

COLUMBINE (*screams*):   My God!
  What's that there under the table?

PIERROT: It is the bodies
  Of the two shepherds from the other play.

COLUMBINE (*slowly*): How curious to strangle him like that,
  With colored paper ribbons.

PIERROT: Yes, and yet
  I dare say he is just as dead. (*Pauses. Calls.*) Cothurnus!
  Come drag these bodies out of here! We can't
  Sit down and eat with two dead bodies lying
  Under the table! . . . The audience wouldn't stand for it!

COTHURNUS (*off stage*): What makes you think so? Pull down
    the tablecloth
  On the other side, and hide them from the house,
  And play the farce. The audience will forget.

PIERROT: That's so. Give me a hand there, Columbine.
        (PIERROT *and* COLUMBINE *pull down the table cover in
          such a way that the two bodies are hidden from the
          house, then merrily set their bowls back on the table,
          draw up their chairs, and begin the play exactly as
          before.*)

COLUMBINE: Pierrot, a macaroon! I cannot *live*
  Without a macaroon!

PIERROT: My only love,
  You are *so* intense! . . . Is it Tuesday, Columbine?
  I'll kiss you if it's Tuesday. (*Curtains begin to close slowly.*)

COLUMBINE: It is Wednesday,
If you must know. . . . Is this my artichoke,
Or yours?
PIERROT: Ah, Columbine, as if it mattered!
Wednesday . . . Will it be Tuesday, then, tomorrow,
By any chance? . . .

THE LOTTERY

SHIRLEY JACKSON was born in San Francisco, in 1920, and received her A.B. at Syracuse University. *The Lottery*, which appeared as a short story in *The New Yorker* in 1948, brought her instant fame. Miss Jackson has written many short stories and novels, such as *Hangsaman, The Sundial*, and *The Bird's Nest*, all of them as eerie, chilling, and shocking as *The Lottery*. But she can also write deliciously humorous works, such as *Life Among the Savages* and *Raising Demons*, which deal with the activities of her five children.

The Lottery cannot be described. It must be read. As with any good literature, the play will have different meanings for different people. The emotional effect of the play, however, will be virtually the same—absolutely overwhelming.

THE LOTTERY

Adapted by Brainerd Duffield
From a story by Shirley Jackson

The scene is a bare stage with a few stones lying here and there. It represents a village square on the 27th of June of the present year. The stage is in darkness. Gradually a pool of amber light comes up at stage center. Two boys, TOMMY and DICKIE, enter, looking about on the ground. From time to time, one of them picks up a stone and puts it in his pocket. The search should continue for about a minute before either of them speaks.

TOMMY: I'm keepin' the best ones right in my pocket.

DICKIE: Me, too.

TOMMY (*indicating right stage*): We oughta make an extra pile over here. Then we could take turns guardin'.

DICKIE: Sure. Then if some other kids tried to swipe any, we'll be ready for 'em. (*He and* TOMMY *begin to build a stockpile of stones at right.*)

(*A* GIRL *somewhat younger enters and crosses to watch them, but the boys ignore her. During this leisurely pantomime, a steeple bell has begun to chime, and*

Copyright, 1953, by The Dramatic Publishing Company. Based upon the story "The Lottery," by Shirley Jackson. Copyright, 1948, by The New Yorker Magazine, Inc. All rights reserved. Permission for an amateur performance of the play may be obtained upon the payment of a royalty fee of ten dollars ($10.00) for each performance when an admission is charged or five dollars ($5.00) when no admission is charged. These fees must be paid in advance of the performance to The Dramatic Publishing Company, Chicago, Ill. Copyright covers, among other rights, the right to make copies; and the copying by hand, by typewriter, or by any other process, of "parts" or of any portion of a copyrighted play is dishonest and illegal.

the amber light widens, gradually illuminating the full stage.)

DICKIE (*muttering*): Girls always got to be hangin' around.

TOMMY: I know it. They spoil everything.

(*The little* GIRL *has attempted to assist* DICKIE *and* TOMMY *by adding a stone or two to the pile, but they turn their backs on her and, feeling hurt,* GIRL *goes out.*)

(*During the preceding, two men,* MARTIN *and* DELACROIX, *enter and cross to center, conversing quietly.*)

MARTIN (*glancing over*): Children are always the first to gather.

DELACROIX: Sure—but everybody'll be comin' now, soon as they hear the bell.

MARTIN (*scanning sky*): Beautiful day for it.

DELACROIX: Yes, fine. I don't care if it *is* my home town, we got the purtiest village green of any in the state.

(*Another man,* HUTCHISON, *has entered, leading his small son,* DAVY, *by the hand. They cross to join the others.*)

DELACROIX (*to* HUTCHISON): How are you, Bill?

HUTCHISON: Fred . . . Horace . . . (*Shakes hands with both men.*) Good to see you. You both know Davy?

MARTIN (*patting* DAVY *on head*): Well, I should hope so. How are you, Davy? (*To* HUTCHISON.) This is his first year, ain't it?

HUTCHISON: That's right. Never seen a Lottery before, have you, Dave?

(DAVY *nods.*)

MARTIN: Gonna grow up and be a good farmer like your dad? (DAVY *nods.*) That's the boy.

DELACROIX (*amiably*): My son, Chester, wants to go off to the Agricultural School and learn a lot of book rubbish. I tell him he'd do better to stay home and learn of his father, same as I did of mine.

MARTIN: That's right, too. Pitch in and help pay the taxes.

DELACROIX: I told him a farmer don't need to develop his mind, long as he builds up his muscles.

HUTCHISON: A strong back, that's what you need when you take up farmin'.

DELACROIX: Where's the wife, Bill?

HUTCHISON (*slight pause*): Oh, she'll be along. (*Frowns and looks about anxiously.*)

> (MRS. DUNBAR *and* MRS. WATSON *enter and cross toward the children. The men continue to talk in pantomime.*)

MRS. DUNBAR (*as they cross*): How does the weather suit you, Stella?

MRS. WATSON: Couldn't be better.

MRS. DUNBAR: We always seem to get good weather for the twenty-seventh. Never knew it to fail.

MRS. WATSON: Been right cold and wet for June.

> (MISS BESSOM *enters and starts toward the other women.*)

MRS. DUNBAR: Oh, that rain done us lots of harm. (*Shakes her head.*) Too *much* rain!

MRS. WATSON: Guess the Lottery ought to change our luck.

MRS. DUNBAR: That's how the sayin' goes. (*Sees* MISS BESSOM.) Look who's here. Howdy, Miss Bessom. Why, you ain't changed a particle!

MISS BESSOM (*slightly piqued*): Who ever said I had?

MRS. DUNBAR (*scrutinizing her*): They told me you were gettin' real fleshy, and it ain't so.

MRS. WATSON: Course it ain't. Hear you had a weddin' in the family.

MISS BESSOM: Yes, my sister Nina's girl got married to young Sam Gilliatt over to Rigby township.

MRS. WATSON: I s'pose that means she'll be drawin' over there from now on?

MISS BESSOM: Oh, sure! She's got to draw with *his* family now. (*To* MRS. DUNBAR.) I declare, Janey, it's been a month of Sundays since I seen you. Don't you *never* come into town?

MRS. DUNBAR: Not if I can help it. Ain't been further than m'own chicken yard—not since Decoration Day, and that's a fact.

MRS. WATSON: One thing about the Lottery, it does bring everyone out, like it or not.

MISS BESSOM: Well, Janey's got Clyde to wait on, too. How's he makin' out?

MRS. DUNBAR: Oh, he'll be fine! Except he's terrible mad to have to stay home and miss the excitement.

MISS BESSOM: I'll bet. (*She and* MRS. WATSON *cluck sympathetically, and the women continue to converse silently.*)

    (DICKIE *and* TOMMY *have drifted away by now to continue their search for stones off stage. Other* VILLAGERS *now drift in. They chat ad lib, building to a general murmur.*)

MARTIN (*on spoken cue,* "I'll bet"): Now I got that tractor, I was figurin' I might make the switch from grass to hay silage.

HUTCHISON: Costs about the same to harvest an acre, don't it?

MARTIN: Just about. Cattle don't seem to mind what they're eatin', and I thought I could get away from the risk of bad weather—

DELACROIX (*slight chuckle*): Don't you fret about the weather, Horace. "Lottery in June, corn be heavy soon."

HUTCHISON (*nodding, with a faint smile*): That's what they always told us, ain't it, Fred?

    (DELACROIX *nods.*)

MISS BESSOM (*glancing about*): Don't see Tessie Hutchison anyplace, do you?

MRS. WATSON: No, I don't. Bill's standin' right there, though, and little Davy, too.

MISS BESSOM: Got a recipe I borrowed and want to give back to her. It's for the watermelon pickles she won a prize with at the social.

    (JACK WILKINS *enters and nods to the ladies.*)

JACK: 'Scuse me, ladies. Hi, Miz Dunbar. How's Clyde doin'?

MRS. DUNBAR: Fine, thanks, Jack. Doctor's goin' to take the cast off next week.

JACK: How's he goin' to get the news today?

MRS. DUNBAR: I promised to send Tommy runnin', soon as the drawin's over.

JACK (*grinning*): That's good. (*Goes to join other men.*) (*Women beam at one another.*)

MISS BESSOM: *Such* a nice boy—Jack Wilkins.

MRS. WATSON: He's got his mother's looks and that's a blessin'.

MRS. DUNBAR: So many of the young ones seem to drift away. This place's gettin' smaller every year.

MISS BESSOM: I know it. Joe Summers told me there's less'n two hundred names on the registration this time.

MRS. DUNBAR: You don't mean it?

MRS. WATSON: Isn't that awful?

(OLD MAN WARNER *has made a slow entrance, crossing to center.* VILLAGERS *have a greeting for him as he passes.*)

DELACROIX: Well, here's Old Man Warner, lookin' spry as ever!

HUTCHISON: How're you feelin', Mr. Warner?

WARNER: Not so bad. (*Winks.*) Rheumatism comes and goes.

MARTIN: How's it seem to be the oldest citizen?

WARNER: You don't hear *me* complainin'.

HUTCHISON (*chuckling*): How many Lotteries does this make?

WARNER: I'm eighty-one last November. Seen my first at the age of five. You figure it out.

DELACROIX: Never missed one in all those years!

JACK: He hears very good, too, don't he?

DELACROIX: Oh, he's a marvel!

WARNER: And I'll be comin' back for a few more!

JACK (*grinning*): You tell 'em, old-timer!

MARTIN (*calling across to women*): Hear that? Old Man Warner says he's good for a few more! (*General murmur of approval from others on stage.*)

MRS. WATSON: He's seen seventy-six of them.

MRS. DUNBAR: Imagine!

WARNER: Oh, you fellers ought to been here in the old days. Not like now. Lottery meant somethin' when I was a boy. (BELVA SUMMERS *has entered, and stops at one side of the stage, opposite the other women. She wears black, and carries some knitting with her, at which she works during the following action. She remains by herself, content to speak to no one.)*

MISS BESSOM: Almost time to get started.

MRS. WATSON (*looking off*): Guess we're goin' to, Miss Bessom. There's Joe Summers now, on the post-office steps.

MRS. DUNBAR: He's bringin' out the box.

MISS BESSOM: Where's his sister? She here?

MRS. DUNBAR (*nodding toward* BELVA): There she is. Off by herself, as usual.

MISS BESSOM (*looking at* BELVA): Beats me how he can stay so cheerful with that one to put up with.

MRS. WATSON: I'd hate to have her in *my* house.

(The murmur of the VILLAGERS *swells.* DICKIE *and* TOMMY *have entered again. They see a stone and both grab simultaneously for it. They tussle with each other to gain possession of the stone.)*

TOMMY: You didn't, neither! I seen it first!

DICKIE: You give that back!

TOMMY: The heck I will! (*Shoves him.*)

DICKIE: Cut it out, will you? Watch who you're shovin'—

(There is a tussle again. MRS. DUNBAR *comes forward and grasps* TOMMY *by the wrist.)*

MRS. DUNBAR: You stop that!

TOMMY: Leggo, Ma! I seen it first, honest!

MRS. DUNBAR: Never you mind. You got stones aplenty!

(MRS. WATSON *attempts to collar* DICKIE, *but he escapes.*)

MRS. WATSON: You come here to me. Wait till I get you home.

MARTIN (*sharply, to* DICKIE): Obey your mother. Mind what I say.

DICKIE (*dutifully*): Yes, Uncle Horace. (*Crosses to* MRS. WATSON, *unwillingly.*)

JACK (*pointing off with gesture of thumb*): Joe Summers is comin'. It won't be long now.

DELACROIX (*good-humoredly*): We'd better line up by families and wait for the bad news.

(VILLAGERS *begin to shift and reassemble according to family groups.*)

HUTCHISON (*to* DAVY): Now, Davy, stick close to me. There's nothin' to be a-scared of.

(JOE SUMMERS *enters, crosses to center. He is carrying a large black wooden box and a wooden paddle. A* TOWNSMAN *follows with a high stool, on which* JOE *places the black box in a dignified and solemn manner.*)

JOE: Thank you, Norbert.

(*During* JOE's *entrance, there has been a growing murmur from* VILLAGERS.)

VILLAGERS (*ad libbing upon* JOE's *entrance*): Here he comes. Howdy, Mr. Summers. There's the head man comin'. He's got the old black box. Howdy, Joe. Let's get goin'.

(JOE *takes a sheaf of papers from his hip pocket and places them on box. He pauses now to mop his forehead with a handkerchief. Most of the* VILLAGERS *are in small groups covering right half of stage. The remainder of the left side of stage is clear, except for* BELVA.)

JOE (*brightly*): Little late today, folks. (*Waves to* JACK.) Here, you! The Wilkins boy. Give me a hand and stir these names up. Stir 'em good and hard. (JACK *stirs box with paddle, which* JOE *hands him. Then* JOE *turns to* TOWNSMAN.) Norbert, you hold it steady for him. Better use both hands. (TOWNSMAN, *using both hands to steady box, helps* JACK *with stirring business.* JOE *notices* BELVA, *and moves toward her, passing others en route.*) How are you, folks?

VILLAGERS: Mr. Summers! Howdy, Joe. How are you? (BELVA, *occupied with her knitting, awaits him with an enigmatic smile. During scene which follows between* JOE *and* BELVA, VILLAGERS *converse in pantomime.*)

BELVA (*drily*): Almost ready, are you, Joe? Hope you haven't forgotten, and left my name out.

JOE: No, Belva. You're down there. I just been checkin' the list.

BELVA (*looking over his shoulder*): Oh, you got a long ways to go yet. A terrible responsibility. Everybody says so. (*Shakes head with mock sympathy.*) Poor Joe Summers. Doin' his duty. And with that naggin' sister, too.

JOE (*grimly*): Well, if everybody says so, Belva, there must be somethin' to it.

BELVA (*knitting as she talks*): I must say *I* enjoy myself. Watchin' an important man at work. Joe Summers—up there runnin' things—devotin' all his time and energy to civic activities. And how you love it!

JOE (*glancing over at* VILLAGERS): You'd oblige me, Belva, by lowerin' your voice a little.

BELVA (*smiling*): Why should I? Nobody asked you to come over and speak to me.

JOE: You might give a thought to the neighbors.

BELVA (*contemptuously*): The neighbors! If everybody wasn't so scared of their neighbors, maybe we'd give up some heathen customs that don't make sense any more. Half the young folks growin' up don't have the faintest notion what a Lottery stands for.

JOE (*turning away*): Oh, what's the use of talkin' to you!

BELVA: There's no tellin' these days where the wisdom stops and superstition begins.

JOE (*turning back to her*): The Lottery has got to be taken serious. People get set in a way of doin' things and you can't change 'em. It's human nature.

BELVA (*stops knitting, speaking softly, but with intensity*): I don't like this town nor anybody in it. But you're the worst of 'em, Joe Summers. You drove him away. Our own brother and you drove him away.

JOE: It was more your doin' than mine. You're the one brought him up to be a weaklin' and a coward. You started him goin' out on the street and preachin' against tradition.

BELVA: You call that cowardly? It takes a *brave* man to say what he thinks, when every hand is against him.

JOE (*doggedly*): He left of his own accord. I didn't send him.

BELVA: It takes real courage to fight prejudice on your own doorstep. (*With contempt.*) It's you and the rest of 'em that are the cowards.

JOE: Every day of my life I have to listen to your craziness. If you want to go off lookin' for him, Belva, I'll give you the money. Take the mornin' train. I'll even draw alone in the Lottery from now on. There—I couldn't offer more'n that, could I?

BELVA: I'm not goin' anywhere. I'm goin' to stay right here and wait. (*Looks up and straight at him.*) Because sooner or later your name might come up. I wouldn't want to miss that day.

> (JOE *turns away abruptly and goes back to center.* BELVA *stands motionless for a moment or two and then resumes her knitting.*)

JOE: All right, Jack, that's good enough, I'm sure.

JACK: Glad to do it, Mr. Summers.

JOE (*to nearby* WOMEN VILLAGERS): Think it's stirred enough, ladies?

MRS. WATSON (*chuckling*): Don't worry, Joe. We trust you.

MRS. DUNBAR: Oh, Joe knows what he's doin', all right.

> (*General laughter from* WOMEN VILLAGERS.)

WARNER: Hear those women hollerin' and cacklin'. They never would have stood for that in the old days.

DELACROIX: Seen some changes, ain't you, Mr. Warner?

WARNER: Bad enough to see Joe Summers up there crackin' jokes. Nobody shows respect for the ceremony. Just go through the motions nowadays.

> (JACK *has crossed to where* WARNER *is standing.*)

JACK: How was it different, Mr. Warner?

WARNER: Oh, it was *some* different. Everybody had to stand just so. And before the drawin', the head man spoke his piece real solemn-like. Had a regular recitation went with it.

HUTCHISON (*scanning* VILLAGERS): Now where in tarnation is my wife?

> (*Chuckle from those near him.*)

MARTIN: Bill Hutchison lost his better half.

HUTCHISON (*to* MRS. DUNBAR): Janey, you seen her?

MRS. DUNBAR: No, I ain't, Bill, and I been lookin', too.

MARTIN: Guess she ain't gonna make it.

MISS BESSOM: Late for the Lottery. Can you beat that?

HUTCHISON: I don't know what's got into the woman.

DELACROIX: That black box has seen a lot of service.

WARNER: Yessir. That box was here afore I was born, and afore my father was.

JACK: Just imagine.

WARNER: Story goes it was made out of the pieces of the first box that ever was used.

DELACROIX: Makes you think, don't it?

WARNER: Goes way back to the days when they first settled down to make a village here.

JACK: Seems like we ought to be ready to build us a new one.

WARNER (shocked): No, boy! Don't say that. Not even jokin'.

DELACROIX: No, Jack. We don't want to upset tradition more'n we have to. Long as it holds together, we ain't gonna change it.

WARNER: I can recollect when they used to use wooden chips 'stead of paper to write the names on.

JACK: What do you know? Wooden chips!

WARNER (nodding): I was real little, but I remember.

(JOE has been busy checking his list, looking about and making notations on the sheets of paper. Occasionally he consults with one of the VILLAGERS close by him.)

JOE (raising voice): Now, folks, I'm just about ready to declare this Lottery open. But you know how I always got this last-minute fussin' to do. Want to make sure the list is accurate—with all the heads of families and members of each household in each family.

MRS. DUNBAR: You go right ahead, Mr. Summers.

MRS. WATSON: Joe never made a mistake yet.

(TESSIE HUTCHISON, wearing an apron over her house dress, enters.)

MRS. DUNBAR: Why, Tessie! Where you been?

TESSIE: Clean forgot what day it was. (Other women close by laugh softly.) Thought Bill was out back stackin' wood. But I looked out the window and seen little Davy was gone. Then I remembered it was the twenty-seventh—and come a-runnin'. (She is drying her hands on her apron as she speaks.)

MRS. DUNBAR: You made it all right, though. Joe is still checkin' his list.

TESSIE: Seems like there's no time at all between Lotteries any more. Seems like we barely got through with the last one.

MRS. DUNBAR: Time sure goes fast.

TESSIE (*glancing around*): Where's Bill at? Oh, I see him. 'Scuse me, Janey.

    (VILLAGERS *make way for her as she moves to join* HUTCHISON.)

VILLAGERS: Hey, Hutchison! Here she comes! Here's your missus, Bill! Look, Bill! She made it after all!

TESSIE (*bending down, to* DAVY): Give Mama a kiss. (DAVY *kisses her.*) That's my good boy. (*Looks at* HUTCHISON *for a moment. He smiles faintly and takes her hand.*)

HUTCHISON: So you got here, did you?

JOE (*calling amiably*): Thought we were goin' to have to get on without you, Tessie.

TESSIE (*with forced pleasantness*): Wouldn't have me leave my dishes in the sink, would you, Joe?

JOE: No, ma'am.

    (*General ripple of laughter from* VILLAGERS.)

HUTCHISON: You stay put, Dave, while I talk with your mother. (DAVY *joins other children, as* HUTCHISON *brings* TESSIE *to a spot where they talk somewhat apart from other* VILLAGERS. *He is not angry, but seems deeply concerned and worried.*) What ever kept you?

TESSIE: I don't know, Bill. I just wasn't thinkin', I guess.

HUTCHISON: That story's all right for the women. I know better. You knew the Lottery was today.

TESSIE: Well, it don't matter now. So long as I'm here.

HUTCHISON: What about Davy? Why'd you try to hide him?

TESSIE: Hide him? I didn't hide him. What makes you say that?

HUTCHISON: I found him in the stable loft. He said you told him to wait there—

TESSIE: Yes, but I was goin' to get him, Bill. I was goin' to bring him—honest.

HUTCHISON: What reason did you have to put him there?

TESSIE: Oh, Bill, he's such a little boy! And his birthday just last month. I hate to see the children takin' part in grown-up ructions before they've even put aside their toys.

HUTCHISON: I went through it when I was little.

TESSIE: I know, Bill. I guess I was born and brought up with it, same as yourself.

HUTCHISON: Then how did you think you could get away with such a thing? You know Davy's name has to be there along with ours. And you know how careful Joe Summers is. Why, we'd have been a laughin'stock in front of everybody.

TESSIE: But I told you I intended to bring him. You got to believe me, Bill.

HUTCHISON: Talkin' a lot of sentimental tommyrot. I always gave you credit for more sense than some of these other females. What's come over you lately, anyway?

TESSIE: I told you—nothin'.

HUTCHISON: Next thing you'll be sayin' we ought to give up Lotteries altogether—like poor Joe Summers' sister.

TESSIE: Well, I've not come to that yet. But some places have given them up. Lots of little towns up to the north—

HUTCHISON: No good'll come of it, either. You wait and see.

TESSIE: I don't say it will. No, I reckon the Lottery serves its useful purpose. When a custom's been handed down from generation to generation, there must be good in it.

HUTCHISON (wagging head, grinning): Then you shouldn't be so cussed busy, findin' fault.

JOE (clearing throat): Well, now, guess we better get started —get this over with—so's we can get back to work. Anybody ain't here?

VILLAGERS: Dunbar! Clyde Dunbar! Dunbar ain't here!

JOE (glancing at list): Clyde Dunbar—that's right. He's broke his leg, hasn't he? Who's drawin' for him?

MRS. DUNBAR: Me, I guess.

JOE: Wife draws for husband. Don't have a grown boy to do if for you, Janey?

MRS. DUNBAR: Ralph's not but sixteen yet. Guess I got to fill in for the old man this year.

(Mild chuckle from VILLAGERS.)

JOE (*making note*): Right. Jack Wilkins, you're drawin' this year?

JACK (*blinking nervously*): Yessir. I'm drawin' for my mother and me.

MARTIN: Good fellow, Jack. Glad to see your mother's got a man to do it.

JOE: Well, I guess that's everyone. (*With a wink.*) Old Man Warner make it?

WARNER (*raising hand*): Here!

JOE (*nodding*): Knew you would. (*Raps on box.*) All ready? (*Whisper runs through* VILLAGERS; *then a hush follows. Everyone is quite serious now. There is no more laughter.*) Now, I'll read off the names—heads of families first—and the men come up and take a paper out of the box. Keep the paper folded in your hand without lookin' at it until everyone has had a turn. Everything clear? (*VILLAGERS are silent, but nervous, wetting their lips, not looking around or moving.* JOE *reads from list.*) Adams. (*A man disengages himself from crowd, comes forward, reaches into black box and takes out a folded paper.* JOE *greets him.*) Hi, Steve. (*Holding paper firmly, the man goes back to his place and stands, not looking down at his hand.* JOE *calls next name.*) Allen. (*Another man comes to box, repeating same business.*) How are you, Mr. Allen? (*Now, as scene continues,* JOE *continues to call out names. Each time, someone comes forward, reaches into box, takes out folded piece of paper and returns to his place, not looking down at hand holding paper. As dialogue of* VILLAGERS *breaks into scene, overlapping* JOE's *voice, calling of the names becomes less distinct, becoming sort of a muted background to* VILLAGERS' *dialogue.*) Appleby . . . Barrows . . . Burgess . . . Caswell . . . Collins . . .

DELACROIX: They do say that over in the north village, they're talkin' of givin' up the Lottery.

WARNER: Pack of crazy fools! Listenin' to the young folks— nothin's good enough for *them*. Next thing you know, they'll want to go back to livin' in caves—nobody work any more—live *that* way for a while.

DELACROIX: That's right, Mr. Warner.

WARNER: First thing you know we'd all be eatin' stewed chickweed and acorns. There's *always* been a Lottery.

JOE: Dunbar . . .

MRS. WATSON: Go on, Janey. That's you.

MISS BESSOM (*as* MRS. DUNBAR *crosses to draw*): There she goes. . . .

JOE: Foster . . . Graves . . . Hutchison . . .

MRS. WATSON: Where do they keep the black box in between times?

MISS BESSOM: It varies. Sometimes one place—sometimes another.

MRS. WATSON: I heard it spent one whole winter in Mr. Graves's barn.

MISS BESSOM: Another year, Clem Martin put it on a shelf in his grocery and left it set there.

MRS. WATSON: Yep. I recall that time.

JOE: Tatum . . . Townsend . . . Tuttle . . . Vincent . . .

MRS. DUNBAR (*to* TOMMY): I wish they'd hurry.

TOMMY: They're almost through, Ma.

MRS. DUNBAR: You get ready to run and tell Dad.

JOE: Warner . . . Howdy, Mr. Warner.

(WARNER *takes slip and returns to his place.*)

WARNER: Got mine. Seventy-seventh year I been in the Lottery.

JOE: Watson . . . Hi, Stella.

MRS. WATSON (*drawing*): Hi, Joe.

JOE: Wilkins . . .

MISS BESSOM (*as* JACK *crosses to draw*): Don't be nervous, Jack.

JOE (*kindly*): Take your time, son.

JACK (*drawing*): Thanks, Mr. Summers.

JOE (*checking off list*): Now, that's all. (*A breathless pause.* JOE *draws and holds up his hand with his slip of paper in it.*) All right, fellows. (*For a moment, no one moves; then there is a rustle as all the slips are opened.*)

VILLAGERS (*whispering*): Who is it? Who's got it? Is it the Dunbars? Is it the Watsons? (*Then, louder ad libs are heard, building to an excited climax.*) It's Hutchison! It's Bill! Bill Hutchison's got it! Hutchison!

    (*The* HUTCHISONS *break away from others and form a small group.*)

MRS. DUNBAR (*excitedly*): Go tell your father!

    (TOMMY *takes a last awestruck look at* BILL HUTCHISON, *where he stands quietly flanked by* TESSIE *and* DAVY, *then* TOMMY *runs out.* HUTCHISON *is staring at bit of paper in his hand.* VILLAGERS *are silent again, all eyes on* HUTCHISON *family.*)

TESSIE (*shouting suddenly*): Joe Summers! You didn't give him time enough to take any paper he wanted. I saw you. It wasn't fair!

MRS. WATSON: Be a good sport, Tessie.

MISS BESSOM: All of us took the same chance.

HUTCHISON: You hush up, Tessie.

JOE: Well, everyone, that was done pretty fast, and now we've got to be hurryin' a little more to get done in time. (*Consulting list.*) Bill, you draw for the Hutchison family. You got any other households in the Hutchisons?

TESSIE (*shrilly*): There's Don and Eva! Make *them* take their chance!

JOE (*gently*): Daughters draw with their husbands' families. You know that as well as anyone, Tessie.

TESSIE: It wasn't fair!

HUTCHISON: I guess there's just the three of us, Joe. Eva draws with her husband. That's only as it should be.

JOE: Then, as far as drawin' for families is concerned, it's you, and, as far as drawin' for households is concerned, that's you, too. Right?

HUTCHISON: Right.

JOE: How many kids, Bill?

HUTCHISON: Just the one. Little Davy here. Bill, Jr., he died when he was a baby.

JOE: All right, then. Jack, you got some blank tickets back? (JACK *holds up two blank slips of paper which he has taken from some of the* VILLAGERS.) Put them in the box, then. Take Bill's and put it in. (JACK *does so.*)

TESSIE (*out of the ensuing silence*): I think we ought to start over. (*As quietly as she can.*) I tell you, it wasn't fair! You didn't give him time enough to choose. Everybody saw that. (*Appealing.*) Listen, everybody!

> (JACK *has stepped back from box. Other* VILLAGERS *have crumpled their own slips and let them drop to ground.*)

JOE: Ready, Bill? (HUTCHISON *takes a quick glance at his wife and son and then nods.*) Remember, take the slips and keep them folded until each of you has taken one. Jack, you help little Davy. (JACK *takes* DAVY's *hand and leads him to box.*) Take a paper out of the box, Dave. Take just *one* paper. (DAVY *does so.*) That's right. Jack, you hold it for him. (JACK *takes paper and holds it carefully.*) Tessie next. (TESSIE *hesitates for a moment, looking around defiantly, then she sets her lips and goes to box. She snatches out a paper and holds it behind her.*) Bill . . . (HUTCHISON *reaches into box and brings out last slip of paper. The* VILLAGERS *are silent and tense.*)

MISS BESSOM (*breaking silence*): I hope it isn't little Dave.

> (VILLAGERS *begin to whisper.*)

WARNER (*clearly*): It's not the way it used to be. People ain't the same way they used to be.

JOE: All right. Open the papers. Jack, you open little Dave's. (JACK *opens paper, holds it up, and a sigh of relief goes through* VILLAGERS *as they see that it is blank.* JOE *turns to* TESSIE.) Tessie . . . (*There is a pause.* TESSIE *does not move to open her slip of paper.* JOE *turns to* HUTCHISON, *who unfolds his paper and shows it. It is blank.* JOE *speaks to* TESSIE *in a hushed voice.*) It's Tessie. Show us her paper, Bill. (HUTCHISON *turns to* TESSIE *and forces her slip of paper out of her hand. It has a black spot on it. He holds it up. A murmur goes through* VILLAGERS. JOE *comes forward.*) All right, folks. Let's finish quickly.

> (JACK *carries black box, paddle, and stool off and presently returns to rejoin* VILLAGERS.)

MRS. WATSON (*excitedly*): Come on, Janey. Hurry up! Come on, Miss Bessom.

MISS BESSOM: I can't move as fast as I used to.

> (VILLAGERS *move toward front of stage, some of them picking up stones as they come.* DICKIE *gives little* DAVY *a fistful of stones. As* VILLAGERS *shift about,* TESSIE *backs away, like a trapped animal, until she is alone at the center of a cleared space at rear.* VILLAGERS *are grouped at both sides of stage. Now* TESSIE *holds out her hands in a desperate appeal, as* VILLAGERS *turn to face her and begin slowly to close in.*)

TESSIE: It isn't fair! It wasn't done fair!

HUTCHISON: Be quiet, Tess. We got to do this. (*Throws a stone, and* TESSIE *flinches, putting her hand to her brow.*) Come on. Come on, everyone.

> (DAVY *throws his fistful of stones.* TESSIE *utters a cry and sinks to her knees.* VILLAGERS *throw stones.*)

TESSIE: It isn't fair! It isn't right! (*Shields her face as* VILLAGERS *continue to throw stones at her.*)

> (BELVA *has crossed the stage, thrusting* JOE *aside in passing. She goes out without looking at spectacle on stage. By now,* VILLAGERS *have hemmed in their victim, cutting her off from view. The clamor of voices builds, as does the ferocity of the stone-throwing.*)

VILLAGERS: Come on! Get it over with! Hit her! That's the way! Hit her, everybody! Get it over! (*Lights dim out, and with darkness comes a low rumble of thunder. Voices of the* VILLAGERS *stop abruptly. Silence.*)

RED CARNATIONS

GLENN HUGHES, head of the department of drama at the University of Washington, was born in Cozad, Nebraska, in 1894, and received his education at Stanford and the University of Washington. He has taught at the State Normal School, in Bellingham, Washington, and at Scripps College. At the University of Washington he operates an arena theatre and a showboat theatre, which are open all year round. Mr. Hughes has written poetry and several plays. A recent book is *A History of the American Theatre*.

Red Carnations is a pleasant comedy built around three enjoyable people. The play reads well because the characters are intelligent and because the plot unfolds quickly and logically. The sheik costume mentioned in the play was popular during the "roaring twenties," when this play was written. Rudolph Valentino played the title role in *The Sheik*, a silent movie. He affected a great many people—even young men, who grew long sideburns and danced slinky tangos as Valentino did.

RED CARNATIONS

Glenn Hughes

The scene is a secluded corner in a city park. It is about four o'clock in the afternoon. The MAN is seated at one end of a bench in the center of the stage, smoking a cigar. He is middle-aged, prosperous in appearance, and wears a red carnation in his lapel. The BOY enters immediately after rise of curtain. He is about twenty, well dressed without being foppish. He, too, wears a red carnation in his lapel. He looks around as if expecting to meet someone. He and the MAN exchange glances, none too friendly. The BOY assumes an easy posture. He lights a cigarette.

MAN: Might as well sit down. Plenty of room on the bench.

BOY (*starting suddenly, as though thinking of other things*): Oh, thanks. Thanks very much. I don't mind standing. It will only be for a minute or two.

MAN (*looking quizzically at him*): You're not expecting to meet a woman, then?

BOY (*diffidently*): Well—why, yes, as a matter of fact, I am.

MAN (*wisely*): You are an optimist.

Copyright, 1925, by Samuel French, in *One-Act Plays for Stage and Study*, 2nd Series; copyright, 1953 (in renewal), by Samuel French. All rights reserved. CAUTION: Professionals and amateurs are hereby warned that *Red Carnations*, being fully protected under the copyright laws of the United States of America, the British Empire, including the Dominion of Canada, and all other countries of the Copyright Union, is subject to a royalty. All rights, including professional, amateur, motion pictures, recitation, public reading, radio and television broadcasting and the rights of translation into foreign languages are strictly reserved. Amateurs may give stage production of this play upon payment of royalty of Five Dollars for each performance, one week before the play is to be given, to Samuel French, Inc., at 25 West 45th St., New York 36, N.Y., or 7623 Sunset Blvd., Hollywood 46, Cal., or if in Canada to Samuel French (Canada) Ltd., at 27 Grenville St., Toronto, Ont.

BOY: Pardon me?

MAN: I merely remarked that you were an optimist.

BOY: I'm afraid I don't understand.

MAN: No; but you will later on, when your one or two minutes have turned into one or two hours. I see you don't know very much about the feminine sex.

BOY: Perhaps not. On the other hand, it strikes me that your remarks are rather personal.

MAN: Well, the only remarks worth making *are* personal. However, if you prefer talking about the *weather*—

BOY (*who is looking at his watch*): Five minutes past . . . (*Looks off stage, then vaguely remembers the* MAN's *speech.*) I—ah, yes, quite right. I am sorry. I was thinking of something else.

MAN: So I perceive. She is already five minutes late.

BOY (*surprised*): How did you know that?

MAN: Experience. Experience. Romance is like history; it repeats itself. Besides, I am in the same boat with you. My appointment was for five minutes ago, also. The only difference is that I am not worrying about it, and you are.

BOY (*crossing to bench*): I think I will sit down, if you don't mind. It's a devil of a bore standing first on one foot and then on the other. (*He sits down on opposite end of bench.*)

MAN: Have a cigar?

BOY: No, thanks; I'll just finish this cigarette. (*He turns directly to the* MAN, *and as he does so, his eye lights on the carnation in the other's lapel. He shows annoyance. He takes the one from his own lapel, hesitates a moment, then replaces it. The* MAN, *noticing the action, smells his.*)

MAN: Pretty flowers, carnations, aren't they? Wonderful fragrance they have, too. I am very fond of them, and I see your taste runs in the same direction.

BOY (*disturbed*): Yes, indeed. Very fine flower. But I—well, I hope you won't think me silly, but as a matter of fact, if it doesn't make any difference to you, would you mind keeping your carnation out of sight for a while, until—well, just to be a good sport, if you would hide it for a few minutes, I'd be very grateful.

MAN (*good-naturedly*): Now, I'd like nothing better than to do you a favor, Mr.—Mr.—

BOY: Smith.

MAN: Thank you. Mr. Smith. That's strange. Very strange!

BOY: What is strange? The name of Smith?

MAN: Yes, strange that you should have it, when that is my name, too.

BOY: Oh, your name is Smith, too? Well, after all, there are lots of us in the world—lots of us Smiths, I mean—so there is no reason why such a coincidence—

MAN: Of course not, of course not—only, I was thinking about the red carnations.

BOY: Well, I don't see—

MAN: I may be mistaken, of course. But two Smiths, meeting in the same spot at the same hour, both wearing red carnations! You must confess it's a bit—

BOY: By Jove! So it is! (*He looks intently, suspiciously, at the* MAN.) I wish you could move to another spot, or take that flower out of your lapel, or— It isn't absolutely necessary for you to wear it, is it?

MAN: But it is! Absolutely! And you are going to cause me all sorts of trouble if *you* don't move, or change your name, or at least throw away your carnation.

BOY: I shall do nothing of the kind. I can't! My Lord, man, she doesn't know me! That is, she doesn't know what I look like. That is why she asked me to wear a red carnation.

MAN: But that is exactly *my* predicament. The woman *I* am to meet does not know *me* by sight. She asked *me* to wear a red carnation. So you see, I can't help you out. After all, a man must look to his own affairs first.

BOY: What beastly coincidence! (*Brightening.*) Oh, well, it may not matter. One of them will arrive before the other does. If you recognize her as your—ah—friend, you can speak up at once, and get on out of the way. If mine should arrive first, I shall do the same.

MAN (*thinking deeply*): Hmmm! You know your—ah—*friend*, when you see her, do you?

BOY (*startled*): Why—well—in a way. That is, her eyes. I would know her eyes anywhere.

MAN: Her eyes! Good heavens!

BOY: Well, you must understand that when a woman is in costume, and wears a mask—

MAN: In costume, and masked!

BOY: Certainly. Why not? I met her at a masked ball. There is nothing unusual about that, is there?

MAN: This is uncanny! Positively uncanny! (*Dramatically.*) Tell me one thing: what kind of costume did she wear?

BOY: She was dressed as the Queen of Sheba.

MAN: My gosh!

BOY: What's the matter?

MAN (*trying to recover*): Nothing! Nothing. (*More to himself.*) I won't believe it! It's impossible!

BOY: What is impossible?

MAN: Nothing is impossible!

> (*The GIRL trips briskly in. She is dressed smartly in afternoon clothes, and wears a hat which shades her eyes, with perhaps a little veil dangling from the brim. She pauses, looks shyly at the MAN and BOY, who turn and stare at her, bewildered. Neither the MAN nor the BOY makes a move. They eye each other. The GIRL, with an embarrassed little cough, walks on past them, not stopping until she has crossed the stage. The MAN and BOY look after her, then at each other.*)

MAN: Is she—?

BOY (*looking hard at the girl*): I think so. But confound it! I couldn't see her eyes.

MAN: I am certain she is my friend.

BOY: What? You are!

MAN: From the way she holds her head.

BOY: But I am quite sure I recognize her as my friend. If I could only get a glimpse of her eyes!

MAN: The only way to settle the matter, as I see it, is to call her by name. I suggest you try first.

BOY: I can't. I don't know her name.

MAN: You mean you don't know the name of the woman you were to meet here?

BOY: She wouldn't tell me what her name was. You'll have to go ahead and see if she belongs to you.

MAN: I must confess, this grows more and more unbelievable. The truth of the matter is, I don't know the name of the one *I* was to meet.

BOY: Good heavens! This is awful! Look here. We can't stand around all day debating the question. One of us must go ahead and break the ice. If he makes a mistake, he can retire and give the right one a chance.

(*The* GIRL, *meanwhile, has been powdering her nose, looking at herself in a tiny mirror, and from time to time glancing over her shoulder at the* MAN *and* BOY.)

MAN: A very good solution. You, having suggested the plan, should have the privilege of trying it out. I shall wait here where I can keep an eye on you, though. Good luck to you!

BOY (*starting toward the* GIRL, *then turning back to the* MAN): But what the deuce am I to say to her?

MAN: Ask her if you are the man she expected to meet here.

BOY: But what if she doesn't know?

MAN: What?

BOY: She may not know whether I am the one or not.

MAN: That is her worry—not yours. You can at least give her a chance to claim you.

BOY: But she might make a mistake!

MAN: Oh, Lord! Are you going or aren't you?

BOY: Yes, I am. (*Starts again toward her. Turns back.*) Don't leave until I've found out, will you?

MAN: No, no! Of course not! Go on!

BOY: I'm going. (*He crosses to within a couple of steps of the* GIRL. *Pauses. She looks around at him and smiles prettily. He clears his throat and speaks.*) How do you do!

GIRL (*sweetly*): How do you do?

BOY (*cautiously*): I beg your pardon, but were you—that is— am I—what I mean to say is—I was expecting to meet someone here, and—I was wondering—

GIRL: Yes, I noticed you were wondering.

BOY (*disconcerted*): I suppose you think I am an idiot, but you see—well, with both of us wearing red carnations, and being here at the same spot at the same time, and—

GIRL: Yes, I observed that both of you were wearing red carnations. I think they are quite becoming.

BOY (*embarrassed*): Thanks very much, but— Well, that isn't exactly the point. (*He laughs nervously.*)

GIRL (*laughing with him*): No, I suppose it isn't.

BOY: It's awfully difficult to explain.

GIRL (*sympathetically*): Yes, isn't it? (*She laughs again prettily.*)

BOY: Of course, if you really are the *one*—that is, the one I was to meet here, then maybe you will understand. Do you?

GIRL: No; I don't think I do.

BOY (*crestfallen*): Oh! Then, I suppose you aren't the one?

GIRL: The one—what?

BOY: The one—I was to meet. Are you?

GIRL: Why, I'm sure I don't know.

BOY (*brightening*): Then you *were* to meet someone?

GIRL: Oh, yes.

BOY: That helps some. And would you know him if you were to see him?

GIRL (*shyly*): I'm afraid not. That is why I asked him to wear a red carnation.

BOY: Ah! That much is settled. But, of course, *he* (*pointing to* MAN) is wearing a red carnation, too.

GIRL: Yes. That does make it rather complicated, doesn't it?

BOY: Rather! So, you see, we'll have to think of some other way to identify him.

GIRL: Identify which? You or him?

BOY (*after a moment of bewilderment*): Me. No, not necessarily. Either one. The one you were intending to meet.

GIRL: That's it! We must identify the one I was intending to meet.

BOY: Can't you think of some way?

GIRL. I don't know. (*She thinks.*) Oh, of course! Why didn't

I think of that before? (*Her face lights up.*) I can ask you your name.

BOY: Splendid! Go ahead and ask me.

GIRL: Well, then, is your name Smith?

BOY (*eagerly*): Yes!

MAN (*who has been standing apart, watching the scene with amusement, now speaks up loudly and emphatically*): So is mine!

BOY (*turning quickly, startled, to look at* MAN): Yes, yes. (*Then to* GIRL.) You see, that is another trouble I—

GIRL: What? Is his name Smith, too? Good heavens!

BOY: That's the point. (*Excitedly.*) If his name wasn't Smith there wouldn't be any difficulty at all.

GIRL (*to* BOY): But how do you know *you* aren't the one to blame?

MAN (*coming forward slightly*): Exactly. If *your* name (*to* BOY) wasn't Smith, there would be no trouble whatever. I insist that you share the blame, at least.

GIRL: It's all a question of who is the original Smith.

BOY: What do you mean by the original Smith?

MAN: From the standpoint of time, I certainly am the original Smith. I carried the name long before *you* (*to* BOY) were born.

BOY: Ridiculous! What has that to do with it? The original Smith in this instance is the one who had the appointment with Miss— I beg your pardon, but you never told me your name.

GIRL: No; I didn't, did I? (*She laughs contagiously.*) It seems a bit odd, but—as a matter of fact, I am not sure that I ever told *you* anything. Perhaps it was *him* (*pointing to* MAN) that I talked with.

BOY: Where? When?

GIRL: At the masked ball Friday night.

MAN: Why, of course, I am the one you talked with.

BOY (*looking at* MAN *in amazement*): You! You were there, too! This is unbearable!

GIRL: Why shouldn't he have been there? He had as much right to be there as you had.

MAN: Certainly. Why should one Smith have preference over another?

BOY: I'll go mad in a minute! Look here! (*To the* GIRL.) You have got to settle this one way or the other. I refuse to stand here all day being made a fool of.

MAN: If you feel that way, you should leave at once. That would clear things up considerably.

BOY (*pugnaciously*): I shan't leave. Don't think you can get rid of me as easily as that! (*To the* GIRL.) There is some way for you to solve this problem. If you talked with one of us last Friday at the masked ball, you must remember something that would tell you which of us it was. We are nothing alike. Look at him! (*Points to* MAN, *who assumes a heroic pose for a moment.*) How could you mistake him for me?

GIRL: But you forget that you were both in costume, and wore masks.

MAN: Quite true. Costumes and masks make a very complete disguise.

BOY: But costumes aren't all alike. I was dressed as a *sheik!*

MAN: So was I!

BOY: What! (*He is almost crying with rage.*) You weren't! This is too much! I won't believe it!

MAN: But I tell you I was. There is nothing remarkable about going to a fancy-dress ball in a sheik's costume. So far as I know, no one has a patent on that idea.

GIRL: Now that you mention it, I distinctly remember noticing more than one sheik at that ball.

BOY (*vehemently to* GIRL): And I suppose you talked to every sheik you saw!

GIRL: Well, naturally, I couldn't be sure. It would be very easy to mistake one sheik for another.

BOY: And you told them all the same thing, I suppose?

GIRL: What do you mean?

BOY (*sarcastically*): You invited every sheik you talked with to meet you here in this corner of the park at four o'clock, and to wear a red carnation in his coat lapel?

GIRL (*with spirit*): I did no such thing. The idea! He was the one who asked *me* to meet *him*.

MAN: Certainly. I asked her to meet me here today.

BOY: But so did I!

GIRL: You are both sure you asked me?

MAN: Positive!

BOY: Certain!

GIRL: But how *can* you be? How do you know that one of you didn't ask some other girl?

BOY: Weren't you dressed like the Queen of Sheba?

GIRL: Yes. That's right.

MAN: Of course she was. That's how she caught my eye.

BOY: Oh, damnation! I can't stand this! (*Turning on the* MAN, *savagely.*) How do you know there wasn't another Queen of Sheba at the ball?

MAN: Perhaps there was. But the point is that there is only *one* Queen of Sheba *here*.

BOY: And you think you asked *this* Queen of Sheba (*indicating the* GIRL) to meet you here in the park at four o'clock today?

MAN (*sarcastically*): Your mind grows clearer every minute!

BOY: And you told her you would wear a red carnation in your coat lapel?

MAN: That is my customary method of identifying myself.

BOY: Well, I *know* this is the Queen of Sheba that I talked with. I can tell by her eyes. I would know those eyes anywhere. It means that she has made fools of us both, for I made the same proposals to her that you did, and she certainly accepted them.

GIRL: Oh, I am sorry! I thought you two were the same man.

BOY (*to the* MAN, *dryly*): She thought we were the same man!

MAN: The compliment was mutual, at any rate.

BOY: Did you think we stuttered, that we should ask you the same thing twice?

GIRL: I thought you were a little—absent-minded, perhaps.

MAN: Very tactful of you to put it so mildly.

GIRL: You must realize how sorry I am! But in the excitement of dancing—and the music—and everything—I must have—well, I am sorry!

BOY: Oh, we realize that.

MAN: Certainly.

GIRL: And you can see how easy it was to make a mistake, when both of you were named Smith, and were dressed like sheiks, and were partial to red carnations?

BOY: Of course.

MAN: Naturally.

GIRL: I suppose the question now is what to do about it.

MAN: It *is* a rather embarrassing situation.

BOY: There is only one way to settle it: she must choose between us.

MAN: We might flip coins to see which of us stays.

BOY: No. I refuse to treat the matter in such a trivial way. If I leave, it will be at the request of the lady. (*He folds his arms defiantly.*)

MAN: Well, that relieves *us* of the responsibility. (*To the* GIRL.) What does "the lady" say?

GIRL: Oh, dear! I suppose I am caught now. What shall I do? Both of you are so *attractive*, and so very honorable about it! I never met two more charming men. (*To the* BOY.) If I were to ask you to leave, would you go?

BOY: Yes. I would stick to my word. But I would find you again sometime.

GIRL (*teasing him*): But how could you? You wouldn't know where to find me. You don't know my name or where I live, or anything about me. And the next time I go to a masked ball, I might not dress as the Queen of Sheba.

BOY: Never mind. I'll find you. And when I do, I'll make sure there isn't any other Smith around to interfere.

MAN: What an unkind remark!

GIRL: Oh, but there would be another Smith around. There always is when I am present. You see, Smith is *my* name, too.

BOY (*bewildered*): What! It can't be!

GIRL: But it is. That's why I remembered *your* name so easily, (*to the* MAN) and *yours*. One can nearly always remember one's own name, even when it is attached to a stranger.

BOY (*angrily*): I quit. I'm through! I've been wasting my time with a pair of lunatics. Good-by, Mr. Smith—and Miss Smith! (*He starts out.*)

GIRL (*in sudden panic*): Oh, don't go! Please don't go! You mustn't desert us!

BOY (*almost off stage*): Good-by!

GIRL (*turning to* MAN): Father! Stop him, please!

BOY (*stopping suddenly and turning back*): What was that?

GIRL (*pulling at the* MAN's *elbow*): Father, don't stand there like a stick!

MAN (*torn between amusement and confusion*): Well, I—really, my dear, I think I have done my part. If you will excuse me, I think I'll— (*He breaks away and makes for opposite side of stage.*)

BOY (*coming back swiftly to the* GIRL, *center*): What does this mean? Who *are* you, and who is that man?

GIRL (*penitently*): I am Miss Smith, and he is—Mr. Smith.

BOY (*sternly*): He is your father?

GIRL (*nodding her head vigorously*): Um-hm! (*The* BOY *utters an exclamation and moves away. She watches him out of the corner of her eye.*) Are you *awfully* mad? (*No reply.*) Will you forgive me? (*No reply.*) Please! (*She slips over to his side and plucks at his coat sleeve.*) I am sorry. But if *you* were my father, *you* wouldn't want me to meet strange men in the park without a chaperon, would you? Even the Queen of Sheba must use discretion. And wasn't Father a sport to act his part so nicely? Just think: I planned the whole thing so it would be most exciting, and it *was* exciting, wasn't it?

BOY (*whirling around suddenly, seizes her, and kisses her*): You little devil! I could strangle you!

MAN (*throwing up his hands, cries out*): The sheik!

GIRL (*trying to disengage herself*): Help! Father, he kissed me!

MAN (*coming over to them*): Serves you right. Bring him

home to dinner with us, and maybe he'll kiss you again. (*To the* Boy.) Mr. Smith, will you accept an invitation to dinner at the Smith residence with Miss Smith and myself?

Boy (*gaily*): Delighted, Mr. Smith. (*To the* Girl.) Miss Smith, will you take my arm? (*He bows. The* Girl *takes his arm and they start off. But the* Boy *stops suddenly, and turning back, addresses the* Man.)

Boy: But see here! Aren't you taking rather a chance? You don't know a thing about me.

Man: My boy, I know enough about you to write your biography.

Boy: But how could you?

Man: I've known your father, J. Rodney Smith, for twenty years, and I've seen you on the golf course with him many a time. And even if I hadn't, I'd have known you; you're a dead ringer for your dad.

Girl: How perfect it all is!

Boy: Well, I'll be—!

Man: Yes, we'll all be—late for dinner! And I want to get home in time to mix the cocktails. Mr. Smith, I hope you drink?

Boy: Oh, yes, indeed! All the Smiths do!

(*They go out arm in arm, the* Girl *between the* Man *and the* Boy.)

FEATHERTOP

MAURICE VALENCY was born in New York, in 1903, and was educated at the College of the City of New York, at Columbia University, and at the Sorbonne. Although admitted to the bar in New York, he chose a career as a philosopher, critic, teacher, and dramatist. Among his writings are the books *The Tragedies of Herod and Mariamne* and *In Praise of Love,* and the plays *The Thracian Horses* and *Battleship Bismarck.* He has added greatly to the reputation of Jean Giraudoux by adapting many of the French writer's plays for the American stage, among them *The Madwoman of Chaillot, Ondine, The Enchanted, The Virtuous Island* and *The Apollo of Bellac.* Recently, Professor Valency adapted Duerrenmatt's *The Visit* for Alfred Lunt and Lynn Fontanne and composed new English librettos for *La Périchole* and *The Gypsy Baron* for the Metropolitan Opera of New York.

Feathertop is a very good example of how a talented dramatist can make a play out of a familiar story. Nathaniel Hawthorne wrote the original short story in the nineteenth century. Now we can read it as a play for television. Stage directions will help the reader "get the picture."

FEATHERTOP

Adapted for television by Maurice Valency
From a story by Nathaniel Hawthorne

FADE IN: A shot of MOTHER RIGBY's fireplace. Dancing flames. An iron pot on a crane seething over. Weird shadows.

SOUND: MOTHER RIGBY is singing an old ballad as she bends over her work.

DOLLY BACK: The kitchen is a low-beamed room, the largest room in a small New England house of colonial design. It is the year 1770. There are cobwebs in the corners. Bunches of herbs and other witch's gear hang from the ceiling. On the wall hangs an old brass astrolabe alongside an old cutlass, a magic square on old parchment, etc. MOTHER RIGBY puts the finishing touches to the scarecrow she has made. This has a ramshackle grandeur about it. It is plainly enough stuffed with straw. The head is a pumpkin. The tattered silk stockings fall lankly over the sticks that serve it for legs. But the embroidered coat and the doeskin breeches were once the last word in fine tailoring and the head has an oddly appealing look to it. An old tiewig gives the figure a raffish cockiness as it sits sprawled out in the chimney corner.

MOTHER RIGBY (*sings as she puts the last touches to it*):
Late, late yestreen I saw the new moon
    With the old moon in her arm,
And I fear, I fear, my master dear,
    That we will come to harm. . . .

(*When she has finished, she takes her pipe from the mantel shelf, fills it from an old tobacco pouch. She gazes at her work with satisfaction. A battered three-cornered hat hangs on a nail nearby. She fetches it down, chuckling, and sets it on the scarecrow's head. Then she stands her creation up in the corner. She stops humming her ballad, and speaks in a sharp, professional tone.*) Diccon! (DICCON, *her helper, appears at once.*) DICCON, a coal for my pipe! (*A glowing coal appears in* DICCON'S *hand. He touches it to her pipe.* MOTHER RIGBY *puffs abstractedly.*) Thank you. Sit down, Diccon. What think you of my scarecrow? He's worth looking at, eh? (*She turns to the scarecrow.*) And you are the fine gentleman, my boy. Fine enough to scare any crow in New England. Ah, there. Ah, there. (*She fishes an old feather out of the trash and mischievously sticks it in his hat.*) There, Feathertop, that's you. Now you're perfect. (*She stares at the fire-light playing over* FEATHERTOP'S *honest features.*) Diccon, that puppet yonder is too good a piece of work to stand all summer long in a cornfield. Just because I'm a witch, I've half a mind to send him forth into the world to take his chance among other straw men of my acquaintance. (*She sets down her glass, chuckling.*) Judge Gookin, for instance—the richest as well as the biggest fool in the Colonies. Wouldn't that be a fine joke? (*She laughs.*) For two coppers, I'd do it. (*Two coins fall mysteriously, one after the other, on the table before her. She picks them up, laughing.*) So. So. The joke begins. Master Gookin wants very much to rise in the world—that I know. Well, I shall give him a leg up—I shall send him the finest gentleman ever seen in these parts—by far. (*Laughs again.*) What for, you wonder? I'll tell you, boy—but first I'll turn you into a man—and then—ah, then you'll hear the joke I've planned for Master Gookin! (*She sticks her pipe into the scarecrow's mouth.*) Come now, puff, darling! Puff! Puff just once. Breathe in a little smoke. Puff, I say! Puff! (*A little smoke trickles out of the pumpkin's mouth. She laughs exultantly.*) Ah, there! That's it, boy. Once more—puff! It's breath I'm giving you. Puff for your life, boy, puff! (*He begins puffing in earnest. The face changes. Upon the innocent and cheerful features of the scarecrow is superimposed a human face of the same contours. This shimmers into focus with each puff and then withdraws.* MOTHER RIGBY *claps her hands.*) Ah, now it takes! Again, boy! Once more! Once more! (FEATHERTOP *emits a cloud of smoke that envelops the head completely. When it clears, the head is human.*) And now fetch us a puff to the very bottom of your bellows. There— (*The figure straightens up miraculously, the utmost in an elegant gentleman.*) See what a fine boy you've become? (FEATHERTOP *smiles, pleased that he's done so well.*) But why are you skulking like a mouse in the corner? You've nothing to be ashamed of. (*She beckons.*) Step forth. The world awaits you. (*He looks frightened and eager by turns but ends by shaking his head. She beckons imperiously.*) Walk, pumpkin head! Walk, Feathertop! I say, walk! (*He hitches forward uncertainly and stands tottering. The rising sun streams in through the window, setting off his figure. He lifts his hand, trying to touch the sunlight.*) Steady! Steady, boy! (*He steadies himself. He steps out.*) That's it. That's splendid! (*He is now enjoying himself. He steps out with an impish grin, pretends to totter, then regains balance, and struts about comically. She is delighted by these unsolicited antics.*) Yes. Yes. Yes. Ha-ha-ha-ha. You're a proper marvel. And now that you're properly puffed up— (*She raises a hand. Her eye flashes. He shrinks back in terror.*) Speak! (*He takes the pipe from his lips, and opens his mouth, trembling. He shakes his head. She insists.*) Speak! (*He gasps desperately.*) Speak or I'll—

FEATHERTOP (*in terror*): Ah—

MOTHER RIGBY: I beg your pardon?

FEATHERTOP (*piteously*): Par-don.

MOTHER RIGBY (*laughs*): Pardon? What for? You haven't done anything yet. Well? Speak!

FEATHERTOP: What—must—I—say?

MOTHER RIGBY: Whatever comes into your head.

FEATHERTOP (*makes an effort to think. Then puts the pipe to his lips and sucks in some smoke. A thought comes with it*): Who—am—I?

MOTHER RIGBY: You? You're my little Feathertop, that's who you are. You're the best witch's puppet ever seen in this world. I'm going to make a man of you.

FEATHERTOP (*pleased*): A man?

MOTHER RIGBY: And no ordinary man. A man among men. Lift up your head, boy. Chin high.

FEATHERTOP: Chin high. (*He laughs with delight.*)

MOTHER RIGBY: Ah, what sparkle! What grace! (*Suddenly she fetches him a slap on the ear. Tears come into his eyes.*)

FEATHERTOP: That hurt.

MOTHER RIGBY: It was your birth pang. No man is complete without one. Congratulations, boy. You're born. Well? How do you like it?

FEATHERTOP: I like it.

MOTHER RIGBY: Do you so? Well, I'm delighted to hear it. Come then, say "Thank you, Mother."

FEATHERTOP: Thank you, Mother.

MOTHER RIGBY: With a proper bow. (*He tries.*) No, no—not like a pump handle. Like a fine gentleman. Like this. (*She bows.*)

FEATHERTOP (*imitates her with impish humor*): Thank you, Mother.

MOTHER RIGBY: That's better. Bit homespun still. Back still creaks a bit. But many a fine gentleman's back creaks worse than yours and no one's the worse for it.

FEATHERTOP (*bows with the utmost grace*): Thank you, ma'am.

MOTHER RIGBY (*curtseys*): Ah, that's something like. You're a real wonder, I declare. So life interests you, does it? Well, there's quite a bit to it in one way or the other.

FEATHERTOP: Where, ma'am?

MOTHER RIGBY: Why, all about you, boy. Just open your eyes and you're certain to see it. (*He steps to the fire.*) That's fire. It burns. Don't touch.

FEATHERTOP: No, ma'am. (*His coat catches a highlight. He passes a timid hand over its surface.*)

MOTHER RIGBY: That's velvet.

FEATHERTOP: It's smooth, ma'am.

MOTHER RIGBY (*smiles*): Not half as smooth as you, pet. (*He smells a bunch of dried herbs.*)

FEATHERTOP: Thank you, ma'am.

MOTHER RIGBY: Them's herbs. Sweet?

FEATHERTOP (*gallantly*): Not half as sweet as you, ma'am.

MOTHER RIGBY (*laughing*): Well, now that's something I didn't expect to hear! Diccon, do you mark the boy? What a piece of work he's turned out, to be sure. (*Admiringly.*) Lad, I count myself a better witch because of you.

FEATHERTOP: You're a wonderful witch, ma'am.

MOTHER RIGBY: Listen to him, now. A feather and a puff of smoke, and he's all compliments and manners. Well, my handsome boy, you've come a long way since sunrise, there's no denying it. You should be quite a man by night-fall at this rate, if you have scope.

FEATHERTOP: Scope, ma'am?

MOTHER RIGBY: And scope you shall have. I'm going to send you forth into the world—what do you say to that—the great, wide, the wonderful world, boy.

FEATHERTOP: Will I like it, Mother?

MOTHER RIGBY: I think so, aye. For I've given you great natural advantages, boy, including a coat that once belonged to a French duke—that was scalped, I believe, by the Indians; 'tis no ordinary garment. Besides, you're tall and slender and you have modesty. You're bound to cut a fine figure among the other stuffed shirts that go strutting and posing about the world.

FEATHERTOP: I shall endeavor to live up to it, ma'am.

MOTHER RIGBY: Oh, you will, you will, never fear. You've a well-turned leg. Your chest is full. And your head's empty.

There's a perfect natural endowment for any sort of career. Without any more, you could be a general and command an army. And as for your heart—there's more heart in that waistcoat, depend on it, than you'll find in many a banker or statesman. Yes, yes, boy—barring accidents, you will go far in this world. (*He puffs fruitlessly.*) Only mind—your pipe's out.

FEATHERTOP (*distressed*): Oh.

MOTHER RIGBY: Knock out the ashes. (*He does so. She hands him her pouch.*) Fill it, boy. Quickly. (*He begins filling it.*) Mark me now, you do stand in some need of education, for you're young, though remarkably grown for your age. I can't send you to Harvard College, there's no time, and besides they'd only stuff your head with rubbish. Well, there are but three things a man needs to know, and I'll teach you those directly. Diccon! (DICCON *appears.*) For the rest, what passes for learning in this world is mostly smoke, and you'll find plenty of that in your pipe. Diccon, a coal! (DICCON *lights the pipe and goes.* FEATHERTOP *puffs away contentedly.*) Now, boy, mark me well—

FEATHERTOP: With all my heart, ma'am.

MOTHER RIGBY: If you wish to get on in this world, look wise, ask no questions, tell no lies.

FEATHERTOP: Look wise. Ask no questions. Tell no lies.

MOTHER RIGBY: Can you remember that? (*He nods.*) With that much learning, you can hold your own with the wisest heads in the New World, nay, in the Old World, too.

FEATHERTOP: But, Mother, how if I'm asked—

MOTHER RIGBY: What, boy?

FEATHERTOP: Where I hail from, who I am?

MOTHER RIGBY: Gentlemen never answer such questions, and 'tis rude to ask. Keep your mouth shut, and others will tell your lies for you. Only see you don't get caught up in them yourself.

FEATHERTOP: Never fear, Mother. I'm no scatterbrain.

MOTHER RIGBY: Oh, you're not? That's good to know. And now, we must look to your fortune, my innocent, for in this world a man without money might as well be dead. Here's two coppers for you.

FEATHERTOP: What am I to do with them, ma'am?

MOTHER RIGBY: You may jingle them together in your pocket, but on no account spend them.

FEATHERTOP: But what if I should have need?

MOTHER RIGBY: You won't. You're a rich man, by the looks of you, and that's all that matters. The rich have no need of money—they have credit. 'Tis a type of witchcraft I don't deal in, but you'll find out soon enough how it goes.

FEATHERTOP (*pockets the money*): Trust me for that, ma'am.

MOTHER RIGBY: I do, boy, I do. You have a good head on your shoulders, a clear, fine, empty head, that's the point. The rest will come. In the meantime, bow and smile. And, above all, listen. So long as you listen, people will consider that you're a marvelously witty fellow.

FEATHERTOP: One never tires of listening to *you*, ma'am.

MOTHER RIGBY (*smiles*): I know. I know. (*Admiringly.*) 'Twouldn't surprise me a bit if you rose to be governor and ruled us all.

FEATHERTOP: I'm not so ambitious, ma'am. 'Twill be enough if I learn to rule myself. But I've a strange longing to see the world.

MOTHER RIGBY: So? And where do you wish to begin, my fine gentleman?

FEATHERTOP: 'Tis all one to me, Mother. I have seen none of it yet.

MOTHER RIGBY: Boston? No, 'tis too big; you'd be lost in Boston. Philadelphia? 'Tis too grand. (*She thinks.*) Feathertop, my boy—

FEATHERTOP: Mother?

MOTHER RIGBY: Straight down that path, a half hour's walk will bring you to Judge Gookin's house. 'Tis a fine, big house.

FEATHERTOP: Finer than this, ma'am?

MOTHER RIGBY (*chuckles*): A little. Master Gookin's the richest, as well as the biggest, fool in the Colonies. And he wants to rise in the world. Well, you shall give him a leg up.

FEATHERTOP: I, ma'am?

MOTHER RIGBY: You, lad. No one in these parts is good enough for his daughter, so he says. She must have a fine gentleman from abroad. Well, we shall send him one—the finest gentleman from abroad that ever was seen. Wait a bit, now— (*She picks an old garter out of a drawer and pins it to his coat. It turns into a jeweled cross.*) There! You're a Knight of the Garter. Lord Feathertop!

FEATHERTOP (*strutting about*): How I glitter! (*Suddenly weak.*) Mother—

MOTHER RIGBY: Why, what ails you? Oh— (*His pipe has gone out.*) Diccon! (DICCON *appears.*) Quick! A coal for his pipe. (DICCON *obliges.*) Puff, lad, puff! (*He brightens up at once.*) Better now?

FEATHERTOP: Much better, thank you. (*In the grand manner.*) A trifling indisposition. Nothing at all, really.

MOTHER RIGBY (*hands him her tobacco pouch; chuckles*): I understand. All the same, remember, boy, stick to your pipe—your life is in it. A puff from time to time and you'll be as fit as a fiddle. There's nothing else but smoke holds you together. Here—there's tobacco in this pouch will keep you glittering a lifetime, and for a light all you need to do is to call for Diccon to bring you a coal.

FEATHERTOP (*gaily*): Diccon! A coal for my pipe! (DICCON *appears, glances at the burning pipe, then goes.* FEATHERTOP *laughs.*) Why, it works like a charm, Mother.

MOTHER RIGBY: Yes, it does. And now, hark ye, lad, while I think of it. When you see Polly Gookin—she's a pretty lass and she's certain to turn your head. Mind you don't lose it completely.

FEATHERTOP: Trust me for that, Mother. I'm no fool.

MOTHER RIGBY: Come, then, off you go. (*The door swings open by itself.*) 'Tis a beautiful morning, and the world's before you.

FEATHERTOP (*peers out dubiously*): Is that it there, Mother?

MOTHER RIGBY: That's it there, boy.

FEATHERTOP (*jauntily*): Why then, I'm off.

MOTHER RIGBY: Here, take my staff with you. (*She hands him her old stick. It turns into a gold-topped cane.*) This will lead you straight to Judge Gookin's door.

FEATHERTOP: Good-by, Mother. (*He wipes away a tear.*)

MOTHER RIGBY: Why, the lad's sentimental.

FEATHERTOP: I've my feelings, ma'am, like other people, I hope.

MOTHER RIGBY: Have you so? Well—mind you don't show them too often. (*Blows him a kiss.*) Good luck, boy. Good luck, my darling.

FEATHERTOP (*waves his hat gallantly as he goes*): Good-by, Mother, good-by. (*He goes.*)

> DISSOLVE TO: *Silhouette of* FEATHERTOP *striding down a road against the morning sun, with* DICCON *behind him.*

> DISSOLVE TO: *Close-up of* FEATHERTOP's *hat and stick on* JUDGE GOOKIN's *hall table.* POLLY GOOKIN *and* BOB ENDICOTT *are standing near them, speaking in low tones.*

BOB: Polly— (POLLY *takes up the hat and perches it on her head.*) Take that off, Polly. 'Tis the stranger's hat.

POLLY: I'll not take it off.

BOB: Polly, listen to me.

POLLY: I'll not listen to you, Bob Endicott. I've listened to you enough.

BOB: But, Polly, I mean to ask your father this very night—

POLLY: You do? Oh, Bob! (*She throws her arms about his neck gaily and kisses him.*) And why not now, pray?

BOB: Oh, Polly, can I ask him for his daughter's hand in front of this Lord—Lord—what's-his-name?

> JUDGE GOOKIN's *voice* (*off stage*): Polly!

POLLY (*puts down hat*): It's Father.

GOOKIN (*off stage*): Polly!

POLLY: I must go.

BOB: I'll come back tonight, Polly, and I'll ask him, never fear.

POLLY: Mind you do, Bob Endicott, or I'll—

GOOKIN (*off stage*): Polly!

POLLY: Good-by.

DISSOLVE TO: JUDGE GOOKIN's *living room. Windsor chairs are drawn up to the fire.* FEATHERTOP *sits in one at his ease, pipe in hand.* GOOKIN *is standing. The décor is colonial, elegant and comfortable.*

GOOKIN: No, no, I won't hear of it! My Lord stay at the inn? What would they say of me in Boston? (*Calls.*) Polly! Polly, I say! I'm naught but a poor widower, sir, as you may know, but my daughter will see to it that whatever poor comforts this house can afford— (*Calls.*) Polly! Where the devil is the girl? (*A servant comes in with a tray, decanter, and glasses.*) Where's your mistress?

ADAM: Miss Polly begs you will be patient. She will be down directly she's dressed.

GOOKIN: Primping, primping. Tell her she's wanted here. (*He pours a glass for* FEATHERTOP.) And now, My Lord— (*He pours himself one.*) Pray tell me (*he clinks glasses with* FEATHERTOP, *who is not too sure of the procedure*) what brings a man of your position to our town?

FEATHERTOP (*takes a sip of the wine thoughtfully; the taste astonishes him*): What d'ye call this liquid?

GOOKIN: What? 'Tis wine, my lad. Port wine.

FEATHERTOP: It makes the head spin.

GOOKIN: Surely you don't disapprove of spirits, My Lord.

FEATHERTOP: Not in the least, sir. In this world you need to drink things to make the head spin. (*Holds out his glass.*) Another drop, Master Gookin.

GOOKIN: My Lord is here on no ordinary business, I'm sure.

FEATHERTOP: I come only to see the world, Master Gookin.

GOOKIN (*laughs knowingly*): Ah, indeed. To be sure. (*Winks.*) Secret business. Private business?

FEATHERTOP: By no means. Public.

GOOKIN: Ah! On public business. Trust me, My Lord, I'll say nothing of it. Not a word. And the nature of— (FEATHERTOP *gets up, his eye caught by a portrait of George III on the wall.*) I confess, I have been expecting this visit for some time.

FEATHERTOP (*pointing to the picture in wonder*): Why is that man so angry?

GOOKIN: Eh? Oh, I take your meaning, My Lord, yes. Ah, My Lord, you're right. His Majesty has good cause to be angry. Thank heaven you've come, My Lord. We look to you for deliverance.

FEATHERTOP (*in astonishment*): To me?

GOOKIN: Come, now, 'tis as plain as a pikestaff. My Lord, be open with me. You were sent here, were you not?

FEATHERTOP: Yes, I was indeed. But—

GOOKIN: Enough, My Lord, say no more. I understand. And look you, sir. (*He unlocks a casket.*) I have not been idle. Here, My Lord. The evidence.

FEATHERTOP: The evidence—

GOOKIN: Enough to hang the lot of them, My Lord. A letter from Major Whitby offering to sell his fortress to the French whenever they desire it. Here he threatens to send his Hessians to sack a farm unless he is paid fifty pounds. Letters. Affidavits. Depositions. All as clear as day. You may open the hearings at once. Tomorrow. The sheriff takes bribes. The selectmen are perjurers. His Majesty's Collector is a knave. Major Whitby is a traitor. The preacher has traffic with witches—

FEATHERTOP: But are there no honest men in the land?

GOOKIN: All rogues. All blackguards. You must make a clean sweep, My Lord. I can see you are shocked.

FEATHERTOP: I am astonished.

GOOKIN: My Lord, can you leave treachery unpunished? Can you permit honest folk to be abused? Can you look on idly while these wolves batten on the blood of the people?

FEATHERTOP: No, certainly I can't do that.

GOOKIN (*pours him out another glass*): My Lord, I say no more. The evidence is in your hands. You may sift it at your leisure.

FEATHERTOP: You wish me to?

GOOKIN: I beg you to.

FEATHERTOP: Very well, I shall.

GOOKIN: And when you see who the guilty are, My Lord, heads will roll, will they not?

FEATHERTOP: Upon my word, they may. They may. (*Inflating*

visibly.) I did not ask to be sent forth into your world, Master Gookin. But now that I'm here (*he blows out a cloud of smoke*) perhaps I shall be of some use in it. (*At this moment*, POLLY GOOKIN *comes in. He sees her. He gasps with amazement.*)

GOOKIN: Be guided by me, My Lord. Hang a dozen of them first. After that—

FEATHERTOP (*rises*): Oh, lovely creature!

GOOKIN: What? (*He turns.*) Why, 'tis only my daughter, Polly.

FEATHERTOP: How beautiful she is, your daughter!

POLLY (*curtseys*): My Lord.

FEATHERTOP (*bows*): My lady.

GOOKIN: The lass is to your taste, eh?

FEATHERTOP: Aye, very much. Very much.

GOOKIN: She's a good girl, My Lord, and has a sweet singing voice. And she'll bring five hundred a year to the man she marries. (ADAM *comes in.*) What is it, Adam?

ADAM: Major Whitby and the King's Collector to present their compliments.

GOOKIN: I'll come out to them. By your leave, My Lord. (*He goes out with* ADAM.)

FEATHERTOP: Your name is Polly, lovely creature?

POLLY: Polly Gookin, My Lord.

FEATHERTOP: Polly Gookin. 'Tis a beautiful name, is it not?

POLLY: It's mine.

FEATHERTOP: 'Tis music in the ear. All of you is lovely, Mistress Polly. Your name, your eyes, your hair— (*He reaches out timidly and touches her hair.*) 'Tis softer than velvet. But your cheek is softer still— (*He strokes her cheek. She draws back.*)

POLLY: My Lord, by your leave—!

FEATHERTOP: Mistress Polly— (*He bends forward very naturally and kisses her on the lips.*)

POLLY: Oh!

FEATHERTOP: You are angry with me?

POLLY: But what do you take me for, My Lord?

FEATHERTOP: I have done something wrong?

POLLY: Pray let me pass.

FEATHERTOP: On my word, I meant no harm. And you're really none the worse for it. Don't be angry, Mistress Polly.

POLLY: I'm not accustomed to your courtly ways, My Lord. We are simple country folk. All the same—

FEATHERTOP: Among country folk, it is not permitted to kiss a lovely face?

POLLY: Only if one intends to marry it, My Lord.

FEATHERTOP: But I intend to marry it, Miss Polly. I very much intend to marry it.

POLLY: You're but mocking me, My Lord. 'Tis not very gallant.

FEATHERTOP: On my word, I'm not.

POLLY: Let me go! Please! (*She breaks away.*)

FEATHERTOP: Wait, Miss Polly, wait— (*She crosses to the door.* GOOKIN *comes in.*)

GOOKIN: My Lord, these scoundrels insist— What's amiss here? Where are you going?

POLLY (*brushing past*): I beg your pardon.

FEATHERTOP: I have made your daughter angry, Master Gookin.

GOOKIN: What? Oh, bother the child—she's high-spirited. I'll bring her round. Major Whitby and the Collector desire to be received. You'll not see them, I hope? (MAJOR WHITBY *and the* COLLECTOR *come in.*)

WHITBY: I'm sure My Lord will see us, Master Gookin, if only out of curiosity. (*He bows.*) My Lord, your most humble and obedient servant, Major Whitby. In command of His Majesty's garrison. (FEATHERTOP *bows curtly.*) And this is Mr. Graham Bell, His Majesty's Collector.

MR. BELL: My Lord.

FEATHERTOP: I am much concerned for Miss Polly, Master Gookin.

GOOKIN: I'll see to it directly. (*Calls.*) Polly! I'll fetch her back. Polly! One moment, My Lord. (*He goes.*)

WHITBY: Hark ye, My Lord—this Gookin . . .

FEATHERTOP: Eh?

WHITBY: A most pernicious liar, sir.

Mr. Bell: A thief, sir. A notorious knave. Not to be trusted for a moment. (*He whispers.*)

Whitby: Whatever he may have told you, My Lord—

Mr. Bell: Whatever he may have said—

Whitby: Believe no word of it—

Mr. Bell: Be guided by us, My Lord. We've been waiting for you night and day.

Whitby: Sh! Mum's the word! (Gookin *comes in.*)

Mr. Bell: Your girl has spirit, Master Gookin.

Gookin: Aye. But what could My Lord have said to her to make her fly off like a jack rabbit?

Feathertop (*putting his pipe to his lips*): Only that I intend to marry her.

Gookin: To marry her! But, My Lord—!

Feathertop: Diccon! A coal for my pipe! (Diccon *appears, adding to the general astonishment.* Feathertop *puffs calmly.*)

> Dissolve to: *A room in* Gookin's *house adjoining the ballroom, where a dance is in progress.* Polly *is standing before a long mirror, admiring her ball gown.* Gookin *stands behind her. There is a sound of string music.*

Gookin (*exasperated*): "But, Father! But, Father! But, Father!" Can you sing no other tune? You want to travel in your own coach, I suppose, with your servants in livery and your house in town?

Polly: Oh, Father, I don't want anything like that.

Gookin: Well, I do. And here's the man can give them to you. Aye, and sent from heaven! A baron!

Polly: But, Father—

Gookin: "But, Father!" Now listen to me, girl, your father knows best, and we'll have no more of this nonsense. I shall send My Lord Feathertop in to you, and mind you cross him in nothing. Wait here.

> (*He goes off. The girl walks back to the mirror and makes a face at his retreating back.* Bob *comes in silently.*)

BOB: Polly— (*Camera on his reflection in the mirror. She turns.*)

POLLY (*in his arms*): Oh, Bob, Bob! I'm frightened!

BOB: Frightened? Of what?

POLLY: This man. This baron.

BOB: Feathertop?

(*Camera on* FEATHERTOP. *He has just walked into the doorway. He stops on hearing his name.*)

POLLY: He's not like other people. He's strange.

BOB: But what's it to you, Polly?

POLLY: Father—Father wants me to marry him.

BOB: Marry him? But you don't even know him. He's scarcely been here a day.

POLLY: I know. I know. But Father— Oh, Bob, Bob, what are we going to do?

BOB: Do? Why, I'll—

(FEATHERTOP *blows out a cloud of smoke. They see him and turn. He comes in, bows.*)

FEATHERTOP (*ignores* BOB): Miss Polly, your father bids me come and fetch you. It seems the dancing is about to begin. (*To* BOB.) By your leave. (*He offers his arm to* POLLY, *who takes it with a helpless look at* BOB.)

BOB: Sir.

FEATHERTOP (*stops*): Yes?

BOB: Nothing. Nothing.

(FEATHERTOP *smiles. He takes* POLLY *out.* BOB *stares after them in desperation. The music strikes up.*)

DISSOLVE TO: *The dance floor. Several couples take places to dance a figure dance of the minuet variety.* FEATHERTOP *and* POLLY *join them.*

FEATHERTOP (*as the dance begins*): I may be a little awkward at this just at first, Miss Polly—

POLLY (*dancing*): Our New World dances must seem strange.

FEATHERTOP: Your New World seems strange. (*He steps on her foot.*) Ah. Forgive me.

POLLY: 'Tis no matter.

FEATHERTOP: The young man yonder— Mr. Endicott—

POLLY: Yes, My Lord?

FEATHERTOP: He takes your fancy, Miss Polly?

POLLY: We grew up together.

FEATHERTOP (*his dancing greatly improved*): He's not for you, Miss Polly. (*He draws her away from the other dancers.*)

POLLY: How do you mean, My Lord?

(*Camera on a lady dancing with* WHITBY.)

THE LADY: Mark My Lord, how he dances, Major.

WHITBY: 'Tis doubtless the latest fashion from Paris.

(FEATHERTOP *dances out of the room with* POLLY *and into the adjoining room. The camera dollies after them.*)

FEATHERTOP (*still dancing*): Miss Polly, I am but lately come into this world. I understand little enough of it.

POLLY: It must seem trivial, My Lord, compared to the world you know.

FEATHERTOP: It seems beautiful and wonderful beyond belief. Yet it bewilders me.

POLLY: How bewilders you, My Lord?

FEATHERTOP: Until I look at you, Miss Polly. Then all is clear.

POLLY: What is clear, My Lord?

FEATHERTOP (*stops dancing; takes her hand*): What it is, and what I am, and what I have to do.

POLLY: I don't understand, My Lord.

FEATHERTOP: 'Tis a beautiful world, this world of yours, with its hills and its plains, its sunlight poured like a blessing from the sky, and its water bubbling like laughter from the depths. There should be joy in such a world, Miss Polly. It should be peopled with happy and lovely beings. Like you, Miss Polly. Not with miserable creatures, like Judge Gookin.

POLLY: My Lord!

FEATHERTOP (*nods*): Or Major Whitby. Or Mr. Bell, His Majesty's Collector. Why should this beautiful world be filled with liars and hypocrites?

POLLY: Is that not human nature, My Lord?

FEATHERTOP: I had begun to think so. But then I saw you, Miss Polly. And then I understood. Men are beautiful. They are good. But they are unhappy. They are afraid. And that makes them hateful and ugly. No matter. They shall be so no longer.

POLLY: But, My Lord—

FEATHERTOP (*more and more exalted*): I came among them in my innocence, and at once they turned to me for help. Very well. (*He takes her other hand.*) I shall not fail them.

POLLY: Let me go, if you please, sir!

FEATHERTOP: For your sake I shall help them. I shall heal them. I shall make all men equal and all men good. I shall exalt the humble. I shall abase the proud. I shall feed the hungry. Aye, the world will be the better for me.

POLLY (*frightened*): Please let me go.

FEATHERTOP: But I shall need help, Miss Polly. I shall need inspiration, more than this poor pipe of mine can give. I shall need a vision of beauty to guide me. I shall need a hand to lead me. I shall need you—

POLLY: You're hurting me.

FEATHERTOP: I love you. (*He moves to take her in his arms. At this moment, half acceding, she sees his image in the glass. It is the scarecrow, pumpkin head and all. She screams.*) I love you. (*But now he sees it also, and recoils in horror. He speaks to the image.*) Go away! (*He makes a threatening gesture. The image steps toward him with the same gesture. His words echo back from it, as he shouts.*) Go away!

    (POLLY *faints. The music stops. People rush in.*)

GOOKIN: My Lord—

WHITBY: My Lord—

BOB: What have you done to her? (*He kneels beside her.*) Polly!

MR. BELL: She's fainted.

    (POLLY *opens her eyes.*)

FEATHERTOP: Miss Polly—

POLLY (*sees him and starts up*): The scarecrow!

WHITBY: Scarecrow?

GOOKIN: Pull yourself together, girl. Have you lost your wits?

BOB (*to* GOOKIN): If she has, the fault is yours!

GOOKIN: Be so good as to leave my house, Mr. Endicott. My Lord, forgive the girl. She's yours.

FEATHERTOP (*totters; he speaks in a choked voice*): Fools! Fools!

GOOKIN: My Lord?

FEATHERTOP: Give the girl to the man she loves. (*He takes up a massive candlestick and draws* GOOKIN *to the mirror.*) Or—do you prefer—

GOOKIN: What, My Lord?

FEATHERTOP: Your lord? There's your lord for you! There! (*They stare in horror at the reflection. He hurls the candlestick at the glass. It shatters.*) There. (*He makes a supreme effort and draws himself up. He surveys them each in turn. Then he puts his pipe in his mouth defiantly.*) Diccon. A coal for my pipe. (DICCON *appears.*)

GOOKIN: But, My Lord—My Lord—where are you going?

    (FEATHERTOP *pauses at the door, looks at them, and blows a puff of smoke at them.*)

    DISSOLVE TO: MOTHER RIGBY's *kitchen. She sits placidly rocking by her fire. The door flies open.* FEATHERTOP *comes in, dejected.*

MOTHER RIGBY: Well, well, boy! And I thought you'd make the whole world over!

FEATHERTOP: So did I, Mother. But then I looked in a glass.

MOTHER RIGBY: I know. I know.

FEATHERTOP: And I saw myself as I am.

MOTHER RIGBY: Alas, boy, I should have warned you.

FEATHERTOP: I don't want to live!

MOTHER RIGBY: Nonsense, boy—you're no different from the rest of them.

FEATHERTOP: I don't want to live! I don't want to live!

    (*He hurls his pipe against the wall. He falls in a heap.*)

MOTHER RIGBY: What a pity! (*She picks up her pipe and fills it slowly.*) Poor little Feathertop! Of all the straw men who go bustling about this world, why should you alone have to know yourself, and die for it? (*She sighs.*) Poor lad! Who knows what mighty thoughts passed through that pumpkin head in its little hour. And how you must have suffered!

(*He looks up at her.*) Well, 'twas not in vain—at least you've put one thing right in the world. (*A flicker of interest appears in his eyes.*) Old Gookin has learned his lesson and the girl will have her boy. 'Tis not much—one good deed and that done unwillingly, but more than most people can boast of in a lifetime of iniquity. Well— (*She stares at her pipe a moment, then puts it to her lips.*) You shall be a scarecrow after all. 'Tis a useful and innocent vocation and will bring you no grief. (*She stares reflectively at the scarecrow lying in a heap on the floor, and prods it with her toe.*) Diccon! (*She sits back in her rocker.*) A coal for my pipe! (DICCON *lights it. She puffs out a cloud which obscures the picture.*)

SORRY, WRONG NUMBER

LUCILLE FLETCHER (1913–   ) wrote *Sorry, Wrong Number* in 1948. Agnes Moorehead made it one of the most popular and oft-repeated plays in the history of radio. Barbara Stanwyck played the role of Mrs. Stevenson in a movie version. The play is available in a version for the stage but the original radio version, which is reproduced here, is better theatre because it makes the reader or listener use his imagination to the limit.

Sorry, Wrong Number is more than a superb hair-raising episode about a useless, neurotic woman. With dramatic force it shows how we can rely too much on a mechanical crutch for maintaining contact with people. The play is unforgettable; so is the heroine and each of the unseen, disinterested people whose voices alone build pictures of total human beings in our minds.

SORRY, WRONG NUMBER

A radio play by Lucille Fletcher

SOUND: *Number being dialed on phone; busy signal.*

MRS. STEVENSON (*a querulous, self-centered neurotic*): Oh—dear! (*Slams down receiver. Dials* OPERATOR.)

OPERATOR: Your call, please?

MRS. STEVENSON: Operator? I've been dialing Murray Hill 4-0098 now for the last three-quarters of an hour, and the line is always busy. But I don't see how it *could* be busy that long. Will you try it for me, please?

OPERATOR: Murray Hill 4-0098? One moment, please.

MRS. STEVENSON: I don't see how it could be busy all this time. It's my husband's office. He's working late tonight, and I'm all alone here in the house. My health is very poor —and I've been feeling so nervous all day—

OPERATOR: Ringing Murray Hill 4-0098.

(SOUND: *Phone buzz. It rings three times. Receiver is picked up at the other end.*)

MAN: Hello.

MRS. STEVENSON: Hello? (*A little puzzled.*) Hello. Is Mr. Stevenson there?

Copyright, 1952, 1948, by Lucille Fletcher. All rights reserved under the International and Pan-American Conventions. *Sorry, Wrong Number* is reprinted by permission of the author and of Dramatists Play Service, Inc. The use of the play in present form must be confined to study and reference. Attention in particular is called to the fact that this play, being duly copyrighted, may not be publicly read or performed or otherwise used without permission from the author's representative. All inquiries should be addressed to Dramatists Play Service, 440 Park Avenue South, New York, N.Y. 10016.

MAN (*into phone, as though he had not heard*): Hello. (*Louder.*) Hello.

SECOND MAN (*slow, heavy quality, faintly foreign accent*): Hello.

FIRST MAN: Hello. George?

GEORGE: Yes, sir.

MRS. STEVENSON (*louder and more imperious, to phone*): Hello. Who's this? What number am I calling, please?

FIRST MAN: We have heard from our client. He says the coast is clear for tonight.

GEORGE: Yes, sir.

FIRST MAN: Where are you now?

GEORGE: In a phone booth.

FIRST MAN: Okay. You know the address. At eleven o'clock the private patrolman goes around to the bar on Second Avenue for a beer. Be sure that all the lights downstairs are out. There should be only one light visible from the street. At eleven fifteen a subway train crosses the bridge. It makes a noise in case her window is open and she should scream.

MRS. STEVENSON (*shocked*): Oh—*hello!* What number is this, please?

GEORGE: Okay. I understand.

FIRST MAN: Make it quick. As little blood as possible. Our client does not wish to make her suffer long.

GEORGE: A knife okay, sir?

FIRST MAN: Yes. A knife will be okay. And remember—remove the rings and bracelets, and the jewelry in the bureau drawer. Our client wishes it to look like simple robbery.

GEORGE: Okay, I get—

(SOUND: *A bland buzzing signal.*)

MRS. STEVENSON (*clicking phone*): Oh! (*Bland buzzing signal continues. She hangs up.*) How awful! How unspeakably—

(SOUND: *Dialing. Phone buzz.*)

OPERATOR: Your call, please?

MRS. STEVENSON (*unnerved and breathless, into phone*): Operator, I—I've just been cut off.

OPERATOR: I'm sorry, madam. What number were you calling?

MRS. STEVENSON: Why—it was supposed to be Murray Hill 4-0098, but it wasn't. Some wires must have crossed—I was cut into a wrong number—and—I've just heard the most dreadful thing—a—a murder—and— (*Imperiously.*) Operator, you'll simply have to retrace that call at once.

OPERATOR: I beg your pardon, madam—I don't quite—

MRS. STEVENSON: Oh—I know it was a wrong number, and I had no business listening—but these two men—they were cold-blooded fiends—and they were going to murder somebody—some poor innocent woman—who was all alone—in a house near a bridge. And we've got to stop them—we've got to—

OPERATOR (*patiently*): What number were you calling, madam?

MRS. STEVENSON: That doesn't matter. This was a *wrong* number. And *you* dialed it. And we've got to find out what it was—immediately!

OPERATOR: But—madam—

MRS. STEVENSON: Oh, why are you so stupid? Look, it was obviously a case of some little slip of the finger. I told you to try Murray Hill 4-0098 for me—you dialed it—but your finger must have slipped—and I was connected with some other number—and I could hear them, but they couldn't hear me. Now, I simply fail to see why you couldn't make that same mistake again—on purpose—why you couldn't *try* to dial Murray Hill 4-0098 in the same careless sort of way—

OPERATOR (*quickly*): Murray Hill 4-0098? I will try to get it for you, madam.

MRS. STEVENSON (*sarcastically*): *Thank* you.
    (*Sound of ringing; busy signal.*)

OPERATOR: I am sorry. Murray Hill 4-0098 is busy.

MRS. STEVENSON (*frantically clicking receiver*): Operator. Operator.

OPERATOR: Yes, madam.

MRS. STEVENSON (*angrily*): You *didn't* try to get that wrong number at all. I asked explicitly. And all you did was dial correctly.

OPERATOR: I am sorry. What number were you calling?

MRS. STEVENSON. Can't you, for once, forget what number I was calling, and do something specific? Now I want to trace that call. It's my civic duty—it's *your* civic duty—to trace that call—and to apprehend those dangerous killers—and if *you* won't—

OPERATOR: I will connect you with the Chief Operator.

MRS. STEVENSON: *Please!*

  (*Sound of ringing.*)

CHIEF OPERATOR (*coolly and professionally*): This is the Chief Operator.

MRS. STEVENSON: Chief Operator? I want you to trace a call. A telephone call. Immediately. I don't know where it came from, or who was making it, but it's absolutely necessary that it be tracked down. Because it was about a murder. Yes, a terrible, cold-blooded murder of a poor innocent woman—tonight—at eleven fifteen.

CHIEF OPERATOR: I see.

MRS. STEVENSON (*high-strung, demanding*): Can you trace it for me? Can you track down those men?

CHIEF OPERATOR: It depends, madam.

MRS. STEVENSON: Depends on what?

CHIEF OPERATOR: It depends on whether the call is still going on. If it's a live call, we can trace it on the equipment. If it's been disconnected, we can't.

MRS. STEVENSON: Disconnected?

CHIEF OPERATOR: If the parties have stopped talking to each other.

MRS. STEVENSON: Oh—but—but of course they must have stopped talking to each other by *now*. That was at least five minutes ago—and they didn't sound like the type who would make a long call.

CHIEF OPERATOR: Well, I can try tracing it. Now—what is your name, madam?

MRS. STEVENSON: Mrs. Stevenson. Mrs. Elbert Stevenson. But —listen—

CHIEF OPERATOR (*writing it down*): And your telephone number?

MRS. STEVENSON (*more irritated*): Plaza 4-2295. But if you go on wasting all this time—

CHIEF OPERATOR: And what is your reason for wanting this call traced?

MRS. STEVENSON: My reason? Well—for heaven's sake—isn't it obvious? I overhear two men—they're killers—they're planning to murder this woman—it's a matter for the police.

CHIEF OPERATOR: Have you told the police?

MRS. STEVENSON: No. How could I?

CHIEF OPERATOR: You're making this check into a private call purely as a private individual?

MRS. STEVENSON: Yes. But meanwhile—

CHIEF OPERATOR: Well, Mrs. Stevenson—I seriously doubt whether we could make this check for you at this time just on your say-so as a private individual. We'd have to have something more official.

MRS. STEVENSON: Oh, for heaven's sake! You mean to tell me I can't report a murder without getting tied up in all this red tape? Why, it's perfectly idiotic. All right, then. I *will* call the police. (*She slams down receiver.*) Ridiculous! (*Sound of dialing.*)

SECOND OPERATOR: Your call, please?

MRS. STEVENSON (*very annoyed*): The Police Department— *please.*

SECOND OPERATOR: Ringing the Police Department. (*Rings twice. Phone is picked up.*)

SERGEANT DUFFY: Police Department. Precinct 43. Duffy speaking.

MRS. STEVENSON: Police Department? Oh. This is Mrs. Stevenson—Mrs. Elbert Smythe Stevenson of 53 North Sutton Place. I'm calling up to report a murder.

DUFFY: Eh?

MRS. STEVENSON: I mean—the murder hasn't been committed yet. I just overheard plans for it over the telephone . . . over a wrong number that the operator gave me. I've been trying to trace down the call myself, but everybody is so stupid —and I guess in the end you're the only people who could *do* anything.

DUFFY (*not too impressed*): Yes, ma'am.

MRS. STEVENSON (*trying to impress him*): It was a perfectly *definite* murder. I heard their plans distinctly. Two men were talking, and they were going to murder some woman at eleven fifteen tonight—she lived in a house near a bridge.

DUFFY: Yes, ma'am.

MRS. STEVENSON: And there was a private patrolman on the street. He was going to go around for a beer on Second Avenue. And there was some third man—a client—who was paying to have this poor woman murdered— They were going to take her rings and bracelets—and use a knife— Well, it's unnerved me dreadfully—and I'm not well—

DUFFY: I see. When was all this, ma'am?

MRS. STEVENSON: About eight minutes ago. Oh . . . (*relieved*) then you *can* do something? You *do* understand—

DUFFY: And what is your name, ma'am?

MRS. STEVENSON (*impatiently*): Mrs. Stevenson. Mrs. Elbert Stevenson.

DUFFY: And your address?

MRS. STEVENSON: 53 North Sutton Place. *That's* near a bridge, the Queensborough Bridge, you know—and *we* have a private patrolman on *our* street—and Second Avenue—

DUFFY: And what was that number you were calling?

MRS. STEVENSON: Murray Hill 4-0098. But—that wasn't the number I overheard. I mean Murray Hill 4-0098 is my husband's office. He's working late tonight, and I was trying to reach him to ask him to come home. I'm an invalid, you know—and it's the maid's night off—and I *hate* to be alone —even though he says I'm perfectly safe as long as I have the telephone right beside my bed.

DUFFY (*stolidly*): Well, we'll look into it, Mrs. Stevenson, and see if we can check it with the telephone company.

MRS. STEVENSON (*getting impatient*): But the telephone company said they couldn't check the call if the parties had stopped talking. I've already taken care of *that*.

DUFFY: Oh, yes?

MRS. STEVENSON (*highhanded*): Personally I feel you ought to do something far more immediate and drastic than just check the call. What good does checking the call do, if they've stopped talking? By the time you track it down, they'll already have committed the murder.

DUFFY: Well, we'll take care of it, lady. Don't worry.

MRS. STEVENSON: I'd say the whole thing calls for a search—a complete and thorough search of the whole city. I'm very near a bridge, and I'm not far from Second Avenue. And I know *I'd* feel a whole lot better if you sent around a radio car to *this* neighborhood at once.

DUFFY: And what makes you think the murder's going to be committed in your neighborhood, ma'am?

MRS. STEVENSON: Oh, I don't know. The coincidence is so horrible. Second Avenue—the patrolman—the bridge—

DUFFY: Second Avenue is a very long street, ma'am. And do you happen to know how many bridges there are in the city of New York alone? Not to mention Brooklyn, Staten Island, Queens, and the Bronx? And how do you know there isn't some little house out on Staten Island—on some little Second Avenue you've never heard about? How do you know they were even talking about New York at all?

MRS. STEVENSON: But I heard the call on the New York dialing system.

DUFFY: How do you know it wasn't a long-distance call you overheard? Telephones are funny things. Look, lady, why don't you look at it this way? Supposing you hadn't broken in on that telephone call? Supposing you'd got your husband the way you always do? Would this murder have made any difference to you then?

MRS. STEVENSON: I suppose not. But it's so inhuman—so cold-blooded—

DUFFY: A lot of murders are committed in this city every day, ma'am. If we could do something to stop 'em, we would. But a clue of this kind that's so vague isn't much more use to us than no clue at all.

MRS. STEVENSON: But surely—

DUFFY: Unless, of course, you have some reason for thinking this call is phony—and that someone may be planning to murder *you?*

MRS. STEVENSON: *Me?* Oh, no, I hardly think so. I—I mean—why should anybody? I'm alone all day and night—I see nobody except my maid Eloise—she's a big two-hundred-pounder—she's too lazy to bring up my breakfast tray—and the only other person is my husband Elbert—he's crazy about me—adores me—waits on me hand and foot—he's scarcely left my side since I took sick twelve years ago—

DUFFY: Well, then, there's nothing for you to worry about, is there? And now, if you'll just leave the rest of this to us—

MRS. STEVENSON: But what will you *do?* It's so late—it's nearly eleven o'clock.

DUFFY (*firmly*): We'll take care of it, lady.

MRS. STEVENSON: Will you broadcast it all over the city? And send out squads? And warn your radio cars to watch out—especially in suspicious neighborhoods like mine?

DUFFY (*more firmly*): Lady, I *said* we'd take care of it. Just now I've got a couple of other matters here on my desk that require my immediate—

MRS. STEVENSON: Oh! (*She slams down receiver hard.*) Idiot. (*Looking at phone nervously.*) Now, why did I do that? Now he'll think I *am* a fool. Oh, why doesn't Elbert come home? *Why* doesn't he?

(*Sound of dialing operator.*)

OPERATOR: Your call, please?

MRS. STEVENSON: Operator, for heaven's sake, will you ring that Murray Hill 4-0098 number again? I can't think what's keeping him so long.

OPERATOR: Ringing Murray Hill 4-0098. (*Rings. Busy signal.*) The line is busy. Shall I—

MRS. STEVENSON (*nastily*): I can hear it. You don't have to tell me. I know it's busy. (*Slams down receiver.*) If I could only get out of this bed for a little while. If I could get a breath of fresh air—or just lean out the window—and see the street— (*The phone rings. She darts for it instantly.*) Hello. Elbert? Hello. Hello. Hello. Oh, what's the *matter* with this phone? *Hello? Hello?* (*Slams down receiver.*) (*The phone rings again, once. She picks it up.*) Hello? Hello— Oh, for heaven's sake, who *is* this? Hello, Hello. *Hello.* (*Slams down receiver. Dials operator.*)

THIRD OPERATOR: Your call, please?

MRS. STEVENSON (*very annoyed and imperious*): Hello, operator. I don't know what's the matter with this telephone tonight, but it's positively driving me crazy. I've never seen such inefficient, miserable service. Now, look. I'm an invalid, and I'm very nervous, and I'm *not* supposed to be annoyed. But if this keeps on much longer—

THIRD OPERATOR (*a young, sweet type*): What seems to be the trouble, madam?

MRS. STEVENSON: Well, everything's wrong. The whole world could be murdered, for all you people care. And now, my phone keeps ringing—

OPERATOR: Yes, madam?

MRS. STEVENSON: Ringing and ringing and ringing every five seconds or so, and when I pick it up, there's no one there.

OPERATOR: I am sorry, madam. If you will hang up, I will test it for you.

MRS. STEVENSON: I don't want you to test it for me. I want you to put through that call—whatever it is—at once.

OPERATOR (*gently*): I am afraid that is not possible, madam.

MRS. STEVENSON (*storming*): Not possible? And why, may I ask?

OPERATOR: The system is automatic, madam. If someone is trying to dial your number, there is no way to check whether the call is coming through the system or not—unless the person who is trying to reach you complains to his particular operator—

MRS. STEVENSON: Well, of all the stupid, complicated—! And meanwhile *I've* got to sit here in my bed, *suffering* every time that phone rings, imagining everything—

OPERATOR: I will try to check it for you, madam.

MRS. STEVENSON: Check it! Check it! That's all anybody can do. Of all the stupid, idiotic . . . ! (*She hangs up.*) Oh— what's the use . . . (*Instantly* MRS. STEVENSON's *phone rings again. She picks up the receiver. Wildly.*) Hello. HELLO. Stop ringing, do you hear me? Answer me? What do you want? Do you realize you're driving me crazy? Stark, staring—

MAN (*dull, flat voice*): Hello. Is this Plaza 4-2295?

MRS. STEVENSON (*catching her breath*): Yes. Yes. This is Plaza 4-2295.

MAN: This is Western Union. I have a telegram here for Mrs. Elbert Stevenson. Is there anyone there to receive the message?

MRS. STEVENSON (*trying to calm herself*): I am Mrs. Stevenson.

WESTERN UNION (*reading flatly*): The telegram is as follows: "Mrs. Elbert Stevenson. 53 North Sutton Place, New York, New York. Darling. Terribly sorry. Tried to get you for last hour, but line busy. Leaving for Boston 11 P.M. tonight on urgent business. Back tomorrow afternoon. Keep happy. Love. Signed. Elbert."

MRS. STEVENSON (*breathlessly, aghast, to herself*): Oh—no—

WESTERN UNION: That is all, madam. Do you wish us to deliver a copy of the message?

MRS. STEVENSON: No—no, thank you.

WESTERN UNION: Thank you, madam. Good night. (*He hangs up phone.*)

MRS. STEVENSON (*mechanically, to phone*): Good night. (*She hangs up slowly, suddenly bursting into tears.*) No—no—it isn't true! He couldn't do it. Not when he knows I'll be all alone. It's some trick—some fiendish— (*She dials operator.*)

OPERATOR (*coolly*): Your call, please?

MRS. STEVENSON: Operator—try that Murray Hill 4-0098 number for me just once more, please.

OPERATOR: Ringing Murray Hill 4-0098. (*Call goes through. We hear ringing at other end. Ring after ring.*)

MRS. STEVENSON: He's gone. Oh, Elbert, how could you? How could you—? (*She hangs up phone, sobbing pityingly to herself, turning restlessly.*) But I can't be alone tonight. I can't. If I'm alone one more second— I don't care what he says—or what the expense is—I'm a sick woman—I'm entitled— (*She dials* INFORMATION.)

INFORMATION: This is Information.

MRS. STEVENSON: I want the telephone number of Henchley Hospital.

INFORMATION: Henchley Hospital? Do you have the address, madam?

MRS. STEVENSON: No. It's somewhere in the seventies, though. It's a very small, private, and exclusive hospital where I had my appendix out two years ago. Henchley. *H-E-N-C—*

INFORMATION: One moment, please.

MRS. STEVENSON: Please—hurry. And please—what *is* the time?

INFORMATION: I do not know, madam. You may find out the time by dialing Meridian 7-1212.

MRS. STEVENSON (*irritated*): Oh, for heaven's sake! Couldn't you—?

INFORMATION: The number of Henchley Hospital is Butterfield 7-0105, madam.

MRS. STEVENSON: Butterfield 7-0105. (*She hangs up before she finishes speaking, and immediately dials number as she repeats it.*)

    (*Phone rings.*)

WOMAN (*middle-aged, solid, firm, practical*): Henchley Hospital, good evening.

MRS. STEVENSON: Nurses' Registry.

WOMAN: Who was it you wished to speak to, please?

MRS. STEVENSON (*highhanded*): I want the Nurses' Registry at once. I want a trained nurse. I want to hire her immediately. For the night.

WOMAN: I see. And what is the nature of the case, madam?

MRS. STEVENSON: Nerves. I'm very nervous. I need soothing—and companionship. My husband is away—and I'm—

WOMAN: Have you been recommended to us by any doctor in particular, madam?

MRS. STEVENSON: No. But I really don't see why all this catechizing is necessary. I want a trained nurse. I was a patient in your hospital two years ago. And after all, I *do* expect to *pay* this person—

WOMAN: We quite understand that, madam. But registered nurses are very scarce just now—and our superintendent has asked us to send people out only on cases where the physician in charge feels it is absolutely necessary.

MRS. STEVENSON (*growing hysterical*): Well, it *is* absolutely necessary. I'm a sick woman. I—I'm very upset. Very. I'm alone in this house—and I'm an invalid—and tonight I overheard a telephone conversation that upset me dreadfully. About a murder—a poor woman who was going to be murdered at eleven fifteen tonight—in fact, if someone doesn't come at once—I'm afraid I'll go out of my mind— (*Almost off handle by now.*)

WOMAN (*calmly*): I see. Well, I'll speak to Miss Phillips as soon as she comes in. And what is your name, madam?

MRS. STEVENSON: Miss Phillips. And when do you expect her in?

WOMAN: I really don't know, madam. She went out to supper at eleven o'clock.

MRS. STEVENSON: Eleven o'clock. But it's not eleven yet. (*She cries out.*) Oh, my clock *has* stopped. I thought it was running down. What time is it?

WOMAN: Just fourteen minutes past eleven.

    (*Sound of phone receiver being lifted on same line as* MRS. STEVENSON'S. *A click.*)

MRS. STEVENSON (*crying out*): What's *that?*

WOMAN: What was what, madam?

MRS. STEVENSON: That—that click just now—in my own telephone? As though someone had lifted the receiver off the hook of the extension phone downstairs—

WOMAN: I didn't hear it, madam. Now—about this—

MRS. STEVENSON (*scared*): But I *did.* There's someone in this house. Someone downstairs in the kitchen. And they're listening to me now. They're— (*Hangs up phone. In a suffocated voice.*) I won't pick it up. I won't let them hear me. I'll be quiet—and they'll think— (*With growing terror.*) But if I don't call someone now—while they're still down there—there'll be no time. (*She picks up receiver. Bland buzzing signal. She dials operator. Ring twice.*)

OPERATOR (*fat and lethargic*): Your call, please?

MRS. STEVENSON (*a desperate whisper*): Operator, I—I'm in desperate trouble—I—

OPERATOR: I cannot hear you, madam. Please speak louder.

MRS. STEVENSON (*still whispering*): I don't dare. I—there's someone listening. Can you hear me now?

OPERATOR: Your call, please? What number are you calling, madam?

MRS. STEVENSON (*desperately*): You've got to hear me. Oh, please. You've got to help me. There's someone in this house. Someone who's going to murder me. And you've got to get in touch with the— (*Click of receiver being put down in* MRS. STEVENSON'S *line. Bursting out wildly.*) Oh, there it is—he's put it down—he's put down the extension—he's coming— (*She screams.*) He's coming up the stairs— (*Hoarsely.*) Give me the Police Department— (*Screaming.*) The police!

OPERATOR: Ringing the Police Department.

(*Phone is rung. We hear sound of a train beginning to fade in. On second ring,* MRS. STEVENSON *screams again, but roaring of train drowns out her voice. For a few seconds we hear nothing but roaring of train, then dying away, phone at police headquarters ringing.*)

DUFFY: Police Department. Precinct 43. Duffy speaking. (*Pause.*) Police Department. Duffy speaking.

GEORGE: Sorry. Wrong number. (*Hangs up.*)

THE STILL ALARM

GEORGE S. KAUFMAN (1889–   ) is a versatile man of the theatre. He can write, produce, and direct plays and he can ad-lib during television interviews with the greatest ease. He began his career by writing humorous columns for Washington and New York newspapers. He wrote several plays by himself, including *The Still Alarm,* but his chief contribution to the American theatre lies in the plays he has written with collaborators: *Beggar on Horseback, Of Thee I Sing, Stage Door, You Can't Take It with You,* and *The Solid Gold Cadillac,* to name a few. Lynn Fontanne became a star in *Dulcy,* the first play Mr. Kaufman wrote. Moss Hart, in his book *Act One,* describes with affectionate, humorous detail Mr. Kaufman's working habits.

The Still Alarm was written for a musical revue and immediately became popular. The sketch is not as satiric as one would expect from Mr. Kaufman; instead it is an excellent example of his dry, offbeat humor. It must be read in the spirit intended by the author. The humor lies in the completely unexpected, untypical behavior of the characters. Only Mr. Kaufman could have developed so unbelievable a situation in so believable a way.

THE STILL ALARM

George S. Kaufman

(VITAL NOTE: *It is important that the entire play should be acted calmly and politely, in the manner of an English drawing-room comedy. No actor ever raises his voice; every line must be read as though it were an invitation to a cup of tea. If this direction is disregarded, the play has no point at all.*)

The scene is a hotel bedroom. Two windows in the rear wall with a bed between them. A telephone stand is at one end of the bed and a dresser is near the other. In the right wall is a door leading to the hall with a chair nearby. In the left wall is a door to another room; near it is a small table and two chairs.

ED *and* BOB *are on the stage.* ED *is getting into his overcoat as the curtain rises. Both are at the hall door.*

ED: Well, Bob, it's certainly been nice to see you again.

BOB: It was nice to see *you.*

ED: You come to town so seldom, I hardly ever get the chance to—

Copyright, 1925, by George S. Kaufman; copyright, 1930, by Brady & Wiman Productions Corporation; copyright, 1952, 1957 (in renewal), by George S. Kaufman. All rights reserved. CAUTION: Professionals and amateurs are hereby warned that *The Still Alarm*, being fully protected under the copyright laws of the United States of America, the British Empire, including the Dominion of Canada, and all other countries of the Copyright Union, is subject to a royalty. All rights, including professional, amateur, motion pictures, recitation, public reading, radio and television broadcasting and the rights of translation into foreign languages are strictly reserved. Amateurs may give stage production of this play upon payment of a royalty of Five Dollars for each performance, one week before the play is to be given, to Samuel French, Inc., at 25 West 45th St., New York 36, N.Y., or 7623 Sunset Blvd., Hollywood 46, Cal., or if in Canada to Samuel French (Canada) Ltd., at 27 Grenville St., Toronto, Ont.

BOB: Well, you know how it is. A business trip is always more or less of a bore.

ED: Next time you've got to come out to the house.

BOB: I want to come out. I just had to stick around the hotel this trip.

ED: Oh, I understand. Well, give my best to Edith.

BOB (*remembering something*): Oh, I say, Ed. Wait a minute.

ED: What's the matter?

BOB: I knew I wanted to show you something. (*Crosses to table. Gets roll of blueprints from drawer.*) Did you know I'm going to build?

ED (*follows to table*): A house?

BOB: You bet it's a house! (*Knock on hall door.*) Come in! (*Spreads plans.*) I just got these yesterday.

ED (*sits*): Well, that's fine! (*The knock is repeated—louder. Both men now give full attention to the door.*)

BOB: Come! Come in!

BELLBOY (*enters*): Mr. Barclay?

BOB: Well?

BELLBOY: I've a message from the clerk, sir. For Mr. Barclay personally.

BOB (*crosses to boy*): I'm Mr. Barclay. What is the message?

BELLBOY: The hotel is on fire, sir.

BOB: What's that?

BELLBOY: The hotel is on fire.

ED: This hotel?

BELLBOY: Yes, sir.

BOB: Well—is it bad?

BELLBOY: It looks pretty bad, sir.

ED: You mean it's going to burn down?

BELLBOY: We think so—yes, sir.

BOB (*a low whistle of surprise*): Well! We'd better leave.

BELLBOY: Yes, sir.

BOB: Going to burn down, huh?

BELLBOY: Yes, sir. If you'll step to the window you'll see. (BOB *goes to a window.*)

BOB: Yes, that is pretty bad. H'm (*To* ED.) I say, you really ought to see this—

ED (*crosses to window, peers out*): It's reached the floor right underneath.

BELLBOY: Yes, sir. The lower part of the hotel is about gone, sir.

BOB (*still looking out—looks up*): Still all right up above, though. (*Turns to boy.*) Have they notified the Fire Department?

BELLBOY: I wouldn't know, sir. I'm only the bellboy.

BOB: Well, that's the thing to do, obviously (*nods head to each one as if the previous line was a bright idea*) notify the Fire Department. Just call them up, give them the name of the hotel—

ED: Wait a minute. I can do better than that for you. (*To the boy.*) Ring through to the Chief, and tell him that Ed Jamison told you to telephone him. (*To* BOB.) We went to school together, you know.

BOB: That's fine. (*To the boy.*) Now, get that right. Tell the Chief that Mr. Jamison said to ring him.

ED: *Ed* Jamison.

BOB: Yes, *Ed* Jamison.

BELLBOY: Yes, sir. (*Turns to go.*)

BOB: Oh! Boy! (*Pulls out handful of change; picks out a coin.*) Here you are.

BELLBOY: Thank you, sir. (*Exit* BELLBOY.)

    (ED *sits at table, lights cigarette, and throws match on rug, then steps on it. There is a moment's pause.*)

BOB: Well! (*Crosses and looks out window.*) Say, we'll have to get out of here pretty soon.

ED (*going to window*): How is it—no better?

BOB: Worse, if anything. It'll be up here in a few moments.

ED: What floor *is* this?

BOB: Eleventh.

ED: Eleven. We couldn't jump, then.

BOB: Oh, no. You never could jump. (*Comes away from window to dresser.*) Well, I've got to get my things together. (*Pulls out suitcase.*)

ED (*smoothing out the plans*): Who made these for you?

BOB: A fellow here—Rawlins. (*Turns a shirt in his hand.*) I ought to call one of the other hotels for a room.

ED: Oh, you can get in.

BOB: They're pretty crowded. (*Feels something on the sole of his foot; inspects it.*) Say, the floor's getting hot.

ED: I know it. It's getting stuffy in the room, too. Phew! (*He looks around, then goes to the phone.*) Hello. Ice water in eleven eighteen. (*Crosses to table.*)

BOB (*at bed*): That's the stuff. (*Packs.*) You know, if I move to another hotel I'll never get my mail. Everybody thinks I'm stopping here.

ED (*studying the plans*): Say, this isn't bad.

BOB (*eagerly*): Do you like it? (*Remembers his plight.*) Suppose I go to another hotel and there's a fire there, too!

ED: You've got to take *some* chance.

BOB: I know, but here I'm sure. (*Phone rings.*) Oh, answer that, will you, Ed? (*To dresser and back.*)

ED (*crosses to phone*): Sure. (*At phone.*) Hello— Oh, that's good. Fine. What? Oh! Well, wait a minute. (*To* BOB.) The firemen are downstairs and some of them want to come up to this room.

BOB: Tell them, of course.

ED (*at phone*): All right. Come right up. (*Hangs up, crosses and sits at table.*) Now we'll get some action.

BOB (*looks out of window*): Say, there's an awful crowd of people on the street.

ED (*absently, as he pores over the plans*): Maybe there's been some kind of accident.

BOB (*peering out, suitcase in hand*): No. More likely they heard about the fire. (*A knock at the door.*) Come in.

BELLBOY (*enters*): I beg pardon, Mr. Barclay, the firemen have arrived.

BOB: Show them in. (*Crosses to door.*)

　　　(*The door opens. In the doorway appear two* FIREMEN *in full regalia. The* FIRST FIREMAN *carries a hose and rubber coat; the* SECOND *has a violin case.*)

FIRST FIREMAN (*very apologetically*): Mr. Barclay.

BOB: I'm Mr. Barclay.

FIRST FIREMAN: We're the firemen, Mr. Barclay. (*They remove their hats.*)

BOB: How de do?

ED: How de do?

BOB: A great pleasure, I assure you. Really must apologize for the condition of this room, but—

FIRST FIREMAN: Oh, that's all right. I know how it is at home.

BOB: May I present a friend of mine, Mr. Ed Jamison—

FIRST FIREMAN: How are you?

ED: How are you, boys? (SECOND FIREMAN *nods.*) I know your Chief.

FIRST FIREMAN: Oh, is that so? He knows the Chief—dear old Chiefie. (SECOND FIREMAN *giggles.*)

BOB (*embarrassed*): Well, I guess you boys want to get to work, don't you?

FIRST FIREMAN: Well, if you don't mind. We would like to spray around a little bit.

BOB: May I help you?

FIRST FIREMAN: Yes, if you please. (BOB *helps him into his rubber coat. At the same time the* SECOND FIREMAN, *without a word, lays the violin case on the bed, opens it, takes out the violin, and begins tuning it.*)

BOB (*watching him*): I don't think I understand.

FIRST FIREMAN: Well, you see, Sid doesn't get much chance to practice at home. Sometimes, at a fire, while we're waiting for a wall to fall or something, why, a fireman doesn't really have anything to do, and personally I like to see him improve himself symphonically. I hope you don't resent it. You're not antisymphonic?

BOB: Of course not— (BOB *and* ED *nod understandingly; the* SECOND FIREMAN *is now waxing the bow.*)

FIRST FIREMAN: Well, if you'll excuse me— (*To window. Turns with decision toward the window. You feel that he is about to get down to business.*)

BOB: Charming personalities.

ED (*follows over to the window*): How *is* the fire?

FIRST FIREMAN (*feels the wall*): It's pretty bad right now. This wall will go pretty soon now, but it'll fall out that way, so it's all right. (*Peers out.*) That next room is the place to fight it from. (*Crosses to door in left wall.* BOB *shows ties as* ED *crosses.*)

ED (*sees ties*): Oh! Aren't those gorgeous!

FIRST FIREMAN (*to* BOB): Have you the key for this room?

BOB: Why, no. I've nothing to do with that room. I've just got this one. (*Folding a shirt as he talks.*)

ED: Oh, it's very comfortable.

FIRST FIREMAN: That's too bad. I had something up my sleeve, if I could have gotten in there. Oh, well, may I use your phone?

BOB: Please do. (*To* ED.) Do you think you might hold this? (*Indicates the hose.*)

ED: How?

FIRST FIREMAN: Just crawl under it. (*As he does that.*) Thanks. (*At phone.*) Hello. Let me have the clerk, please. (*To* SECOND FIREMAN.) Give us that little thing you played the night the Equitable Building burned down. (*Back to phone.*) Are you there? This is one of the firemen. Oh, *you* know. I'm in room—ah— (*Looks at* BOB.)

BOB: Eleven eighteen.

FIRST FIREMAN: Eleven eighteen, and I want to get into the next room— Oh, goody. Will you send someone up with the key? There's no one in there? Oh, supergoody! Right away. (*Hangs up.*)

BOB: That's fine. (*To* FIREMEN.) Won't you sit down?

FIRST FIREMAN: Thanks.

ED: Have a cigar?

FIRST FIREMAN (*takes it*): Much obliged.

BOB: A light?

FIRST FIREMAN: If you please.

ED (*failing to find a match*): Bob, have you a match?

BOB (*crosses to table*): I thought there were some here. (*Hands in pockets.*)

FIRST FIREMAN: Oh, never mind. (*He goes to a window, leans out, and emerges with cigar lighted.* BOB *crosses to dresser; slams drawer. The* SECOND FIREMAN *taps violin with bow.*)

FIRST FIREMAN: Mr. Barclay, I think he's ready now.

BOB: Pardon me.

> (*They all sit. The* SECOND FIREMAN *takes center of stage, with all the manner of a concert violinist. He goes into "Keep the Home Fires Burning."* BOB, ED *and* FIRST FIREMAN *wipe brow as lights dim to red on closing eight bars.*)

TRIFLES

SUSAN GLASPELL (1882–1948) was born in Davenport, Iowa, and received her college training at Drake University in Des Moines. As a reporter for a Des Moines newspaper, she covered sessions of the state legislature. From this experience she acquired a great amount of material which she later developed into short stories and novels. In fact, *Trifles* grew out of one of her experiences as a newspaperwoman. Miss Glaspell loved the theatre and supported many theatre groups with her plays and her encouragement. She helped the Provincetown Players become established on Cape Cod and on Macdougal Street, in Greenwich Village, and she worked with the Federal Theatre Project.

Trifles was first produced by the Provincetown Players, who also gave first performances of many of Eugene O'Neill's one-act plays. The theme of *Trifles*—it's the small things that count —is not an unusual one, but Miss Glaspell's treatment is certainly unique. Slowly she builds interest until the reader becomes as deeply involved as the neighbors. Although two important characters never appear in the play, they are so clearly described that we automatically take sides. We understand how sometimes man's loyalty transcends man's laws.

TRIFLES

Susan Glaspell

The scene is the kitchen in the farmhouse of JOHN WRIGHT, a gloomy kitchen, abandoned without having been put in order—the walls covered with a faded wallpaper. A door leads to the parlor at right. On the wall near this door is a built-in kitchen cupboard with shelves in the upper portion and drawers below. In the rear wall, up two steps, is a door opening onto stairs leading to the second floor. In the rear wall there is another door which leads to the shed and from there to the outside. Between these two doors is an old-fashioned black iron stove. Running along the wall at left from the shed door is an old iron sink and sink shelf, in which is set a hand pump, and an uncurtained window. Near the window is an old wooden rocker. In the center of the room is an unpainted wooden kitchen table with straight chairs on either side. There is a small chair near the parlor door. Unwashed pans under the sink, a loaf of bread outside the breadbox, a dish towel on the table—other signs of incompleted work. At the rear, the shed door opens and the SHERIFF comes in, followed by the COUNTY ATTORNEY and HALE, a neighboring farmer. The SHERIFF and HALE are men in middle life, the COUNTY ATTORNEY is a young man; all are much bundled up and go at once to the stove. They are followed by two women—the SHERIFF's wife, MRS. PETERS, first; she is a slight, wiry woman, a thin, nervous face. MRS. HALE is larger and would ordinarily be called

Reprinted by permission of Dodd, Mead & Company from *Plays* by Susan Glaspell. Copyright, 1920, 1948, by Susan Glaspell. For permission to produce *Trifles* write direct to Baker's Plays, Boston 10, Mass. No performance may be given without permission.

more comfortable looking, but she is disturbed now and looks fearfully about as she enters. The women have come in slowly, and stand close together near the door.

COUNTY ATTORNEY (*at stove, rubbing his hands*): This feels good. Come up to the fire, ladies.

MRS. PETERS (*after taking a step forward*): I'm not—cold.

SHERIFF (*unbuttoning his overcoat and stepping away from the stove to table as if to mark the beginning of official business*): Now, Mr. Hale, before we move things about, you explain to Mr. Henderson just what you saw when you came here yesterday morning.

COUNTY ATTORNEY: By the way, has anything been moved? Are things just as you left them yesterday?

SHERIFF (*looking about*): It's just the same. When it dropped below zero last night I thought I'd better send Frank out this morning to make a fire for us. (*Sits down.*) No use getting pneumonia with a big case on, but I told him not to touch anything except the stove—and you know Frank.

COUNTY ATTORNEY: Somebody should have been left here yesterday.

SHERIFF: Oh, yesterday. When I had to send Frank to Morris Center for that man who went crazy—I want you to know I had my hands full yesterday. I knew you could get back from Omaha by today and as long as I went over everything here myself—

COUNTY ATTORNEY: Well, Mr. Hale, tell just what happened when you came here yesterday morning.

HALE (*crossing down to above table*): Harry and I had started to town with a load of potatoes. We came along the road from my place and as I got here I said, "I'm going to see if I can't get John Wright to go in with me on a party telephone." I spoke to Wright about it once before and he put me off, saying folks talked too much anyway, and all he asked was peace and quiet—I guess you know about how much he talked himself; but I thought maybe if I went to the house and talked about it before his wife, though I said to Harry that I didn't know as what his wife wanted made much difference to John—

COUNTY ATTORNEY: Let's talk about that later, Mr. Hale. I do want to talk about that, but tell now just what happened when you got to the house.

HALE: I didn't hear or see anything; I knocked at the door, and still it was all quiet inside. I knew they must be up; it was past eight o'clock. So I knocked again, and I thought I heard somebody say, "Come in." I wasn't sure, I'm not sure yet, but I opened the door—this door (*indicating the door by which the two women are still standing*), and there in that rocker (*pointing to it*) sat Mrs. Wright.

(*They all look at the rocker near the window.*)

COUNTY ATTORNEY: What—was she doing?

HALE: She was rockin' back and forth. She had her apron in her hand and was kind of—pleating it.

COUNTY ATTORNEY: And how did she—look?

HALE: Well, she looked queer.

COUNTY ATTORNEY: How do you mean—queer?

HALE: Well, as if she didn't know what she was going to do next. And kind of done up.

COUNTY ATTORNEY (*takes out notebook and pencil and sits at table*): How did she seem to feel about your coming?

HALE: Why, I don't think she minded—one way or other. She didn't pay much attention. I said, "How do, Mrs. Wright. It's cold, ain't it?" And she said, "Is it?"—and went on kind of pleating at her apron. Well, I was surprised; she didn't ask me to come up to the stove, or to set down, but just sat there, not even looking at me, so I said, "I want to see John." And then she—laughed. I guess you would call it a laugh. I thought of Harry and the team outside, so I said a little sharp: "Can't I see John?" "No," she says, kind o' dull like. "Ain't he home?" says I. "Yes," says she, "he's home." "Then why can't I see him?" I asked her, out of patience. " 'Cause he's dead," says she. "*Dead?*" says I. She just nodded her head, not getting a bit excited, but rockin' back and forth. "Why—where is he?" says I, not knowing what to say. She just pointed upstairs—like that. (*Himself pointing to the room above.*) I started for the stairs, with the idea of going up there. I walked from there to here— then I says, "Why, what did he die of?" "He died of a rope round his neck," says she, and just went on pleatin' at her apron. Well, I went out and called Harry. I thought I might—need help. We went upstairs and there he was lyin'—

COUNTY ATTORNEY: I think I'd rather have you go into that upstairs, where you can point it all out. Just go on now with the rest of the story.

HALE: Well, my first thought was to get that rope off. It looked— (*Stops, his face twitches.*) But Harry, he went up to him, and he said, "No, he's dead, all right, and we'd better not touch anything." So we went back downstairs. She was still sitting that same way. "Has anybody been notified?" I asked. "No," says she, unconcerned. "Who did this, Mrs. Wright?" said Harry. He said it businesslike— and she stopped pleatin' of her apron. "I don't know," she says. "You don't *know?*" says Harry. "No," says she. "Weren't you sleepin' in the bed with him?" says Harry. "Yes," says she, "but I was on the inside." "Somebody slipped a rope round his neck and strangled him and you didn't wake up?" says Harry. "I didn't wake up," she said after him. We must 'a' looked as if we didn't see how that could be, for after a minute she said, "I sleep sound." Harry was going to ask her more questions but I said maybe we ought to let her tell her story first to the coroner, or the sheriff, so Harry went fast as he could to Rivers' place, where there's a telephone.

COUNTY ATTORNEY: And what did Mrs. Wright do when she knew that you had gone for the coroner?

HALE: She moved from the rocker to that chair over there (*pointing to a small chair in the corner*) and just sat there with her hands held together and looking down. I got a feeling that I ought to make some conversation, so I said I had come in to see if John wanted to put in a telephone, and at that she started to laugh, and then she stopped and looked at me—scared. (*The* COUNTY ATTORNEY, *who has had his notebook out, makes a note.*) I dunno, maybe it wasn't scared. I wouldn't like to say it was. Soon Harry got back, and then Dr. Lloyd came, and you, Mr. Peters, and so I guess that's all I know that you don't.

COUNTY ATTORNEY (*rising and looking around*): I guess we'll go upstairs first—and then out to the barn and around there. (*To the* SHERIFF.) You're convinced that there was nothing important here—nothing that would point to any motive?

SHERIFF: Nothing here but kitchen things.

> (*The* COUNTY ATTORNEY, *after again looking around the kitchen, opens the door of a cupboard closet. He brings a small chair over, gets up on it, and looks on a shelf. Pulls his hand away, sticky.*)

COUNTY ATTORNEY: Here's a nice mess.

> (*The women draw nearer to the stove.*)

MRS. PETERS (*to the other woman*): Oh, her fruit; it did freeze. (*To the* COUNTY ATTORNEY.) She worried about that when it turned so cold. She said the fire'd go out and her jars would break.

SHERIFF (*rises*): Well, can you beat the women! Held for murder and worryin' about her preserves.

COUNTY ATTORNEY (*getting down from chair*): I guess before we're through she may have something more serious than preserves to worry about.

HALE: Well, women are used to worrying over trifles.

> (*The two women move a little closer together.*)

COUNTY ATTORNEY (*with the gallantry of a young politician*): And yet, for all their worries, what would we do without the ladies? (*The women do not unbend. He goes to the sink, takes a dipperful of water from the pail, and pouring it into a basin, washes his hands. While he is doing this the* SHERIFF *and* HALE *cross to cupboard, which they inspect. The* COUNTY ATTORNEY *starts to wipe his hands on the roller towel, turns it for a cleaner place.*) Dirty towels! (*Kicks his foot against the pans under the sink.*) Not much of a housekeeper, would you say, ladies?

MRS. HALE (*stiffly*): There's a great deal of work to be done on a farm.

COUNTY ATTORNEY: To be sure. And yet (*with a little bow to her*) I know there are some Dickson County farmhouses which do not have such roller towels. (*He gives it a pull to expose its full length again.*)

MRS. HALE: Those towels get dirty awful quick. Men's hands aren't always as clean as they might be.

COUNTY ATTORNEY: Ah, loyal to your sex, I see. But you and Mrs. Wright were neighbors. I suppose you were friends, too.

MRS. HALE (*shaking her head*): I've not seen much of her of late years. I've not been in this house—it's more than a year.

COUNTY ATTORNEY (*crossing to women*): And why was that? You didn't like her?

MRS. HALE: I liked her all well enough. Farmers' wives have their hands full, Mr. Henderson. And then—

COUNTY ATTORNEY: Yes—?

MRS. HALE (*looking about*): It never seemed a very cheerful place.

COUNTY ATTORNEY: No, it's not cheerful. I shouldn't say she had the homemaking instinct.

MRS. HALE: Well, I don't know as Wright had, either.

COUNTY ATTORNEY: You mean that they didn't get on very well?

MRS. HALE: No, I don't mean anything. But I don't think a place'd be any cheerfuler for John Wright's being in it.

COUNTY ATTORNEY: I'd like to talk more of that a little later. I want to get the lay of things upstairs now. (*He goes past the women to rear wall, where steps lead to a stair door.*)

SHERIFF: I suppose anything Mrs. Peters does'll be all right. She was to take in some clothes for her, you know, and a few little things. We left in such a hurry yesterday.

COUNTY ATTORNEY: Yes, but I would like to see what you take Mrs. Peters, and keep an eye out for anything that might be of use to us.

MRS. PETERS: Yes, Mr. Henderson.

    (*The men leave. The women listen to the men's steps on the stairs, then look about the kitchen.*)

MRS. HALE (*crossing to sink*): I'd hate to have men coming

into my kitchen, snooping around and criticizing. (*She arranges the pans under sink which the* COUNTY ATTORNEY *had shoved out of place.*)

MRS. PETERS: Of course it's no more than their duty. (*Crosses to cupboard.*)

MRS. HALE: Duty's all right, but I guess that deputy sheriff that came out to make the fire might have got a little of this on. (*Gives the roller towel a pull.*) Wish I'd thought of that sooner. Seems mean to talk about her for not having things slicked up when she had to come away in such a hurry. (*Crosses to* MRS. PETERS *at cupboard.*)

MRS. PETERS (*who has been looking through cupboard, lifts one end of a towel that covers a pan*): She had bread set. (*Stands still.*)

MRS. HALE (*eyes fixed on a loaf of bread beside the breadbox, which is on a low shelf of the cupboard*): She was going to put this in there. (*Picks up loaf, then abruptly drops it. In a manner of returning to familiar things.*) It's a shame about her fruit. I wonder if it's all gone. (*Gets up on the chair and looks.*) I think there's some here that's all right, Mrs. Peters. Yes—here. (*Holding it toward the window.*) This is cherries, too. (*Looking again.*) I declare, I believe that's the only one. (*Gets down, jar in her hand. Goes to the sink and wipes it off on the outside.*) She'll feel awful bad after all her hard work in the hot weather. I remember the afternoon I put up my cherries last summer. (*She puts the jar on the big kitchen table. With a sigh, is about to sit down in the rocking chair. Before she is seated, realizes what chair it is; with a slow look at it, steps back. The chair, which she has touched, rocks back and forth.* MRS. PETERS *moves to table and they both watch the chair rock for a moment or two.*)

MRS. PETERS (*shaking off the mood which the empty rocking chair has evoked, now, in a businesslike manner, speaks*): Well, I must get those things from the front-room closet. (*She goes to the parlor door, but, after looking into the other room, steps back.*) You coming with me, Mrs. Hale? You could help me carry them. (*They go in the other room;*

reappear, MRS. PETERS *carrying a dress, petticoat, and skirt,* MRS. HALE *following with a pair of shoes.*) My, it's cold in there. (*She puts the clothes on the big table, and hurries to the stove.*)

MRS. HALE (*at table examining the skirt*): Wright was close. I think maybe that's why she kept so much to herself. She didn't even belong to the Ladies' Aid. I suppose she felt she couldn't do her part, and then you don't enjoy things when you feel shabby. She used to wear pretty clothes and be lively, when she was Minnie Foster, one of the town girls singing in the choir. But that—oh, that was thirty years ago. This all you was to take in?

MRS. PETERS: She said she wanted an apron. Funny thing to want, for there isn't much to get you dirty in jail, goodness knows. But I suppose just to make her feel more natural. (*Crosses to cupboard.*) She said they was in the top drawer in this cupboard. Yes, here. And then her little shawl that always hung behind the door. (*Opens stair door and looks.*) Yes, here it is. (*Quickly shuts door leading upstairs.*)

MRS. HALE (*abruptly moving toward her*): Mrs. Peters?

MRS. PETERS: Yes, Mrs. Hale?

MRS. HALE: Do you think she did it?

MRS. PETERS (*in a frightened voice*): Oh, I don't know.

MRS. HALE: Well, I don't think she did. Asking for an apron and her little shawl. Worrying about her fruit.

MRS. PETERS (*starts to speak, glances up, where footsteps are heard in the room above; in a low voice*): Mr. Peters says it looks bad for her. Mr. Henderson is awful sarcastic in a speech and he'll make fun of her sayin' she didn't wake up.

MRS. HALE: Well, I guess John Wright didn't wake when they was slipping that rope under his neck.

MRS. PETERS (*crossing slowly to table and placing shawl and apron on table with other clothing*): No, it's strange. It must have been done awful crafty and still. They say it was such a—funny way to kill a man, rigging it all up like that.

MRS. HALE (*crossing to* MRS. PETERS *at table*): That's just what Mr. Hale said. There was a gun in the house. He says that's what he can't understand.

MRS. PETERS: Mr. Henderson said coming out that what was needed for the case was a motive; something to show anger, or—sudden feeling.

MRS. HALE (*who is standing by the table*): Well, I don't see any signs of anger around here. (*She puts her hand on the dish towel, which lies on the table, stands looking down at table, one half of which is clean, the other half messy.*) It's wiped to here. (*Makes a move as if to finish work, then turns and looks at loaf of bread outside the breadbox. Drops towel. In that voice of coming back to familiar things.*) Wonder how they are finding things upstairs. I hope she had it a little more red-up up there. You know, it seems kind of *sneaking*. Locking her up in town and then coming out here and trying to get her own house to turn against her!

MRS. PETERS: But, Mrs. Hale, the law is the law.

MRS. HALE: I s'pose 'tis. (*Unbuttoning her coat.*) Better loosen up your things, Mrs. Peters. You won't feel them when you go out.

    (MRS. PETERS *takes off her fur tippet, goes to hang it on chair back left of table, stands looking at the work basket on floor near window.*)

MRS. PETERS: She was piecing a quilt. (*She brings the large sewing basket to the center table and they look at the bright pieces.*)

MRS. HALE: It's a log-cabin pattern. Pretty, isn't it? I wonder if she was goin' to quilt it or just knot it?

    (*Footsteps have been heard coming down the stairs. The* SHERIFF *enters, followed by* HALE *and the* COUNTY ATTORNEY.)

SHERIFF: They wonder if she was going to quilt it or just knot it!

    (*The men laugh, the women look abashed.*)

COUNTY ATTORNEY (*rubbing his hands over the stove*): Frank's fire didn't do much up there, did it? Well, let's go out to the barn and get that cleared up.

    (*The men go outside.*)

MRS. HALE (*resentfully*): I don't know as there's anything so strange. our takin' up our time with little things while we're waiting for them to get the evidence. (*She sits in chair at table, smoothing out a block with decision.*) I don't see as it's anything to laugh about.

MRS. PETERS (*apologetically*): Of course they've got awful important things on their minds. (*Pulls up a chair and joins* MRS. HALE *at the table.*)

MRS. HALE (*examining another block*): Mrs. Peters, look at this one. Here, this is the one she was working on, and look at the sewing! All the rest of it has been so nice and even. And look at this! It's all over the place! Why, it looks as if she didn't know what she was about! (*After she has said this they look at each other, then start to glance back at the door. After an instant* MRS. HALE *has pulled at a knot and ripped the sewing.*)

MRS. PETERS: Oh, what are you doing, Mrs. Hale?

MRS. HALE (*mildly*): Just pulling out a stitch or two that's not sewed very good. (*Threading a needle.*) Bad sewing always made me fidgety.

MRS. PETERS (*with a glance at door, nervously*): I don't think we ought to touch things.

MRS. HALE: I'll just finish up this end. (*Suddenly stopping and leaning forward.*) Mrs. Peters?

MRS. PETERS: Yes, Mrs. Hale?

MRS. HALE: What do you suppose she was so nervous about?

MRS. PETERS: Oh, I don't know. I don't know as she was nervous. I sometimes sew awful queer when I'm just tired. (MRS. HALE *starts to say something, looks at* MRS. PETERS, *then goes on sewing.*) Well, I must get these things wrapped up. They may be through sooner than we think. (*Putting apron and other things together.*) I wonder where I can find a piece of paper, and string. (*Rises.*)

MRS. HALE: In that cupboard, maybe.

MRS. PETERS (*looking in cupboard*): Why, here's a bird cage. (*Holds it up.*) Did she have a bird, Mrs. Hale?

MRS. HALE: Why, I don't know whether she did or not—I've not been here for so long. There was a man around last year selling canaries cheap, but I don't know as she took one; maybe she did. She used to sing real pretty herself.

MRS. PETERS (*glancing around*): Seems funny to think of a bird here. But she must have had one, or why would she have a cage? I wonder what happened to it?

MRS. HALE: I s'pose maybe the cat got it.

MRS. PETERS: No, she didn't have a cat. She's got that feeling some people have about cats—being afraid of them. My cat got in her room and she was real upset and asked me to take it out.

MRS. HALE: My sister Bessie was like that. Queer, ain't it?

MRS. PETERS (*examining the cage*): Why, look at this door. It's broke. One hinge is pulled apart. (*Takes a step down to* MRS. HALE.)

MRS. HALE (*looking, too*): Looks as if someone must have been rough with it.

MRS. PETERS: Why, yes. (*She brings the cage forward and puts it on the table.*)

MRS. HALE (*glancing toward door*): I wish if they're going to find any evidence they'd be about it. I don't like this place.

MRS. PETERS: But I'm awful glad you came with me, Mrs. Hale. It would be lonesome for me sitting here alone.

MRS. HALE: It would, wouldn't it? (*Dropping her sewing.*) But I tell you what I do wish, Mrs. Peters. I wish I had come over sometimes when *she* was here. I (*looking around the room*) wish I had.

MRS. PETERS: But of course you were awful busy, Mrs. Hale— your house and your children.

MRS. HALE (*rises and crosses to window*): I could've come. I stayed away because it weren't cheerful—and that's why I ought to have come. I—(*looking out window*)—I've never liked this place. Maybe because it's down in a hollow and you don't see the road. I dunno what it is, but it's a lonesome place and always was. I wish I had come over to see Minnie Foster sometimes. I can see now— (*Shakes her head.*)

MRS. PETERS: Well, you mustn't reproach yourself, Mrs. Hale.

Somehow we just don't see how it is with other folks until
—something turns up.

MRS. HALE: Not having children makes less work—but it
makes a quiet house, and Wright out to work all day, and
no company when he did come in. (*Turning from window.*) Did you know John Wright, Mrs. Peters?

MRS. PETERS: Not to know him; I've seen him in town. They
say he was a good man.

MRS. HALE: Yes—good; he didn't drink, and kept his word as
well as most, I guess, and paid his debts. But he was a hard
man, Mrs. Peters. Just to pass the time of day with him—
(*Shivers.*) Like a raw wind that gets to the bone. (*Pauses,
her eye falling on the cage.*) I should think she would 'a'
wanted a bird. But what do you suppose went with it?

MRS. PETERS: I don't know, unless it got sick and died. (*She
reaches over and swings the broken door, swings it again;
both women watch it.*)

MRS. HALE: You weren't raised round here, were you? (MRS.
PETERS *shakes her head.*) You didn't know—her?

MRS. PETERS: Not till they brought her yesterday.

MRS. HALE: She—come to think of it, she was kind of like a
bird herself—real sweet and pretty, but kind of timid and—
fluttery. How—she—did—change. (*Silence; then, as if struck
by a happy thought and relieved to get back to everyday
things, crosses to cupboard, replaces small chair used to
stand on to its original place.*) Tell you what, Mrs. Peters,
why don't you take the quilt in with you? It might take up
her mind.

MRS. PETERS: Why, I think that's a real nice idea, Mrs. Hale.
There couldn't possibly be any objection to it, could there?
Now, just what would I take? I wonder if her patches are
in here—and her things.

(*They look in the sewing basket.*)

MRS. HALE (*crosses to table*): Here's some red. I expect this
has got sewing things in it. (*Brings out a fancy box.*) What
a pretty box. Looks like something somebody would give
you. Maybe her scissors are in here. (*Opens box. Suddenly
puts her hand to her nose.*) Why— (MRS. PETERS *bends*

nearer, then turns her face away.) There's something wrapped up in this piece of silk.

MRS. PETERS: Why, this isn't her scissors.

MRS. HALE (*lifting the silk*): Oh, Mrs. Peters—it's—
     (MRS. PETERS *bends closer.*)

MRS. PETERS: It's the bird.

MRS. HALE: But, Mrs. Peters—look at it! Its neck! Look at its neck! It's all—other side to.

MRS. PETERS: Somebody—wrung—its—neck.
     (*Their eyes meet. A look of growing comprehension, of horror. Steps are heard outside.* MRS. HALE *slips box under quilt pieces, and sinks into her chair. Enter* SHERIFF *and* COUNTY ATTORNEY. MRS. PETERS *stands looking out of window.*)

COUNTY ATTORNEY (*as one turning from serious things to little pleasantries*): Well, ladies, have you decided whether she was going to quilt it or knot it? (*Crosses to table.*)

MRS. PETERS: We think she was going to—knot it.
     (SHERIFF *crosses to stove, lifts stove lid, and glances at fire, then stands warming hands at stove.*)

COUNTY ATTORNEY: Well, that's interesting, I'm sure. (*Seeing the bird cage.*) Has the bird flown?

MRS. HALE (*putting more quilt pieces over the box*): We think the—cat got it.

COUNTY ATTORNEY (*preoccupied*): Is there a cat?
     (MRS. HALE *glances in a quick, covert way at* MRS. PETERS.)

MRS. PETERS (*turning from window*): Well, not *now*. They're superstitious, you know. They leave.

COUNTY ATTORNEY (*to* SHERIFF PETERS, *continuing an interrupted conversation*): No sign at all of anyone having come from the outside. Their own rope. Now let's go up again and go over it piece by piece. (*They start upstairs.*) It would have to have been someone who knew just the—
     (MRS. PETERS *sits down at the table. The two women sit there not looking at one another, but as if peering into something and at the same time holding back. When they talk now it is in the manner of feeling*

*their way over strange ground, as if afraid of what
they are saying, but as if they cannot help saying it.*)

MRS. HALE (*hesitantly and in hushed voice*): She liked the
bird. She was going to bury it in that pretty box.

MRS. PETERS (*in a whisper*): When I was a girl—my kitten—
there was a boy took a hatchet, and before my eyes—and
before I could get there— (*Covers her face an instant.*) If
they hadn't held me back I would have—(*catches herself,
looks upstairs where steps are heard, falters weakly*)—hurt
him.

MRS. HALE (*with a slow look around her*): I wonder how it
would seem never to have had any children around.
(*Pause.*) No, Wright wouldn't like the bird—a thing that
sang. She used to sing. He killed that, too.

MRS. PETERS (*moving uneasily*): We don't know who killed
the bird.

MRS. HALE: I knew John Wright.

MRS. PETERS: It was an awful thing was done in this house
that night, Mrs. Hale. Killing a man while he slept, slipping
a rope around his neck that choked the life out of him.

MRS. HALE: His neck. Choked the life out of him. (*Her hand
goes out and rests on the bird cage.*)

MRS. PETERS (*with rising voice*): We don't know who killed
him. We don't *know.*

MRS. HALE (*her own feeling not interrupted*): If there'd been
years and years of nothing, then a bird to sing to you, it
would be awful—still, after the bird was still.

MRS. PETERS (*something within her speaking*): I know what
stillness is. When we homesteaded in Dakota, and my first
baby died—after he was two years old, and me with no
other then—

MRS. HALE (*moving*): How soon do you suppose they'll be
through looking for the evidence?

MRS. PETERS: I know what stillness is. (*Pulling herself back.*)
The law has got to punish crime, Mrs. Hale.

MRS. HALE (*not as if answering that*): I wish you'd seen
Minnie Foster when she wore a white dress with blue ribbons and stood up there in the choir and sang. (*A look*

around the room.) Oh, I *wish* I'd come over here once in a while! That was a crime! That was a crime! Who's going to punish that?

MRS. PETERS (*looking upstairs*): We mustn't—take on.

MRS. HALE: I might have known she needed help! I know how things can be—for women. I tell you, it's queer, Mrs. Peters. We live close together and we live far apart. We all go through the same things—it's all just a different kind of the same thing. (*Brushes her eyes, noticing the jar of fruit, reaches out for it.*) If I was you I wouldn't tell her her fruit was gone. Tell her it *ain't.* Tell her it's all right. Take this in to prove it to her. She—she may never know whether it was broke or not.

MRS. PETERS (*takes the jar, looks about for something to wrap it in; takes petticoat from the clothes brought from the other room, very nervously begins winding this around the jar; in a false voice*): My, it's a good thing the men couldn't hear us. Wouldn't they just laugh! Getting all stirred up over a little thing like a—dead canary. As if that could have anything to do with—with—wouldn't they *laugh!*

(*The men are heard coming downstairs.*)

MRS. HALE (*under her breath*): Maybe they would—maybe they wouldn't.

COUNTY ATTORNEY: No, Peters, it's all perfectly clear except a reason for doing it. But you know juries when it comes to women. If there was some definite thing. (*Crosses slowly to table.* MRS. HALE *and* MRS. PETERS *remain seated at either side of table.*) Something to show—something to make a story about—a thing that would connect up with this strange way of doing it—

(*The women's eyes meet for an instant. Enter* HALE *from outer door.*)

HALE (*remaining by door*): Well, I've got the team around. Pretty cold out there.

COUNTY ATTORNEY: I'm going to stay here awhile by myself. (*To the* SHERIFF.) You can send Frank out for me, can't you? I want to go over everything. I'm not satisfied that we can't do better.

SHERIFF: Do you want to see what Mrs. Peters is going to take in?

(*The* COUNTY ATTORNEY *picks up the apron, laughs.*)

COUNTY ATTORNEY: Oh, I guess they're not very dangerous things the ladies have picked out. (*Moves a few things about, disturbing the quilt pieces which cover the box. Steps back.*) No, Mrs. Peters doesn't need supervising. For that matter, a sheriff's wife is married to the law. Ever think of it that way, Mrs. Peters?

MRS. PETERS: Not—just that way.

SHERIFF (*chuckling*): Married to the law. (*Moves to parlor door.*) I just want you to come in here a minute, George. We ought to take a look at these windows.

COUNTY ATTORNEY (*scoffingly*): Oh, windows!

SHERIFF: We'll be right out, Mr. Hale.

(HALE *goes outside. The* SHERIFF *follows the* COUNTY ATTORNEY *into the other room. Then* MRS. HALE *rises, hands tight together, looking intensely at* MRS. PETERS, *whose eyes make a slow turn, finally meeting* MRS. HALE's. *A moment* MRS. HALE *holds her, then her own eyes point the way to where the box is concealed. Suddenly* MRS. PETERS *throws back quilt pieces and tries to put the box in the bag she is carrying. It is too big. She opens box, starts to take bird out, cannot touch it, goes to pieces, stands there helpless. Sound of a knob turning in the other room.* MRS. HALE *snatches the box and puts it in the pocket of her big coat. Enter* COUNTY ATTORNEY *and* SHERIFF.)

COUNTY ATTORNEY (*crosses to outer door facetiously*): Well, Henry, at least we found out that she was not going to quilt it. She was going to—what is it you call it, ladies?

MRS. HALE (*standing at table facing front, her hand against her pocket*): We call it—knot it, Mr. Henderson.

THE TRYSTING PLACE

BOOTH TARKINGTON (1869–1946) was born in Indianapolis and, although he traveled widely, a large part of his heart remained loyal to the Hoosier State. Educated at Phillips Exeter Academy, Purdue, and Princeton, he spent his life writing novels and plays. He was awarded five honorary degrees and twice won the Pulitzer prize for literature. He captured the affection of a large American audience with his novels *Penrod, Seventeen, Claire Ambler,* and *The Fighting Littles.* Among his plays are *Clarence,* in which Alfred Lunt played his first starring role, *Beauty and the Jacobin,* and *Monsieur Beaucaire.*

The Trysting Place is a good example of Tarkington's sunny writing. He has contrived a believable situation—people often make dates to meet in a certain corner of a hotel lobby, especially in a vacation hotel. In addition, each of the characters is madly in love. No wonder they do things and say things they would promptly deny if they heard them played back on a tape recorder.

THE TRYSTING PLACE

Booth Tarkington

The scene is a room just off the lounge of a hotel in the country. However, this is not a "country hotel," but, on the contrary, one of those vast and elaborate houses of entertainment that affect an expensive simplicity in what is called the colonial manner, and ask to be visited—by those financially able to do so—in the general interest of health and the outdoor life. The wall at the back of the stage is broken only by symmetrically spaced pilasters of an ivory color; each of the side walls is broken in the same manner; but here the pilasters help to frame two rather broad entrances, one at the right and one at the left, and beyond these entrances, on both sides, we have glimpses of the two corridors that lead to them. There are a few old prints on the walls; and there are flowering plants on stands in the corners. The furniture consists of some chintz-covered easy chairs, a light wicker settee with a chintz cushion, and a valance that reaches the floor; and there are two wicker tables with a vase of jonquils on each of them. In the rear right-hand corner of the room, near the stand of plants, there is a tropical-looking chair, wicker, with a back of monstrous size—a Philippine Island chair—and in the opposite corner is its mate. The time is a summer afternoon in 1920.

Copyright, ©, 1921, 1949, by Curtis Publishing Company. All rights reserved. For permission to produce *The Trysting Place* write direct to Baker's Plays, Boston 10, Mass. No performance may be given without permission.

Dance music is heard from a distant orchestra. Just after the rise of the curtain two people come in together from the left—a Young Woman *of twenty-five, or perhaps she is even a little older, and a slim* Boy *obviously under twenty. She is rather elaborate in her afternoon indoor dress, but none the less effectively pretty; he is of a scrubbed and sleeked youthfulness, in white trousers, a short black coat, and dancing shoes; and from the moment of his first appearance he is seen to be in an extremity of love. He leans as near the* Young Woman *as he can; his eyes search her face yearningly and without intermission; he caroms into her slightly as they come in, and repeats the carom unwittingly. They have evidently just come from the dancing floor and are a little flushed; she fans herself with her handkerchief and he fans her with his. They are heard talking before they enter. "Oh, let's do find some place to sit down!" she is saying; and he, simultaneously: "Oh, wasn't that divine! You dance just simply divinely!" These speeches "bring them on."*

The Young Woman: Here's a place we can sit down! (*She immediately drops into a chair.*)

The Boy: Yes, this is a lovely place, where nobody is at all. It's the only quiet place in the hotel; you never see more than two people here at a time, because it's kind of off, like this. That's why I wanted to walk this way. (*Sitting on a lounge and leaning toward her.*) Isn't it divine to be in a place where nobody is at *all?*

The Young Woman (*still fanning herself*): Why, you and I are here.

The Boy: Yes, but I mean nobody else at all. We're practically all alone, practically.

The Young Woman (*laughing as she waves her hand to indicate the spacious corridors to the right and left*): Alone? Why, there are at least three hundred people in this hotel.

The Boy: Yes, but they're all either outdoors, or dancin', or havin' tea, right now. It's practically the same as being alone. It is—practically, I mean.

THE YOUNG WOMAN: Yes, I've noticed that it was a rather secluded spot myself. (*She glances about the room thoughtfully, then turns to him, smiling.*) Don't you want to run and dance with some of those pretty young girls your own age?

THE BOY (*with pained earnestness*): Them? My goodness, no!

THE YOUNG WOMAN: Oh, but that isn't normal, is it?

THE BOY: I'm not normal. I don't want to be normal.

THE YOUNG WOMAN: Well, but it would only be natural for you to like those pretty young things, so— Well, *do* run and dance with one of 'em. Won't you, please?

THE BOY (*interrupting*): No. They haven't got any experience of life. What I like is a woman that's had some experience of life, like you.

THE YOUNG WOMAN: But at your age—

THE BOY: Age hasn't got anything to do with it. The thing that brings a man and a woman together, it's when they have about the same amount of experience of life.

THE YOUNG WOMAN (*absently*): You think that's it, Mr. Briggs? (*She looks about the room thoughtfully as she speaks.*)

MR. BRIGGS (*with intense seriousness*): I know it is. I had that feeling the minute I was introduced to you, night before last in the lobby—right by the third column beyond the office newsstand, at a quarter after nine o'clock in the evening.

THE YOUNG WOMAN: You did?

MR. BRIGGS: It came over me, and I felt kind of—(*he swallows*)—kind of drawn to you, Missuz—Missuz—Missuz— (*He seems to hesitate somewhat emotionally.*)

THE YOUNG WOMAN: My name is Mrs. Curtis. You seem to have forgotten it.

MR. BRIGGS (*swallowing again*): I haven't. I know it's Curtis. The trouble is, it kind of upsets me to call you *Missuz* Curtis. I thought it was Miss Curtis when I was introduced to you. I didn't know your name was Missuz—Missuz—Missuz Curtis till the clerk told me, early the next morning.

MRS. CURTIS (*frowning a little*): The clerk told you?

MR. BRIGGS: Yes. I asked him if he'd noticed whether you'd gone in to breakfast yet. He said, "You mean Missuz—Missuz Curtis?" Then I knew you must be married. (*He shakes his head ruefully.*)

MRS. CURTIS (*smiling*): Well?

MR. BRIGGS (*thoughtfully*): Well, it can't be helped.

MRS. CURTIS: I suppose not.

MR. BRIGGS (*brightening a little*): Well, anyhow, I had that— that sort of *drawn* feeling toward you, the way I *would* get toward a woman that's had some experience of life; but a hotel like this is no place to explain feelings like that. You can't when you're dancing—not the way you want to—and all the rest of the time you had some o' those *old* men hangin' around, or else my mother and sister wanted me for something; because a hotel like this—why, it's terrible the way a young man's mother and sister want him to do somep'n for 'em *all* the time; so this is the first chance I've had.

MRS. CURTIS (*rather urgently*): Don't you really think you'd better be dancing with some of those young things yonder?

MR. BRIGGS (*puzzled*): Think I'd *better* be?

MRS. CURTIS: Yes; I do really wish you would. Wouldn't it be a lot more fun than explaining something, as you said, to me?

MR. BRIGGS (*hurriedly*): No. No, it wouldn't. I want to explain how I feel about you.

MRS. CURTIS: Please go and dance, Mr. Briggs. I think it would be *much* better if you—

MR. BRIGGS (*rapidly*): No, it wouldn't. I want to explain how I feel about you, so you'll understand. It's like this, Missuz— (*swallowing again*)—Missuz Curtis. I never used to think I'd ever get to feeling this way about—about somebody that was married, but it—it came over me before I knew you *were* married. I already *was* feeling this way before he said, "You mean—you mean Missuz Curtis?" It'd already (*he swallows*) happened to me before I knew you were a—a married woman. (*Shaking his head.*) I certainly never *did* think I'd feel this way about a married woman.

MRS. CURTIS: But I'm not—not as you mean it. I'm a widow, Mr. Briggs.

MR. BRIGGS (*as in a dim perplexity*): A wid— You're a widow? (*He jumps up suddenly, greatly amazed.*) Oh, my!

MRS. CURTIS: What's the matter?

MR. BRIGGS: Oh, my!

MRS. CURTIS: What is it?

MR. BRIGGS: I guess I've got to get used to the idea of it. First I thought you weren't married, and then I was just gettin' used to the idea that you *were,* and now—well, I s'pose it's a good deal better, your bein' a widow, though, except—except for—

MRS. CURTIS: Except for?

MR. BRIGGS (*hurriedly*): Oh, I didn't mean except for your *husband!* I didn't mean your bein' a widow was better for— (*He checks himself and swallows.*)

MRS. CURTIS: Oh!

MR. BRIGGS (*frowning with thought*): No. I meant more on account of the way my family treats me. My mother and sister—well, to tell the truth, they always seem to think I'm about four years old. They can't seem to *realize;* and when I go and tell 'em you're a *widow*—

MRS. CURTIS: You think they'll be interested in hearing it? I haven't even met them.

MR. BRIGGS: No, but—but of course they've been *talkin'* about you quite a good deal.

MRS. CURTIS: They have?

MR. BRIGGS: You know how people are in a hotel like this: wondering who everybody else *is,* and whether some woman's some old man's wife or his daughter or just a trained nurse, and so on. Of course my family noticed *you* right away and then after I *met* you of course then they said a *lot* more about you. Golly! (*He shakes his head, indicating that the comment has been unfavorable.*)

MRS. CURTIS: Oh, indeed!

MR. BRIGGS (*ruefully*): They watch me like a hawk, and I

know what they'll say now! When I tell 'em you're a widow,
I mean.

MRS. CURTIS: Do you?

MR. BRIGGS (*shaking his head*): I certainly never thought myself I would ever get to feeling this way about a widow,
either!

MRS. CURTIS: Don't you *really* think you'd better run and
dance with one of those—

MR. BRIGGS (*absently*): No. (*Turning to her suddenly.*) I
was goin' to ask you—well, of course, in a—a technical way,
so to speak, I mean in a strictly technical way, so to speak;
I'm not exactly of age yet, and I suppose I'd have to get my
mother's consent, because *she's* a widow, too, and got herself appointed my guardian besides; and the truth is she's
a pretty coldhearted, bossy kind of a woman, and it's goin'
to be a big difficulty gettin' her to see this thing right.

MRS. CURTIS: To see *what* right?

MR. BRIGGS: The way I feel about you. I know it's goin' to be
difficult, because I started to talk a little about it last night
to my mother and my sister—her name's Jessie—and they
behaved--well, they behaved a good deal like two fiends.

MRS. CURTIS: They did?

MR. BRIGGS: I told 'em they didn't know you, and they *haven't*
even *met* you, but they treated me like a—like a mere *jest;*
and then they got so critical, the way they talked about you,
it might be better if they didn't see me with you again for
a few days. I can't stand the way they talk after they see
me with you.

MRS. CURTIS: Indeed!

MR. BRIGGS: Well, what I was saying: I can't touch my prin-
cipal till I'm twenty-one on account of the way my father
went and tied up his will; but of course my mother and
sister think a good many'll be after me on account of it;
but, anyhow, I *have* got to feeling this way, and I know I'll
never get over it, so what I wanted to ask you—well, it's—it's
—(*he swallows*)—it's just this: I know you *are* a widow and
everything like that, but would you be willing to (*he swal-*

lows) well, of course I don't know how long since you lost your first husband—

MRS. CURTIS (*incredulously*): What! (*She rises.*)

MR. BRIGGS: I mean, I—I don't know how you *would* feel about gettin' married again yet, even if I didn't have my own difficulties about it, but—but—

MRS. CURTIS (*with increased incredulity*): Are you *proposing* to me, Mr. Briggs?

MR. BRIGGS: Well—uh—yes. (*Then, looking beyond her down the corridor on the right.*) Oh, goodness. They watch me like a hawk! Here comes my mother! (*Dismayed, he turns to the left.*)

MRS. CURTIS (*as he turns*): Perhaps it was time!

MR. BRIGGS (*dismally*): There's my sister Jessie!

MRS. CURTIS: What of it?

MR. BRIGGS (*hastily*): I told you they behave like two fiends when they see me with you. (*Glancing right and left nervously.*) Well, excuse me. (*With perfect gravity he kneels at one end of the settee, which is in the rear.*) It'll be a good deal better if they don't see me, I expect. (*He promptly crawls under the settee, and the valance conceals him entirely. From this invisibility he appeals with pathetic urgency in a hoarse whisper.*) They'll prob'ly go right on. *Please* wait! Or—if you *haf* to go, come *back!*

(MRS. CURTIS *stands dumfounded for a moment; and then, controlling a tendency to laugh immoderately, she turns to examine a print on the left wall as* MR. BRIGGS's *mother enters from the right.* MRS. BRIGGS *is a handsome woman of forty-five or fifty, not now in a gracious mood. She comes in decisively, halts, and stares at* MRS. CURTIS's *back. Then she looks over the room in an annoyed and puzzled manner.* MR. BRIGGS's *sister,* JESSIE, *comes in from the left. She is a pretty girl of about twenty, but her expression is now rather cross. Her dress and equipment show that she has just come in from the golf course.*)

JESSIE (*calling as she comes in*): Lancelot! (*She halts, puz-*

zled, and looks inquiringly at her mother.) Mama, where's
Lancelot? I was sure I saw him in here just a second ago.

MRS. BRIGGS (*grimly*): So was I. (*After looking at each other,
they turn their heads simultaneously and stare at* MRS. CUR-
TIS, *who appears to be interested in the print.*) It's very
odd!

JESSIE: Yes, very.

> (*The two again look at each other, and at a little dis-
> tance appear to consult telepathically, without any
> change of expression; then they turn once more to
> look at* MRS. CURTIS.)

MRS. BRIGGS: I beg your pardon, but I'm under the impression
that you have met my son.

MRS. CURTIS (*turning*): Yes?

JESSIE: Wasn't he here just now?

MRS. CURTIS: Yes, he was.

MRS. BRIGGS: Would you be good enough to tell me, did he
leave here to go to his room?

MRS. CURTIS (*casually*): I don't think so; he didn't say so.
(*She gives them a little nod, smiling politely, and goes out
at the left. They stare after her.*)

JESSIE (*still staring after* MRS. CURTIS): She's a very bold
type.

MRS. BRIGGS (*seating herself on the settee*): Very.

JESSIE (*turning to her*): I don't see how that little goose got
away. You were coming from that direction and I from just
yonder. I suppose he thought we'd say something that
would embarrass him before her.

MRS. BRIGGS: I suppose she's thirty-five. I've heard of such
people, but I never saw one before.

JESSIE: I regard her as distinctly the dangerous type of ad-
venturess.

MRS. BRIGGS: Certainly. In the first place, her not having told
the child frankly that she's a widow. One of the clerks told
me she *was.*

JESSIE: Oh, she did that to flatter him into believing he's a real
grown-up "man of the world" having an "affair"!

MRS. BRIGGS: So that when he's sufficiently entangled she can tell him she's a widow—and by that time we don't know *what* he'd do! A country justice of the peace, probably!

JESSIE: Last night, when we were trying to teach him a little common sense about strange people in hotels, what was it he said she was? "An angel!"—oh, yes!—"One of heaven's highest angels."

MRS. BRIGGS (*grimly*): He said he wouldn't "listen to one of heaven's highest angels gettin' talked against by a lot o' women!" I'm sure they heard him in the next suite. (*She rises.*) I suppose you'd better go and see where he slipped out to, Jessie. Of course, he'll try to find *her* again as soon as he can.

JESSIE (*dropping into a chair*): I played three times round the course. Do you mind if I just sit here a while and rest?

MRS. BRIGGS: Then why don't you go to your room?

JESSIE (*laughing feebly*): I'm just too tired. I will in a minute. (*With a gesture toward the left entrance.*) Hadn't you better—

MRS. BRIGGS: Keep her in sight? Yes. That's easier than trying to keep *him* in sight. You're going up to your room right away, aren't you?

JESSIE: Yes, in only a minute. I really think you'd better go, Mama. He might—

MRS. BRIGGS: No, I'll see to that! (*She goes out.*)

(JESSIE *stares after her for a moment, glances at a wrist watch, then rises and looks down the corridor beyond the entrance at the right. She appears to derive some satisfaction from what she sees there, returns to her chair and sits in a carefully graceful attitude, her expression demure. A moment later a* YOUNG MAN—*he is about twenty-five—comes in rather nervously from the right. He pauses near the entrance.*)

THE YOUNG MAN: You!

JESSIE (*softly*): You!

THE YOUNG MAN: Is your mother—

JESSIE: She's gone.

THE YOUNG MAN (*nervously advancing*): I—I—

JESSIE: I was afraid maybe we couldn't have this nook to our-selves, after all. My absurd little brother was in here, hang-ing about that dreadful Mrs. Curtis, and I was afraid they wouldn't go away; but Mama scared 'em both off provi-dentially.

THE YOUNG MAN (*moving a chair close to hers and sitting*): And so we're alone! (*He speaks with a sentimental hushed-ness.*) All alone!

JESSIE: All alone, Rupert! This is the only place in the hotel where you *can* be by yourself awhile. That's why I said to meet here.

RUPERT (*nervously*): You don't think your mother'll be back for a while?

JESSIE: No; she won't.

RUPERT: She hasn't found out I've come, has she?

JESSIE: She hasn't the remotest idea, thank heaven! Nobody dreams you're within hundreds of miles of here. That's one advantage of a big hotel.

RUPERT: Darling—

JESSIE: Yes, darling?
(*The settee moves slightly at this, but it is behind them and they do not see it.*)

RUPERT: I can't understand why your mother dislikes me so.

JESSIE (*gravely*): Well, I suppose her feeling about you is—well, she *says* it's because you're rather poor and I'm—not.

RUPERT: But what makes her think I care about you because you're not?

JESSIE: Well—

RUPERT (*leaning toward her and lowering his voice*): Darling, there's something I want to ask you—

JESSIE (*leaning toward him and almost whispering*): Yes, dearest, what is it?
(*The settee slowly moves nearer them as their voices become more indistinct.*)

RUPERT: I want to ask you—

JESSIE: Yes?

RUPERT (*with hushed tenderness*): Do you *really* love me, dearest?

JESSIE (*gazing upward, tranced*): Oh, dearest, I do!
  (*The settee goes back to where it came from.*)

RUPERT: But you don't think your mother'll ever change her mind about me?

JESSIE: She never does change her mind.

RUPERT: Then what can we do?

JESSIE (*in a low voice*): Darling, there's something I wouldn't say for anything in the world to anybody but you.
  (*The settee again approaches slightly.*)

RUPERT: Yes?

JESSIE: I think Mama really knows you're not mercenary, but the *real* reason for her opposition to you is pretty selfish. I think it's because she doesn't want me to marry and go away and leave her alone in the world.

RUPERT: But she wouldn't be. She'd still have the companionship of your young brother.

JESSIE (*shaking her head*): That'd be the same as none. Lancelot seems to have scarcely *any* sense, you see.
  (*The settee once more retires.*)

RUPERT: Then I don't see what possible hope—

JESSIE (*warning him as she sees someone approaching in the corridor to the right*): Sh-h-h!

RUPERT (*following her gaze*): Who *is* that old chap?

JESSIE: It's old Mr. Ingoldsby. He's some old friend of Mama's that happened to turn up here.

RUPERT (*moving as if to withdraw*): I'd better—

JESSIE (*quickly*): No; he doesn't know you. Sit still. (*She turns toward* MR. INGOLDSBY *with a smile as he enters.*) Good afternoon, Mr. Ingoldsby. Did you do it in eighty-five again today?

  (INGOLDSBY *is a man of fifty-five or, possibly, sixty. He wears neat knickerbockers and is otherwise sprightly in his outdoor attire. He smiles rather absently as he replies.*)

INGOLDSBY: Eighty-five? No, I—ah—no. I didn't go around today. Ah—has Mrs. Briggs been here?

JESSIE: Here?

INGOLDSBY: Yes, I mean—ah—here.

JESSIE: I think she's somewhere looking for Lancelot.

INGOLDSBY: Yes? Ah—I—

JESSIE: Is there something you'd like me to tell her when I see her?

INGOLDSBY (*going toward the left entrance*): No, I—I— (*He glances at his watch, and looks absently at* JESSIE.) No, I believe I—ah— (*He departs.*)

RUPERT: Well, I *do* hope nobody else'll come poking about like that, because I—

JESSIE: No, darling; we're alone again now.

RUPERT: Darling—

JESSIE: Yes, darling?

RUPERT: We've had such difficulties in managing our little interviews; it does seem a precious thing to be near you again.

JESSIE: Oh, it does!

RUPERT: If we could only go away together, where it could *always* be like this—

JESSIE (*dreamily*): Yes, with the world shut out.

RUPERT: Why can't we—

JESSIE: Hush, darling.

    (*She sees someone approaching in the corridor on the left. He looks dolefully in that direction.*)

JESSIE: It's that dreadful woman.

RUPERT: I don't know her.

JESSIE: She's been trying to entangle Lancelot, and he's completely lost what slight intelligence he *had*, the little ninny! She's old enough to be his mother.

    (*The settee makes a slight convulsive movement.*)

RUPERT: Sh! She'll hear you.

    (MRS. CURTIS *enters from the left. She looks about, with a faint embarrassment.* JESSIE *stares at her, then speaks coldly.*)

JESSIE: I beg your pardon. Did you leave something when you were here with my little brother?

MRS. CURTIS (*smiling constrainedly*): Did you happen to see a pair of white gloves?

    (RUPERT *rises and looks in his chair.*)

JESSIE: No. There aren't any here.

MRS. CURTIS: I *may* have left them anywhere, of course. (*To* RUPERT.) Don't bother, please. I thought just possibly— (*She stoops slightly and looks behind the settee, and her expression shows a considerable illumination.*) If I *had* left anything here I just wanted to see if it was still—

JESSIE: No; there aren't any gloves here. (*She speaks in a sharp whisper to* RUPERT.) Sit down! (*He does so. Their backs are toward* MRS. CURTIS.)

MRS. CURTIS: No. They don't seem to be. I'm sorry to have disturbed you. (*She moves toward the left entrance as she speaks. The settee follows her. She checks it with a sudden commanding push.*)

JESSIE: I hardly think my little brother will come back *here.* My mother went to look for him.

MRS. CURTIS (*politely*): No doubt she's found him by this time. (*She looks from the settee to* JESSIE *and* RUPERT, *and back again; and her eyes widen with an intense inward struggle.*)

JESSIE (*turning to look at her coolly*): Was there anything else?

MRS. CURTIS (*after a moment during which her inward struggle prevents her from replying*): Oh—oh, no! I'm so sorry to have disturbed you! (*Her voice threatens to break and she goes out hurriedly, at the left.*)

JESSIE (*staring after her*): Absolutely brazen! She came back after that idiot *boy!* Thought *he'd* probably come back!

RUPERT: Darling—

JESSIE (*turning to him eagerly*): Yes, darling—

RUPERT (*looking over her shoulder*): Oh, my goodness! (*He speaks with intense anguish.*)

JESSIE (*seizing his hand feverishly*): What's the matter, darling?

RUPERT (*rising*): It's your mother! (*He strides hastily backward out of sight from the left entrance.*)

JESSIE: Oh, murder!

RUPERT: She didn't see me, but she will if I try to go out there. (*He points to the right entrance.*)

JESSIE: She's coming!

RUPERT: This is awful! (*His despairing eye falls upon the huge Philippine chair in the left rear corner of the room; he rushes to it, turns it around, with its back toward the front, and sits in it, concealed from view. He speaks in a hoarse whisper.*) Darling—

JESSIE: Hush! (*She has checked an impulse to rise and fly; and now, affecting carelessness, she brushes her left sleeve with her right hand, crosses her knees, swings her foot, whistles an operatic air, and looks at the ceiling.* MRS. BRIGGS *enters at the left, frowning.* JESSIE *addresses her cheerfully.*) Back again, Mama? Where's Lancelot?

MRS. BRIGGS (*in an annoyed tone*): I don't know. I thought you were going straight to your room.

JESSIE: Oh, I am.

MRS. BRIGGS: Have you just been sitting here alone?

JESSIE: Mrs. Curtis came back a minute ago looking for the child.

MRS. BRIGGS: Yes; I saw *her*. Wasn't anyone else—

JESSIE (*carelessly*): Oh, yes; that Mr. Ingoldsby was here, too.

MRS. BRIGGS: He was? (*She looks at her watch and then toward the corridor on the left.*) You told me you were very tired and were going straight to your room.

JESSIE (*casually*): Oh, well, I feel rested now.

MRS. BRIGGS: You should lie down before dressing for dinner.

JESSIE: Why don't *you* do that, Mama? You know how it brightens you up.

MRS. BRIGGS (*frowning*): Brightens me up? Really!

JESSIE: Oh, I don't mean like a *terribly* aged person; but a nap every day's a good thing for everybody.

MRS. BRIGGS (*stiffly*): I *took* a nap after lunch. Really, it's time you went.

JESSIE: Oh, I'll just sit around awhile longer. I rather like to just sit around and do nothing, like this.

MRS. BRIGGS: You *said* you were going, and you ought to do things when you say you're going to do them.

JESSIE: But *why?* Why can't I just sit around here a little longer if I want to?

MRS. BRIGGS: Because you said you—

JESSIE: Oh, what if I did! Haven't I got a right to change my mind?

MRS. BRIGGS: I insist on your lying down for half an hour before you dress for dinner. What makes you so obstinate about it? Have you any *reason* for wishing not to do this simple thing? Is there anything you're trying to conceal from me, Jessie?

JESSIE (*rising hastily*): Certainly not!

MRS. BRIGGS (*severely*): You haven't any particular reason for staying here and not going to your room as you said you would?

JESSIE: No!

MRS. BRIGGS: Then—

JESSIE: Oh, I'll go; but I don't understand why you make such a point of it!

MRS. BRIGGS (*a little flustered*): A point of it? I? I'm not making a point of it! I don't at all, except—except for your health.

JESSIE (*going*): My *health!* (*She halts.*) What nonsense!

MRS. BRIGGS: Your health is the only thing to consider. You've started; why don't you *go?*

JESSIE: But what's the *hurry?*

MRS. BRIGGS: Hurry? Oh, none! I just meant, as you *are* going, why shouldn't you *go* and get it over?

JESSIE: What makes you so queer?

MRS. BRIGGS (*with quiet severity*): Queer? You call your mother queer? It seems to me you're the one that's behaving queerly. Jessie, is there anything you're trying to—

JESSIE: No! Don't get so upset. I'll go!

(*She goes out at the left.* MRS. BRIGGS *stares after her for a moment, looks in the opposite direction, then seats herself upon the settee, and from the midst of a handkerchief which she has crumpled in her hand produces a small gold vanity box. She opens it, gazes in the tiny mirror, touches her hair, glances right and left, and uses a diminutive powder puff quickly; then she closes the box, conceals it in her handkerchief*

again, and hums a song to herself. MR. INGOLDSBY
enters at the left. He has a slightly embarrassed air.)

MRS. BRIGGS (*as if surprised*): Oh!

INGOLDSBY: Ah—I was here a while ago. It was a little earlier
than our—our appointment; if I may call it so. (*He laughs
nervously.*)

MRS. BRIGGS (*smiling*): Well, I suppose it *could* be called an
appointment—in a way.

INGOLDSBY: I—I thought—that is, I've noticed this was about
the only place in the hotel where there aren't usually a lot
of people. I suggested it because—because I had something
to say—ah—I mean that I thought it would be as well to say
it in private—as it were. That is, if we were alone together,
I—ah—that is to say, it's something I couldn't very well say
in—in public, so to speak. I mean it would be difficult with
other people present.

MRS. BRIGGS (*smiling nervously*): Is it something very mysterious, Mr. Ingoldsby?

INGOLDSBY: I wish you wouldn't call me that.

MRS. BRIGGS (*seriously*): You want me to call you Henry?

INGOLDSBY: You did once.

MRS. BRIGGS (*rising in some agitation*): Yes, but that was
pretty long ago.

INGOLDSBY (*sharply*): I called you Fannie then.

MRS. BRIGGS (*more agitated*): I don't think we should ever
refer to it. When an episode is as long buried as—

INGOLDSBY (*his own agitation increasing*): Episode? See here,
Fannie; you know why I stayed a bachelor. You do know.

MRS. BRIGGS (*protesting quickly*): No, no! I have no responsibility for that!

INGOLDSBY: Haven't you? When you broke your engagement
to me—

MRS. BRIGGS (*crying out, though she suppresses the loudness
of her voice*): It was a misunderstanding, Henry.

INGOLDSBY: It was not. I've held my peace in silence all these
years because of my principles. I wouldn't refer to such
things with you when you had become a married woman.
But I can speak now. You deliberately broke off with me—

Mrs. Briggs (*choking*): I didn't!

Ingoldsby (*with a suppressed passion*): You did! (*He paces the floor as he goes on.*) You decided Lance Briggs was the better man, and you sent me my ring and letters without a single word explaining why you did it.

Mrs. Briggs: Oh!

Ingoldsby: You did!

Mrs. Briggs: Is it fair to attack me with that now?

Ingoldsby: Fair? How *dare* you speak of *fairness* to *me*?

Mrs. Briggs: But you *knew* why I did it.

Ingoldsby (*bitterly*): I did indeed! It was simply because you were of a fickle nature. Of course you didn't have the courage to explain *that.*

Mrs. Briggs (*with great emotion*): But you don't know the pressure, the awful pressure my mother brought to bear on me. She simply *made* me marry him, Henry. It was night and day, day and night, week in, week out—

Ingoldsby: And you never for one moment had the simple bravery, the simple *loyalty* to the man you'd given your word to—

Mrs. Briggs: I was worn out. I was—

Ingoldsby: You didn't care enough for me to—

Mrs. Briggs: I *did!*

Ingoldsby: No! No! No!

Mrs. Briggs (*piteously*): Henry, you *must* listen to me! (*She puts her hand on his arm.*)

Ingoldsby (*moving away from her*): Why didn't you say that *then?* Why didn't—

Mrs. Briggs: I loved you—I did, Henry! I simply let my mother break my will and wreck our two lives.

Ingoldsby: What folly! You were perfectly happy with Briggs. I don't know *how* many people told me you were.

Mrs. Briggs: I did my duty, and I tried to do it cheerfully; but the scar was always there, Henry.

Ingoldsby (*harshly*): I don't believe it!

Mrs. Briggs (*plaintively*): It was, Henry. (*She sinks into the chair* Jessie *has occupied.*)

Ingoldsby (*swallowing*): What?

MRS. BRIGGS (*feebly*): It was, Henry—the scar was always there. (*Her head droops.*)

(*He walks across the room, then returns to her and looks down upon her.*)

INGOLDSBY (*swallowing*): Do you know what my life has been?

MRS. BRIGGS (*tremulously, not looking up*): I—I heard you became very—very prosperous in—in real estate.

INGOLDSBY: Yes. What's that to fill a man's life? Look at the difference! You have children to be a comfort to you in your—your—as you approach middle age. I have nothing.

MRS. BRIGGS (*pathetically, still looking down*): Oh, I'm sure you have something.

INGOLDSBY: I tell you I have nothing—nothing in the world to make life worth living, not a thing on earth! (*He glances about, then sits beside her and speaks in a very low voice.*) Fannie—Fannie—

(*The settee approaches a little nearer.*)

MRS. BRIGGS (*also in a very low voice*): Well?

INGOLDSBY: Fannie—I—I—Fannie—I— (*His emotion is difficult to control and his voice fades out into a murmur of several slight incoherent sounds, whereupon the settee again moves slightly closer.*)

MRS. BRIGGS: Yes, Henry?

INGOLDSBY: You said your life was wrecked, though you bore it dutifully and—and cheerfully. Mine—*my* life—it was withered.

MRS. BRIGGS (*murmuring*): Oh—Henry!

INGOLDSBY: But, after all, our lives aren't over.

MRS. BRIGGS (*shaking her down-bent head and protesting in a weak voice*): Oh, no, no! Don't begin to talk that way.

INGOLDSBY: Fannie, I never got over it. As time went on, I took up my work and tried to do my part in the world, but —but I never got over it, Fannie. I'm not over it now.

MRS. BRIGGS (*turning to him mournfully*): Oh, yes, you are!

INGOLDSBY (*shaking his head*): I'm not. I still—I still—I still—I still—

(*The settee again moves a little nearer.*)

MRS. BRIGGS: No, no.

INGOLDSBY: I do. I still—I still—

MRS. BRIGGS (*in a faint and tearful protest*): No, you don't, Henry. You only think you do.

INGOLDSBY: No, I really do. I—I—I care for you yet, Fannie.

MRS. BRIGGS (*recovering herself enough to smile faintly as she shakes her head*): Oh, my, no!

INGOLDSBY: Fannie, let's—let's save these years that we still have before us. Let's try to make up for that old mistake.

MRS. BRIGGS (*becoming a little brisker*): Why, how—how—why, we—why, I couldn't think of such a thing!

INGOLDSBY (*solemnly*): Fannie, I ask you to marry me.

(*She stares at him; the settee moves an inch nearer.*)

MRS. BRIGGS: What?

INGOLDSBY: I ask you to marry me.

MRS. BRIGGS: Why, good gracious! I wouldn't have my children know that anybody had said such a thing to me for all the kingdoms on earth!

INGOLDSBY (*earnestly*): They needn't know it till afterwards.

MRS. BRIGGS (*breathlessly*): Afterwards? After—after—

INGOLDSBY: You're not going to wreck us both *again*, are you, Fannie?

MRS. BRIGGS (*as in amazement*): Why, if I'd dreamed you were going to say anything like *this* to me when you asked me to meet you here this afternoon—

INGOLDSBY (*solemnly*): Fannie, I want you to give me your answer, and to do it now. What do you say?

MRS. BRIGGS (*feebly, with her hand to her breast*): Oh, my!

INGOLDSBY: Yes; you must.

MRS. BRIGGS: But I haven't had time to *think!* Why, I wouldn't have anybody know about this for—

INGOLDSBY: I want my answer, Fannie—Fannie, *dear!*

MRS. BRIGGS (*blankly*): *Oh,* dear!

INGOLDSBY: Fannie, *dearest!* (*He takes her hand.*)

MRS. BRIGGS: Oh, I wouldn't have anybody know this—

INGOLDSBY: Dearest, dearest Fannie!

MRS. BRIGGS: Why, I wouldn't have anybody know that we—

(*They are interrupted by a voice from a mysterious and*

*invisible source. It is a male and adult voice, loudly
and emphatically affecting to clear the throat of its
origin in the manner of a person wishing to attract
the attention of some other person.*)

THE MYSTERIOUS VOICE: A-hem! A-a-a-*hem!*

MRS. BRIGGS (*leaping in her chair*): Good heavens!

INGOLDSBY (*jumping up*): What was that?

MRS. BRIGGS (*rising*): Why, it was a man's voice.

INGOLDSBY: It was right here in the room with us.

MRS. BRIGGS (*sinking into her chair*): Oh, murder!

INGOLDSBY (*staring about the room, notices the Philippine
chair with its back turned to the front*): There's somebody
sitting in that chair! (*He starts toward it angrily, but is
checked by a suppressed scream from* MRS. BRIGGS.)

MRS. BRIGGS: *Don't!* I'd *much* rather never know who it is.
(*Rising.*) Let's get away! (*She totters.*)

INGOLDSBY (*undecided, but very angry*): We ought to know
who's spying on us like this.

MRS. BRIGGS (*clutching at him*): Oh!

THE MYSTERIOUS VOICE (*indignantly*): I'm not spying! This
is a public room in a public hotel—

MRS. BRIGGS (*moaning*): Oh!

THE MYSTERIOUS VOICE (*continuing*): Any guest of this hotel
has a right to sit here in peace, and if you *will* go on talking about your private affairs in a public room—

MRS. BRIGGS (*leaning on* INGOLDSBY'S *arm*): Oh, my!

THE MYSTERIOUS VOICE (*continuing heatedly*): Why, it's
your own fault, not mine. I was only warning you not to
go any further. I've heard enough of other people's private
affairs for one afternoon, anyhow.

MRS. BRIGGS (*almost hysterically*): Oh, let's go! (*She swings
the reluctant and angry* INGOLDSBY *toward the left entrance.*) Let's go!

INGOLDSBY (*turning to call back angrily*): I don't know who
you are, sir; but when I've seen this lady to a—a place of
safety—I *intend* to know. I'll be *back* here, sir.

THE MYSTERIOUS VOICE: Fine!

MRS. BRIGGS: Oh, mercy! (*She moves hastily away from* IN-

GOLDSBY *as* JESSIE *suddenly comes in, from the left, confronting them.*)

JESSIE (*halting sharply*): What in the world's the matter?

MRS. BRIGGS (*in a shaking voice*): Nothing! Nothing at all, Jessie. Why should you think anything's the matter?

JESSIE: Why, you're all upset!

MRS. BRIGGS (*trying hard to seem lightly amused, and failing*): Not at all—not at all! I was just sitting here a moment with Mr. Ingoldsby, chatting over old times and—and then we decided to leave. We decided to leave—that's all. I— I'm— (*Suddenly she starts, and with an incoherent exclamation looks behind her. Then she faces* JESSIE *and, with a painful effort to smile, completes her sentence.*) I'm all right.

JESSIE: Yes, you seem so. Mr. Ingoldsby, will you kindly tell me what you've been saying to my mother to upset her so?

MRS. BRIGGS: But I'm not—

INGOLDSBY (*checking her sharply*): Miss Briggs, I should not be likely to say anything disrespectful to my old and dear friend, your mother. (*Looking around angrily.*) The truth is, there's an eavesdropping scoundrel concealed in this room, and I—

JESSIE (*alarmed*): What! Oh, I'm *sure* there isn't.

INGOLDSBY: There is! An eavesdropping—

THE MYSTERIOUS VOICE (*angrily*): This is a public room, I told you. How can *I* help it if you—

INGOLDSBY: I can't stand this. He's behind that chair.

(*He breaks away from* MRS. BRIGGS *and* JESSIE, *who both clutch at him.*)

JESSIE (*crying out*): Don't! *Please* don't!

MRS. BRIGGS (*simultaneously*): Henry! *Don't!*

(*But* INGOLDSBY *has already reached the Philippine chair that has its back turned toward the front of the stage; he seizes* RUPERT *by the collar and drags him forth.* RUPERT *is horrified.*)

INGOLDSBY: Come out of there, you scoundrel. Come out to the light of day.

RUPERT (*hastily*): I didn't do it. It wasn't *me.*

MRS. BRIGGS: Rupert Smith!

JESSIE (*dolefully*): Oh, goodness!

INGOLDSBY (*hotly*): What do you mean by terrorizing a lady?

RUPERT: I didn't! I didn't say a *word!* I *was* behind there, but I couldn't help it. It wasn't *my* voice talking to you.

INGOLDSBY: Then who was it?

THE MYSTERIOUS VOICE: If you're anxious for more witnesses, I suggest that you look under the settee.

MRS. BRIGGS (*changing her mind as she is in the act of sinking down upon the settee*): What?

JESSIE: Look at it!

    (MRS. BRIGGS *screams faintly, as the settee moves rapidly to the left entrance, evidently meaning to leave the room.*)

INGOLDSBY (*to* RUPERT): Stop that thing! Catch it!

    (*They seize the settee just as it is disappearing into the corridor. They drag it back into the room.*)

RUPERT (*trying to lift the settee*): Come out from under there!

INGOLDSBY: Come out, now!

THE SETTEE: I won't! You lea' me alone!

INGOLDSBY: Both together now—heave!

    (*They heave, and the settee yields, disclosing* LANCELOT, *with his previously smooth hair disheveled and his clothes well rumpled.*)

MRS. BRIGGS (*astonished*): Lancelot! Oh, gracious me!

INGOLDSBY (*to* LANCELOT): Shame on you!

RUPERT: Yes, shame on you!

LANCELOT (*resentfully*): Well, you *would* get me; but I'll make you sorry you did it, both of you! (*He rises, brushing himself and adjusting his attire.*)

INGOLDSBY (*irritably*): Don't you know better than to frighten ladies and eavesdrop and—

LANCELOT (*warmly*): I was abs'lootly honorable, because I couldn't help it, and you none of you ever gave me a single chance to get away. *My* conduct is the only one here that hasn't got a stain on it or anything. (*He turns hotly upon* MRS. BRIGGS *and* JESSIE.) I got nothing to reproach myself with, but I'd just like to know what either of you got to say for yourselves *now* about the way you been talkin' about Mrs. Curtis! If you either of you ever just *dare* to soil your lips with even her *name* again, why, I know more *things*—

MRS. BRIGGS: Be quiet, Lancelot.

LANCELOT: Quiet? *Me?* (*He laughs shortly with an irony he could not express in words.*) In the first place, don't call me Lancelot any more. You know how I hate that name, and I been tryin' to break you of it long enough—and now I will! I don't care what you call me, but don't call me *that!*

JESSIE (*pointing to the settee*): How long were you under there?

LANCELOT (*sternly*): Long enough to get mighty tired of hearin' people callin' each other "darling"! Good gracious! You don't think I *enjoyed* it, do you? Why, what I heard while I was under there—well, I got a pretty strong constitution, but—

MRS. BRIGGS: Hush! Oh, me!

INGOLDSBY: The voice that spoke didn't sound like Lancelot's voice—

LANCELOT (*turning upon him ominously*): Did you hear me say not to call me Lancelot? I mean you, too.

INGOLDSBY (*with hasty meekness*): I'll call you anything you like; but I want to know who it was that *spoke*. You say it wasn't you—

LANCELOT (*very emphatically*): No, it wasn't. I wouldn't 'a' told you to look under the settee, would I?

INGOLDSBY (*with a gesture toward* RUPERT): And this gentleman says it wasn't he.

RUPERT: Why, it spoke again after I came out.

INGOLDSBY (*quite bewildered*): So it did. Then who—

LANCELOT: I don't care who it was; what I want to point out, right here and now, before we go any further, why, I'm in a position to say that I got some plans for my future life and I don't expect to have any interference with 'em from my family, or from anybody that wants to *join* my family either. All up to now, I've spent my life in a dependent position, so to speak, but after what's happened here lately, and knowin' all the *things* I *do* know— (*His voice has risen during this oration, and* JESSIE, *after a glance to the left entrance, attempts to moderate him.*)

JESSIE: Hush! There's somebody—

LANCELOT: I don't care *who's* comin', I'm goin' to say my say. I expect to settle my own future in my own way, and any lady that I may decide to make *another* member of this family—

JESSIE: *Hush!*

(*The eyes of* LANCELOT *follow hers to the left entrance and his stern manner is instantly softened.*)

LANCELOT: It's her.

(MRS. CURTIS *comes in, but stops uncertainly near the entrance.*)

MRS. CURTIS: Oh! I'm afraid I— (*She turns to go.*)

LANCELOT: Wait. I was just talkin' to 'em about you.

MRS. CURTIS: You were, Mr. Briggs?

LANCELOT (*to the others, reprovingly*): *She* never calls me Lancelot. Missuz—Missuz Curtis, I didn't have to tell 'em; they'd already found out you were a widow. We don't need to bother about that anyway.

MRS. CURTIS: *We* don't?

LANCELOT: I've found out a good *many* things since I saw you, and I'm goin' to tell you the whole biznuss.

MRS. BRIGGS: Shame!

JESSIE (*with a despairing laugh*): What would it matter? There's somebody *else* here that knows "the whole biznuss"!

MRS. CURTIS (*struck by this*): What did you say, Miss Briggs?

INGOLDSBY (*warmly*): She made a sensible remark, madam. There is a person concealed in this room—

MRS. CURTIS (*impulsively*): Oh, dear! How did you know?

ALL THE OTHERS: What?

MRS. CURTIS: Nothing.

INGOLDSBY: All right! (*To* RUPERT.) I think I know now where he is, and I'm going to have him out.

MRS. CURTIS (*gasping, then imploringly*): *Please* stop!

INGOLDSBY (*halting*): Why?

MRS. CURTIS (*weakly*): It's a friend of mine.

LANCELOT (*apprehensively*): A friend of yours?

MRS. CURTIS: I—I'll answer for him. He'll never mention—ah —anything. He really wouldn't be interested. He doesn't know any of you.

THE MYSTERIOUS VOICE: No; and doesn't care to!

INGOLDSBY (*angrily*): Now, I *will*—

MRS. CURTIS: *Please* don't!

INGOLDSBY: I mean to know who he is.

MRS. CURTIS (*pleading*): Please! If you found him, you'd only see a total stranger to you. But he *wouldn't* be a stranger to quite a lot of people in this hotel that *I* know.

INGOLDSBY (*now shaking his head*): I'm afraid I don't see it.

MRS. CURTIS (*in a faltering voice*): He's just here for one day and we—we didn't want anyone to know it. I had so many engagements I could only take a short walk in the country with him this morning and—and promise to meet him here at five this afternoon.

LANCELOT (*who has been staring at her painfully*): But—but —see here!

MRS. CURTIS: Yes, I tried to get you to run away and dance with some nice young thing.

LANCELOT (*pathetically*): So you could be here with—him?

MRS. CURTIS: I—I believe so.

LANCELOT (*dismally*): Oh, my!

INGOLDSBY: Madam, what you say doesn't excuse this person's eavesdropping.

THE MYSTERIOUS VOICE (*belligerently*): Why doesn't it? A lady's got a right to keep her engagement a secret as long as she wants to, hasn't she? There are people in this hotel that would know all about it if they saw her with me. (*With some bitterness.*) That's why she said to meet her here, because it's so quiet!

INGOLDSBY: That doesn't excuse—

THE MYSTERIOUS VOICE: It's more your fault than anybody else's. I was awake all last night on a noisy train, and I was quietly *asleep* here—till you woke me up.

INGOLDSBY: Till *who* woke you up?

THE MYSTERIOUS VOICE: Till *you* did. I never knew a man that made so much noise about proposing a second marriage.

JESSIE (*amazed*): Oh, Mama!

MRS. BRIGGS (*with severe dignity*): I'll speak to you and Mr. Rupert Smith after dinner. Henry, I don't see the propriety of continuing an argument with this interloper, whoever he may be. (*She takes* INGOLDSBY'S *arm.*)

JESSIE: No. Let's *do* get away from here! (*She moves toward the left entrance with* RUPERT.)

INGOLDSBY (*looking back, as he follows with* MRS. BRIGGS; *speaks reprovingly*): I hope you have some shame for your conduct, sir.

THE MYSTERIOUS VOICE: Bless you, my children!

INGOLDSBY (*infuriated*): Now, I'll— (*He turns to go back.*)

MRS. BRIGGS (*restraining him*): Henry!
    (*They go out the left entrance.* JESSIE *and* RUPERT *have passed out into the corridor.*)

LANCELOT: Did he say "a lady's got a right to keep her—her *engagement*—a secret"?

MRS. CURTIS: Yes.

LANCELOT: To—to—to you?

MRS. CURTIS: Yes, dear.

LANCELOT (*piteously*): Oh—oh, pshaw!

MRS. BRIGGS (*calling back*): Lancelot!

LANCELOT (*meekly*): Yes'm.
    (*He goes dismally across to the left entrance and pauses.* INGOLDSBY *and* MRS. BRIGGS *have withdrawn, preceding him.*)

MRS. CURTIS (*as he pauses*): What is it, Mr. Briggs?

LANCELOT (*swallowing*): Noth—nothin'. (*He goes out.*)

MRS. CURTIS (*turning, after a moment's faintly smiling meditation*): You poor thing!

THE MYSTERIOUS VOICE (*in an aggrieved tone*): Well, I should say I am!
    (*She goes to the Philippine chair, near the right rear corner, and, moving a smaller chair close to it, seats*

herself and addresses the invisible person, who is evidently sitting in the shelter of the big chair.)

MRS. CURTIS: After all, there's nobody else here just *now,* darling.

THE MYSTERIOUS VOICE: No. We're alone, darling.

MRS. CURTIS: You poor darling! (*She glances about, then impulsively leans behind the huge back of the Philippine chair.*

THE NEIGHBORS

ZONA GALE (1874–1938) was born in Portage, Wisconsin, and achieved her greatest success writing novels, plays, and poems about Midwestern rural life with sympathy, honesty, and, sometimes, with irony. She received her college training at the University of Wisconsin and was awarded honorary degrees from Rollins and Wooster colleges. For a while Miss Gale worked on Milwaukee and New York newspaper staffs. She helped Thomas H. Dickinson establish the Wisconsin Dramatic Society, one of the first community theatre groups in America. *The Neighbors* was written especially for this organization. Miss Gale won a Pulitzer prize for *Miss Lulu Bett,* which she dramatized from her own novel.

The Neighbors is one of Miss Gale's pleasant, homespun comedies about people she knew all around her. The incidents in the play may seem commonplace but the author has surrounded her characters with an irresistible atmosphere of contagious good will that affects everyone it touches.

THE NEIGHBORS

Zona Gale

The scene is Mrs. Abel's *kitchen. At one side is an ironing board, with full clothes basket on the floor. At the back we see an open door, an open window with blooming plants on its outside sill, and a wide cupboard with a figured calico curtain before it. At the other side of the room is an exit into a shed. In the kitchen are a wooden-bottomed rocker with high back and calico cushion, some wooden-bottomed straight chairs, a table covered with a red cloth and ranged with four or five lamps, and at the corner farthest from the ironing board, clothes bars spread with a few freshly ironed pieces.*

By the window sits Grandma, *who does not leave her chair throughout the play until its end. She is very old. She is in bright-colored calico, with ribbons on her black cap. She is cutting and winding white and black carpet rags, and a basket of the balls is beside her on the floor.* Mis' Diantha Abel *is ironing at the board. She has on a blue calico gown, a long gingham apron, spectacles, and a black hat trimmed with faded flowers and a dilapidated ostrich feather. She irons slowly, as anybody would iron, tests her flatiron, and starts for the shed to renew it at the stove out there.*

Grandma (*looking up*): Seems to me Inez is a terrible long time gettin' that starch.

MIS' ABEL: I wish she'd hurry herself back. I ain't got enough starch to do the collars.

GRANDMA: I'll cold-starch 'em for you, if you want.

MIS' ABEL: No, Grandma, you jest set still and take care o' yourself. Don't you go botherin' about other folks's work.

GRANDMA: I'm terrible tired cutting up carpet rags. (MIS' ABEL *disappears into the shed.* GRANDMA, *sorting her rags, talks on, raising her voice to follow* MIS' ABEL.) 'Tain't as though they was goin' to be rugs. We got rag rugs all over the house now. So has everybody else we know. Everybody's floors is plastered with 'em. I been cuttin' rags ever since I came an' doin' nothin' (MIS' ABEL *returns with her fresh iron, testing it as she comes*) *but* cuttin' rags. Seems like I'd ought to be able to make somethin' else with my fingers. Somethin' human. Where you goin', Dianthy?

MIS' ABEL: I'm a-goin' to get this ironin' out of the way, short off. That is, I am if Inez ever gets back from Mis' Ellsworth's with that cup o' starch.

GRANDMA: What you got your hat on for?

MIS' ABEL: So's if anybody runs in they won't set half the day, henderin' me. They'll think I'm goin' off.

GRANDMA: I know. The neighbors do hender terrible. (*A pause.*) Sometimes, though, I think it must be kind o' nice to have somethin' to be hende ³ *at.*

MIS' ABEL (*ironing, but not fast*): I always say mornin's is wove and cut out for hard work. I don't want Mis' Moran or somebody comin' in an' settin' the whole forenoon. This ironin's got to be got out of the way this mornin', no matter what happens to who. (*Her iron sticks, and she rubs it vigorously on the carpet.*)

GRANDMA (*who has dropped her work and is reaching to pick dead leaves off the plants in the window*): I don't seem to have no go in me no more. I don't know what's come over me. I ain't no more interested in them carpet rags than I am in the dipthery.

    (EZRA WILLIAMS *appears at the open window. He is large and flushed and furious.*)

EZRA: Mis' Abel! *Mis' Abel!*

MIS' ABEL (*looks at him, then turns and goes on ironing*): Well, Ezra, as a family we ain't deef.

EZRA: Is this you folks's wood out here?

MIS' ABEL (*over shoulder*): Wood?

EZRA: I want to know if you folks ordered any cordwood?

MIS' ABEL: No. We didn't order no wood.

EZRA: Well, they've brought you some. Only they've unpiled it in front of my door on the piece that's new-seeded and that I've tended like a baby.

MIS' ABEL: Ezra, you're that reasonable that I s'pose it's reasonin' that keeps you so calm. That wood never heard of us.

EZRA: You sure?

MIS' ABEL: Not as sure as you are about things. You don't often find folks as sure as that. But—sure.

EZRA: Well, it's somebody's fool wood, an' I've got to go an' find the fool that ordered it up— (*He strides off, still talking.*) Whoever heard o' anybody gettin' cordwood in, anyhow, in the middle o' the summer?

 (GRANDMA, *who has stopped picking off dead leaves and has listened attentively during his stay, looks after him till he disappears; then she turns.*)

GRANDMA: What did he say?

MIS' ABEL: Did he talk too soft for you, Grandma?

GRANDMA: He was so mad I couldn't keep my mind on what he *was* saying.

MIS' ABEL: Oh, well, he was just talkin' to hear himself talk. About some cordwood.

GRANDMA: It don't seem as if anybody *could* be so interested in cordwood.

MIS' ABEL: They ain't nothin' in the world for Ezra but just Ezra. Nothin' in the world for him but just—him.

GRANDMA (*looking off*): Don't you s'pose there is? It don't seem like they's enough to *any*body to occupy 'em the whole time.

 (*Up to the open door comes* PETER. *He is tall, awkward, grave; long, uncovered wrists, heavy, falling hands; but he has an occasional wide, pleasant, shy smile.*)

PETER (*on the porch*): Good morning, Mis' Abel.

MIS' ABEL: Oh, good morning, Peter. I just happen to be ironin' a flat piece, so I don't have to put my mind on it. I'm goin' to do the collars next (*pointedly*), and they take thought. What's wanted?

PETER (*shuffling, turning his hat*): Any groceries this morning, Mis' Abel?

MIS' ABEL: Groceries?

PETER (*nods and enters*): I've started takin' orders for Ferguson.

MIS' ABEL: Well, I'm glad to hear that. When do you start?

PETER: Today.

MIS' ABEL: Does many order to the door?

PETER: I dunno. I've just started. I'm just startin'. Now.

MIS' ABEL (*rubbing her iron on the carpet*): I ain't doin' no orderin' today. We've got to eat up what we've got. Unless you want to bring me fif' cents' worth o' granulated sugar. You might do that. Get up there and get me that basket of odds an' ends on the top of the cupboard. Seems to me I see a piece o' beeswax up there.

PETER (*finishes writing down the order for sugar and brings a chair from near GRANDMA's chair*): I thought I'd just stop in an' see. You don't think she— (*He stumbles over the chair he is carrying.*) She wouldn't want anything this morning, would she, Mis' Abel?

MIS' ABEL: Who's she? Who you talking about?

PETER: Why, Inez.

MIS' ABEL: I thought it was Inez. Why didn't you say so in the first place? I hate di-plomacy in man or beast.

PETER (*who has not quite reached the cupboard with the chair, sets it down and turns abruptly*): Well, then, I'll say it now. Mis' Abel! Why don't she treat me right?

MIS' ABEL: Treat *you* right? (PETER, *his momentary courage going, takes the chair on over to the cupboard, turns, nods mutely.*) Why, I don't see how she can. Near as I can make out, you never open your head when you're with her.

PETER (*climbing on chair*): It's funny about me, Mis' Abel. (*From the chair.*) Honest, I dunno what to do about me, sometimes.

MIS' ABEL: Well, *stop* thinkin' about you so much.

PETER (*spreading out his hands*): I do try to. But when I try to think how to stop myself thinking about myself, there's myself thinkin' about me.

MIS' ABEL: Think about somethin' else, then! Get me down that basket. You can stand and talk to me all day. I don't see why you can't talk to her.

PETER (*reaching for basket*): *I* could talk all right enough. But my tongue won't. I could—but my tongue, it won't. (*Turns with the basket.*) Why, some girls I know I can jolly like the dickens. But Inez—when she comes along, Mis' Abel, I can't remember anything I know. (*Has down the basket and turns with it in his hands.*) History, now—I know a real lot of history. And about birds and things. I'd *like* to talk with her about them. But last week, when I took her to the picnic, I couldn't think out any of 'em to say no more'n a *hen*. (*He makes a large gesture with the basket at a perilous angle.*)

MIS' ABEL (*with a quick movement to catch the basket*): Well, don't ask me to tell you how to court. Men that don't know history from a coach-and-four can court successful. (*Hunting for beeswax in the basket.*) But you can't expect Inez to know whether she likes you or not if you sit like a block. Say something—do something, so's she'll know you're alive.

PETER (*despondently, as he climbs down*): I know it. I ain't much. An' what little I am don't show through somehow. (*He drags the chair back to its place beside* GRANDMA *in* MIS' ABEL'S *assenting silence. Sets the chair down with a bang.*) Honest, Mis' Abel, I wouldn't care much what happened to me. (GRANDMA *looks up at him, and drops a ball of carpet rags.* PETER *picks it up and it unrolls away from him toward the door.* GRANDMA *suddenly laughs out, an old woman's laugh, shrill, but not unkindly. Miserably.*) I guess I *am* a joke.

GRANDMA: Joke, nothin'. You're a human. You're a human an' you don't know it. I see a-many in my day.

MIS' ABEL (*waxing her iron*): Well, a body needn't be a fool if they are human. My goodness, if Inez don't get here with that starch—

> (INEZ *comes up on the porch. She is slight, and very girlish. She wears a straight, dull-reddish gown. She is hatless and excited.*)

INEZ (*with marked and slightly ironical sweetness to* PETER, *who is almost at the door*): So sorry to have missed you, Peter. Good-by, then. Mother! Guess!

MIS' ABEL (*ironing*): Guess what? I'm too busy.

INEZ: Well, but listen. It's important. It's awful—

MIS' ABEL (*pausing, iron in hand, and looking over her shoulder*): Well, out with it. What is it? What you making such a fuss about it for?

INEZ: It's Mis' Ellsworth's sister. She's died out West. And they're sending her little boy out here to Mis' Ellsworth.

MIS' ABEL (*setting down her iron*): My land a-living! Carry Ellsworth with a boy on top of everything else!

INEZ: I know it. She just heard last night. And she's home trying to think what to do.

MIS' ABEL: When's he going to get here?

INEZ: Tonight. Tonight on the seven fifty-eight.

MIS' ABEL (*pushing her hair back and taking her hat with it*): Ain't that just the end of everything?

INEZ: And her with nobody to do a thing for her.

PETER (*who has dropped the ball again at sight of* INEZ, *has been making more and more of a tangle of the carpet rags ever since she entered*): They couldn't anybody do anything, could they?

INEZ: Well, of course they could! There'll be things for everybody to do that knows her.

> (PETER *comes toward her, his tangle of carpet rags following him. He and* INEZ *talk apart, he awkward and mostly mute, she evidently mocking him as they try to disentangle the rags.*)

MIS' ABEL (*has walked over toward* GRANDMA *and stands, one arm akimbo*): Did you understand, Grandma? Carry Ellsworth's sister's boy is coming to live with her. (*With disapproving emphasis.*)

GRANDMA: Boy? A little boy?

MIS' ABEL: Yes, sir. Tonight. Comin' tonight on the seven fifty-eight.

GRANDMA (*placidly*): Ain't that nice?

MIS' ABEL: Nice? And her all alone in the world?

GRANDMA: Yes. Him comin' and her all alone. She won't be alone no more. I wisht I was younger and could do for one.

MIS' ABEL: My land, I should think you've had enough to do for. I guess you never had no peace till you come into our family.

GRANDMA (*bursting out*): Peace! That's it. Now I've got peace. Peace an' carpet rags. (*When they are not looking, she gives a big white ball of carpet rags a vicious throw through the shed door.*)

MIS' ABEL (*harking back*): Nice. You think it's nice. Why, Carry Ellsworth won't know what to do with a boy no more than nothing in this world. I dunno what she *is* goin' to do to dress him.

INEZ (*turning with the properly wound ball*): We'll have to think of somebody that'll have some cast-off clothes.

MIS' ABEL (*impatiently*): Boys' duds makes awful good weather strips. Before we got the upstairs plastered I use' to wish I'd had a boy or two. It's goin' to be an awful nuisance, doin' for him. There's some of your pa's clothes she might use. I dunno's it'll need clothes first pop, though. But they's everything to think of—

(PETER *starts forward, his face bright with what he means to try to say.*)

PETER: Oh, Inez . . . That is, oh, Mis' Abel. I'm a boy. I mean I was a boy. I mean I've got some trousers—and a coat—and another coat. Shall I get 'em?

MIS' ABEL: What do you mean—something to cut over? Well, get 'em, of course. What you standing there for? Get 'em and bring 'em here. Inez, you run over an' ask Mis' Trot to come in for a minute. Mind you say a *minute*, or she'll set the whole forenoon.

PETER (*at the door*): Are you comin' now, Inez? I—I go that way too.

INEZ (*airily*): Oh, don't you wait for me, Peter. I've got some things to see to. (*Exit* PETER, *looking at her dumbly.*) Mother, hasn't Peter got any lungs?

MIS' ABEL: Lungs?

INEZ: Or maybe it's brains. He looks nice enough—he looks real nice. But he acts as if he didn't have good sense when it comes to talkin'.

MIS' ABEL: Your pa was the same way.

INEZ (*indignant*): *Father?*

MIS' ABEL: Certainly. After we was married, whenever he begun actin' like he knew it all, an' like I wasn't nothin' but the flyleaf o' things, I used to remember how perfectly simple he did use' to act when I first knew him—when he was first makin' up. An' many's the time I've just laughed to myself, and gone and done like he told me to, sheer through rememberin' how simple and scairt and green he did use to act.

INEZ (*softly*): Father? *Father!*

MIS' ABEL: Him. Now run for Mis' Trot and don't be lettin' me let my spare-room pillow shams dry. I guess I'll carry this one in here out o' the dirt. (*Exit with sham.*)

GRANDMA: Daniel was like that, too. He done things regular greenhorn. I remember the day we was engaged, he almost made such a botch of it I didn't know what he meant. He busts out and says, "*Will you?*" an' I thought he meant would I go to the huskin' bee and I said, "Yes." When I see my mistake—well, I let it go at that. I see what hard work he was makin' of it.

INEZ: That was old Uncle Daniel, wasn't it? I remember him. He was awful old.

GRANDMA: Well, but I bet he was consider'ble more up to snuff than your young popinjays is now!

INEZ (*hastily*): Oh, yes. Oh, I know— (*She retreats to the door and is met on the threshold by* MIS' ELMIRA MORAN.) Oh, good morning, Mis' Moran. Come in. Mother'll be back in a minute. Sit down. (*Exit.*)

MIS' MORAN (*stout, sixty, gets about with difficulty; she has a scarf wound many times about her head, but no shawl. Un-*

winds scarf deliberately and sinks in rocker as she speaks):
I dunno as I can. My leg is so bad I can hardly hobble. And
my left shoulder don't get no better. Nor my head—it don't
act right. I dunno but my time is come and my grave is dig-
gin' around the next corner. I feel that way. I told Jake so.
(*Enter* MIS' ABEL.)

MIS' ABEL: Good mornin', Mis' Moran. Ain't it just perfectly
dreadful about—

MIS' MORAN: Dreadful! I dunno what I am goin' to do if it
keeps up. I was just sayin', I said so to Jake only this mornin', I says, "Jake," I says, "I'm gettin' so that I'm su'prised
whenever I wake up alive. Whenever I do it," I says, "it's
like every blessed mornin' of my life was a genu-ine resur-
rection for me. I feel it."

MIS' ABEL: What you talkin' about?

MIS' MORAN: If that ain't just like Jake's treatment of me.
Right while I was talkin' to him, Jake asked me if I'd remembered to set the pancakes. Said he didn't hear me do
it.

MIS' ABEL: Well, but land, land—what's that got to do—

MIS' MORAN: I'd been goin' to tell him about my back, but I
hadn't the heart. I just laid and cried. Mis' Abel, my back's
been behavin' so queer, I can hardly move it. Why, the last
few days—

MIS' ABEL (*positively*): Just you put your finger on the place,
Elmiry Moran, till I tell you the news. Carry Ellsworth's
got a baby.

MIS' MORAN (*sits bolt upright suddenly and with ease*): A
what?

MIS' ABEL: Yes, sir. It ain't here yet. It's due tonight.

MIS' MORAN (*rises, steps toward* MIS' ABEL *easily and eagerly*): What under the sun do you mean, Dianthy Abel?
Carry Ellsworth's goin' to have a baby—

MIS' ABEL: Tonight. On the seven fifty-eight. Her sister's that
died out West. At least the boy's alive and they're sending
him to her.

MIS' MORAN (*limps slowly back to her chair*): You'd ought
not to give me them turns, Dianthy. The doctor says I

mustn't forget for a single minute the condition I'm in. How old is he?

MIS' ABEL: Well, let me see. . . .

(INEZ *appears in doorway with* MIS' TROT. MIS' TROT *is little and "wiry" and active and alert. She comes in with a collar in one hand and a brooch in the other.*)

INEZ: Here's Mis' Trot, Mother.

MIS' TROT: Well, did you ever *hear* anything like it, ever? Carry Ellsworth, of all the folks under the canopy.

MIS' ABEL: That's just exactly what I said.

INEZ (*going to table where lamps are ranged and beginning to clean them*): How much does she get a month now?

MIS' TROT (*at the mirror over the shelf, putting on her collar, speaks with the brooch between her lips*): Why, she only gets her eight dollars a month pension from her husband's leg.

MIS' ABEL: And then of course whatever she earns substitutin' clerkin', when clerks are sick.

MIS' MORAN: But barrin' Christmas week I don't believe that amounts to shucks for pay.

MIS' TROT (*drawing up as a matter of course to help* INEZ *with the lamp chimneys*): It struck me all of a heap. An' we'd just found a buffalo bug in the parlor carpet. Yes, sir. A buffalo bug. In my *parlor*. I tried to step on it—but you know how they are. No corpse to 'em whatever. I couldn't tell whether I hit it or not—and they always run like horses. I've come right off an' left him there, if he *is* there. I wouldn't of done such a thing, but, thinks I, what's Carry Ellsworth goin' to *do*? How old's this child?

MIS' ABEL: That's what we was figurin' when you come in. Now, Lucretia Ellsworth was married the year we moved out of the Kane house—no, that was Elmira, wasn't it? I guess Lucretia wasn't married till the next year. We was livin' in the Mitchell house.

MIS' MORAN: I thought you lived in the Mitchell house before you lived in the Kane. Wasn't you livin' in the Mitchell house when our barn burned?

MIS' TROT: N-o. (*That peculiar, long-drawn "no," with a*

sound of d *in the* n.) You wasn't. Why (*to* MIS' MORAN) your barn never burned till the winter I was livin' alone. I remember wakin' up alone in the house and seein' the glare.

MIS' ABEL: I *know* we was livin' in the Mitchell house when Lucretia was married because I remember runnin' acrost home for more spoons durin' the ceremony. I know I missed my cry altogether, 'count o' not gettin' back till the congratulations. I'd hid my spoons in the spare-room closet and I come over after 'em, all hurried and rattled an' dressed up and I could *not* remember where I'd put them. Let's see that was six—seven—eight—

MIS' MORAN: Oh, that wasn't more'n seven years ago this summer. Because we bought out the Sparks grocery most eight years ago, an' I remember sellin' Hackett Ellsworth the five pounds o' rice.

MIS' TROT: Why, Mis' Moran—it was *all* of eight years ago. You forget how time flies. I'd 'a' said nine, to be on the safe side.

MIS' ABEL: Yes, it must 'a' been eight years ago. I know it was the year Inez had her first ready-made suit. Yes, Carry's boy must be about six—seven years old. It don't seem possible.

INEZ: Carry? I thought you said Lucretia's wedding?

MIS' ABEL: Well, Carry was married right after. She hadn't meant to be so soon. But her father didn't want to put up the parlor stove so long's the girls wasn't goin' to be home, so she was married in the fall to save the bother of a stove weddin'.

MIS' MORAN: Six—seven years old. Land, land. Just the hard age to take care of, when they begin to be smart. What *is* she goin' to do?

MIS' ABEL: Just his mere victuals is an item.

MIS' TROT (*sighing*): Yes, sir. Another mouth is another mouth excep' when it's a boy's mouth. Then it's a regular bureau drawer.

MIS' MORAN: This is goin' to be an awful pull for the poor thing. She wouldn't take money, though, I don't suppose, even if anybody had any to offer her?

INEZ: Oh, not money!

Mis' Trot: No, the last way to help anybody is to give 'em money.

Mis' Moran: Well, of course Carry'll look to us all to advise her some.

Mis' Trot: Oh, I dunno but advice is next worse than money.

Mis' Abel: Well, it's goin' to be a terrible lot of trouble, whatever way you look at it. I should say the thing she needs is a *job*. But while she's gettin' it she'd ought to have some clothes and some extry bedding and I dunno what all. And you know what that means—attemptin' to get together truck like that.

Mis' Trot: I could 'a' done a little somethin' today if it hadn't been for that buffalo bug. But as it is I mustn't stay a minute longer. That animal'll be up into my lace curtains. How you goin' to go at gettin' the stuff together?

Mis' Abel (*ironing hard*): Well, I do hate to load it onto her in tied-up bundles at the back door. I dunno but we'd ought to go to the trouble of a pound party or somethin' like that.

Mis' Trot (*looking up with changing expression*): That would be kind of nice—wouldn't it?

Mis' Abel: Carry didn't have much of any wedding presents. And she never had a baby. I dunno as I ever set foot in her house to any real occasion excep' a funeral. (*Turns with her iron in her hand.*) S'posin' we was to give her a kind of a shower?

Mis' Moran: A what? A shower?

Mis' Trot: Like they have for babies?

Inez: Oh, no. I know what Mother means. Like they have for brides.

Mis' Abel (*sets down her iron, turns and leans against the ironing board; puts pillow sham on chair back*): I mean a shower—whether for bride, babe, or just anybody. It would be a lot of backaching work, but we could make it real nice for her.

Grandma (*who has worked on, without looking up, until* Mis' Abel *has said "shower"—then she has listened*): So you could. Go on and do it. Seems to me you could make it so sort of sociable and friendly it wouldn't seem a bit nasty, like charity does.

Mis' Trot (*looking away, with expression growing more rapt*): Be kind of nice if you could have it the night the child gets here. But that's tonight. Of course you couldn't do that.

Mis' Moran: Well, of course I can't do a thing on account o' my back. But I should think if you could scrape the things together today so's to take 'em with you when you go, you could have it tonight all right.

Mis' Trot (*sitting upright—not suddenly, but still with her rapt manner, leaning forward with her hands across her knees*): An' be there with 'em when she comes back from the depot with the boy!

Mis' Moran: And you could have all the things she needs piled in the middle of the front-room floor and you be in there with the door shut when she got there—(*edging forward on her chair*)—clothes and groceries an' I dunno but some toys—

Mis' Abel: Be an awful job, managin'. How'd we let ourselves into the house?

Mis' Trot (*really kindling*): Easiest thing in the world. I could go in an' set with her awhile before she starts for the seven fifty-eight. I could take her in a cup o' jell, or somethin'. And then I could tell her I'd set there on the porch so's to have a look at him when she got back.

Mis' Abel: And then you could let us all in. That's the ticket! My land, look at me near settin' on my spare-room pillow sham.

Mis' Trot (*laying down last lamp chimney and going to the door to shake the cloth; speaks over shoulder, shaking cloth*): Well, you do that and you can count on me to be over there when you come. You won't have much trouble gettin' the stuff. (*Giving the cloth to* Inez *and turning toward the door.*) I've got to get back to that buffalo bug now, or it'll be layin' eggs in every pattern in the carpet.

(Inez *carries lamps to their high shelf, puts away cloths.*)

Mis' Abel: You come back here.

MIS' TROT (*looks at her in surprise*): But—

MIS' ABEL: You can't be going home, not with all there'll be to see to.

MIS' TROT: I just can't do it. That buffalo bug—

MIS' ABEL: You forget that buffalo bug, Mis' Trot, an' tell us what to have for refreshments. Strawberries? Or a little canned fruit and loaf cake?

MIS' TROT (*returning*): Why, of course we've got to feed 'em. I never thought o' that. *Canned fruit.* I'd just as soon anybody'd set me down to oatmeal as canned fruit—*when* it's a party. Strawberries—well . . . No, for the land's sakes, if we're going to do it, let's us do it. Let's us have ice cream or nothin'. . . .

MIS' MORAN: Be nice for the little boy, too.

MIS' ABEL: But, my land, it costs so to buy it—

MIS' TROT: Buy it? Who said anything about buying it? I'll freeze it. I can make it cheaper'n anybody in this town.

MIS' ABEL: Well, of course you can. That's what we'll do. You freeze it.

MIS' TROT (*excitedly*): I can make it for fourteen cents a quart and freeze it myself, puttin' in our own cow and chickens. Yes, I'll do it—buffalo bug or no buffalo bug. A gallon'll be enough. We can all chip in—

  (*Stamping up on the porch comes* EZRA. *He is still more exasperated, and he comes in without greeting and with his hat on his head.*)

EZRA: Well, I been to both you folks's houses, huntin' you up. An' I been downtown lookin' for the men. Which one o' you ordered wood? Whoever it was can send your menfolks straight out here and unpile it from in front of my door, a stick at a time.

MIS' ABEL: I've told him we didn't order no wood.

MIS' MORAN: Well, *we* didn't. We been cuttin' wood from the wood lot for years.

MIS' TROT: We don't burn none. We burn soft coal—what we have left over after we've sprinkled the house with it thorough, an' our clothes an' our hands an' our necks.

EZRA (*stands puzzled but still warlike*): Well, it's somebody's fool wood. It must belong somewheres in the block. Just ask your menfolks when they come home this noon. I bet you one of 'em—

MIS' ABEL: Let's tell him. Wait a minute, Ezra. We want—

EZRA: I can't wait. I've got my hands so full they sag.

INEZ: Oh, Mr. Williams! I know whose wood that is. It must be Mis' Ellsworth's. I heard her wonderin' this morning why it hadn't come.

EZRA: Well, of all the snide swindles! I've got too much to do to unpile no cord of wood for no woman, widow or worse. . . . (*He is at the threshold when* MIS' ABEL *stops him.*)

MIS' ABEL (*clapping her hands and following him*): Ezra! Ezra Williams. Stop goin' on and listen hard. Carry Ellsworth's sister's boy is comin' on to her tonight to support.

EZRA (*at the door*): Support? Well, I can't help that. I'm doin' some supportin' myself—working my wings off at it. And when it comes to an extry job for nothin'—

MIS' ABEL: Yes, but Carry Ellsworth ain't you. Here's a boy plumpin' down on her to feed and clothe and lug up to man's estate.

EZRA: Well, ain't that just like a woman! Always gettin' herself come down onto by a lot o' distant relatives to support.

MIS' ABEL: Well, it *is* goin' to make trouble for everybody, but we thought we'd ought to—

MIS' MORAN: We thought it'd be real nice to do for her friendly, at a party—

MIS' TROT: And have 'em have refreshments—ice cream and cake. And have everybody bring things.

MIS' ABEL: Wait till I tell him. And all be there when she gets back from the depot—all waiting, in her house, to s'prise her. Couldn't you get hold of some men and see what they could get together? Us ladies'll see to some clothes but—

MIS' MORAN: You scrape up some money, Ezra. Or some groceries—canned stuff, or like that—

MIS' TROT: And have 'em all sent to one place, hadn't we better?

MIS' ABEL: Have 'em all sent here. Then some of the men can

come and tote 'em over when we see her go off to meet the seven fifty-eight.

EZRA (*who has stood shaking his head, edging away*): Yah-pa'cel o' women. Ain't that just like 'em? Do you think I ain't got anything else to do? Ain't enough o' you women to tend to the society end of this town and its relations? No —don't you expect no time out of me. I might send over some little thing—but I ain't a minute to spare today, I tell you. (*He is out the door with the last words.*)

GRANDMA (*who has been looking up at him with fixed attention*): Well, now, would you think *any*body would be that much interested in cordwood?

MIS' ABEL: No, sir, you wouldn't.

MIS' MORAN: Well, ain't that just awful for him not to do one thing?

MIS' TROT: Him with nothin' but cordwood on his hands, mind you—and me with a buffalo bug!

MIS' ABEL: As near as I can see we've got to put this thing through ourselves. You take upstreet, Mis' Trot, and, Mis' Moran, you take downstreet—and I'll take the business part. Everybody's always after them, so I think you really squirm more askin' though you do get it so easy. Inez, you might be lookin' up some of your old picture books for the boy, or somethin' to amuse him. Come on, ladies.

MIS' TROT, MIS' ABEL, MIS' MORAN (*all talking together as they go out,* MIS' MORAN *having forgotten her limp*): Who'll I get to bake the cakes? Well, I'd get some good cake-makers, for mercy's sakes, and there's only about six in town. I know where I'm going for a cake. I'm goin' straight for Mis' Ezra Williams. (*Exeunt all three.*)

INEZ: I'll iron off a flat piece or two first. (*She goes to the shed to change the iron.*)

GRANDMA (*peering out of the windows, through the plants*): Dum 'em. They've gone off to do things. And I'm so old, so fool old. (*She smites her hands together.*) Oh, God. Can't you make us hurry? Can't you *make* us hurry? Get us to the time when we won't have to dry up like a pippin before we're ready to be took off? Our heads an' our hearts an' our legs an' our backs—oh, make 'em last busy, *busy,* right up to the time the hearse backs up to the door!

INEZ (*returns, picks up a piece from the basket, looks over at her*): What's the matter, Grandma?

GRANDMA: Eh, nothin'. Only, I'm *folks.* That's all. I mean I was folks—me that was folks and now ain't.

(INEZ *looks at her, puzzled, and stands rubbing the iron on a newspaper when* PETER *reappears in the doorway, the sugar under his arm, and in his hand a paper.*)

PETER: Mis' Abel! I forgot to ask you just what things you need for that little boy— Oh, you here, Inez? I thought you was out. I thought— Here's your mother's sugar.

INEZ (*cooling her iron and not looking at him*): I'm sorry Mother isn't in. She'll be back in a few minutes. Won't you come back then?

PETER: Inez! I've got lots of conversation in me. (INEZ *searches his face swiftly. Goes on with ironing. With determination.*) I mean, I don't say half the things I could say.

INEZ (*with a moment of understanding and sympathy, she leans on the board and looks at him*): What about, Peter?

PETER: About—about—oh, things. I think of so many things, Inez, when I'm alone, that I'd like to tell you.

INEZ (*still the same*): Why *don't* you tell me, Peter? What are they about?

PETER: Well, woods things, and about water rats—and gophers —and—and—birds' nests!

INEZ (*still understanding, still patient*): Well, I like these things, too, you know, Peter. Tell me some now.

PETER (*looking wild*): Well . . . Birds' nests. They's—they's quite a few birds' nests in the trees this spring. . . .

INEZ (*bursts into sudden uncontrollable laughter*): In the trees! Oh, come now, Peter! Not birds' nests in the trees! Oh . . . *Peter!* You mustn't tell me things like that!

PETER (*struggling desperately*): Well, orioles now. Orioles. . . . I saw an oriole by Thatchers' barn. Its note was all wavy—

INEZ (*grave again*): I know it. I've heard 'em. I love 'em.

PETER: And I thought—what was it I thought when I heard him call? . . .

INEZ: What . . . Peter? (*Sets down her iron and, an elbow in her hand, the other hand over her mouth, she watches him quizzically and somewhat wistfully.*)

PETER (*simply*): It was something I liked to think. And I know I thought how you'd like it, too. Most folks don't hear 'em call. Lots of folks don't hear lots of things. But you do. And I do. Ain't that kind of nice—like them things was for you and me. . . . (*He catches at a corner of her apron, lifts it, and drops it, disconcerted.*) Mebbe you dunno what I mean.

INEZ: Oh, Peter, Peter, Peter! (*Laughs with her eyes shut.*) Oh, *Peter!*

PETER (*turns away, looks up in another part of the room*): I know it. I don't know why it is I can't talk to you, Inez. I think of things I want to say to you, but when I'm with you I don't seem able to think 'em over again. There's history, now. I was readin' some history last night. There was so many things I wanted to tell you in it. I—I know you'd of thought so, too!

INEZ: Really. You think I would? Well, then, here I am. Try me!

PETER: I can't. I didn't plan it out this way—and you laughing.

INEZ: Oh, tell me—do. Was it about robbers—and princesses—and castles, Peter? Was it about knights and swords and roses—

PETER: Oh, it was better things. One was about Peter the Great, you know. Him. He was a—my, he was just a dandy!

INEZ (*now really at the end of her patience*): Was that what you wished to tell me?

PETER (*miserably*): No. But—

INEZ: Because if it was, I'm not in the least interested in Peter the Great! Not-in-the-least! (*She marches across the floor to the shed door to renew her iron, and on the threshold she turns, overcome again by the sorry figure he has cut.*) Peter, oh, Peter . . . (*Laughs with her eyes shut, and goes into the shed.* PETER *sits where she has left him, and drops his head in his hands.*)

GRANDMA (*suddenly wheels in her chair*): Young man! (PETER *lifts his head.*) Do you call that courtin'? (PETER *makes a helpless gesture.*) Because if I couldn't court no better than that I'd go and batch it and be done with it. You court like a stick of wood.

PETER (*with a hopeless gesture*): What'll I do?

GRANDMA: Do? Do what most everybody in the world has to do before they can fit their skins and skulls. Quit thinkin' about yourself. Dunce!

PETER: Well, but I—I— (INEZ *comes back with the iron.* GRANDMA *subsides.* PETER *rises miserably.*) I guess I'll have to be going.

INEZ: Oh, must you? Well, good-by, Peter.

PETER: I s'pose it's all done there is to do about the little chap —the one that's coming?

INEZ: Why, of course it isn't. Who did you think did it all?

PETER: Do—do you think I could be any use to 'em? (INEZ *amazes him by dropping her flatiron with a clatter on the ironing stand and bursting into sobs.*) Inez! What is it? (*He leaps to her, for the first time unconscious of himself, and puts his arms about her. For just a moment she leans to him, then springs free and speaks angrily.*)

INEZ: It's nothing. It's nothing, I tell you. Go 'way, Peter. Please go 'way.

PETER (*stands still for a moment, then flings up his head and speaks in wonder*): Inez! Inez! Do you *care* because I'm a fool?

INEZ: Go 'way, Peter. Please go 'way.

PETER: Well, I will go—now. But by the great horn spoon, Inez, I'll come back! (*He rushes out.*)

(INEZ *runs to* GRANDMA, *sinks beside her, buries her face in her gown.*)

INEZ: Grandma, Grandma. Why can't he be like other folks? *Why* can't he be like other folks?

GRANDMA (*with great tenderness*): Hush . . . dearie. Hardly anybody ever is. Hardly *any*body is.

(*Moment's pause. The door opens, and* MIS' ABEL *enters sidewise, her arms piled with old clothes. She is calling to somebody over her shoulder.*)

MIS' ABEL: Well, supposin' they *are* too big? Send 'em along—send 'em along. I've cut over more of 'em than I ever made new ones. (*Closes the door behind her by pushing against it.*) My land, that's been a tug. Folks has kept a-givin' me things an' I've kep' sayin' I'd take 'em right along. (*Dropping things on the floor and keeping them together.*) I know 'em. If folks had waited to send the stuff by somebody they'd 'a' took to lookin' it over again an' got to snippin' off the buttons and mebbe decide they was too good to give away at all. You needn't tell me. Folks is *folks.*

GRANDMA (*patting* INEZ's *arms—*INEZ *has risen, and stands surreptitiously drying her eyes*): That's it—that's it. Folks is folks, no matter how different—or similar. They can't fool us. Folks is folks.

INEZ (*turns and sees the garments which her mother is vaguely sorting*): Oh, Mother, how fine. Isn't that a pile? How fine! (*Examines the garments and after a moment goes to the shed with her flatiron.*)

MIS' ABEL: They's everything here. Enough to clothe Carry Ellsworth's nephew till he's black in the face.

(*Enter* MIS' TROT, *breathless.*)

MIS' TROT: I've solicited the rest of the stuff for the ice cream and I've got four cakes promised. (*Seeing the things on the floor.*) What a lot of splendid truck!

MIS' ABEL: Well, I'm 'most dead luggin' it. (*She is stooping, turning over the things.*)

MIS' TROT (*looking toward the door*): And ain't the air nice in the forenoon? It seems like breathin' somethin' else. Comin' along by the wood yard, somethin'—I dunno whether it was the smell of the cedar shingles or the way the fence looked so nice and shady—but (*little laugh*) I ain't never felt so much like when I was a girl since I was born one. If it hadn't been for the thought of that buffalo bug in the house, I declare I would of most enjoyed myself.

MIS' ABEL (*in falsetto*): Did you? Why, I was just thinkin' that out on Main Street—that it seemed somethin' like quite a while ago. I thought it was the smell of the sage where somebody was fryin' pork, but mebbe it wasn't.

(*Enter* MIS' MORAN. *She is walking nearly erect and is hurrying somewhat.*)

MIS' MORAN: It's all right. I just see Carry Ellsworth goin' into the post office, and I turned in on purpose. I told her somebody'd come over tonight and set while she went to the station, and be there when she comes back. She seemed to like the idee. Is this stuff all here?

MIS' ABEL: Yes, and more to come. Don't you think we'd best all be setting in there in the dark when she gets here with him, and all of us yell "Shower," shan't we? Just like they do?

MIS' TROT (*down on the floor beside the things*): Poor little soul—it's him I'm a-thinkin' of. His mother dead and his home broke up and him dragged away from what folks he knows. *Look here!* Well, of course we're glad to have any of these things. (*Holds up a very ragged garment.*) How's this for a contribution? Nobody could patch that without they had a piece of cloth the size of the American flag—and not a button on it. I'll bet you Mis' Hemenway give this—didn't she now?

MIS' ABEL (*looking closely*): Yes, sir, she did. If you'd packed as many missionary barrels as I have you'd 'a' known it was Mis' Hemenway's without lookin'. Mis' Hemenway is a splendid cake-maker, but she *is* nearsighted about gifts she gives the poor.

MIS' TROT (*goes on sorting*): I got to thinkin', supposin' it had been my Jeddie, if I'd been took, and him traipsed off to a strange state, and all. Ain't it real pitiful—well, now, would you think anybody'd give away a thing as good as that is? (*She holds up a garment, and* MIS' MORAN, *who has been shaking her head over the other one, takes it from her.*)

MIS' MORAN: No, I would *not*. Why, it looks like new from the store. They ain't a thread broke in it. *And* the buttons on. Who give this, Mis' Abel?

Mis' ABEL (*who is piling up some things from the lot on the table*): I was wondering what he'd be like. Nice little thing, I guess maybe— Carry's so nice. . . . (*Looks at the garment.*) Oh, that's Mis' Fitch—couldn't you tell? Her that always sends a thirteen-egg angels' food to the church suppers when a loaf o' pound cake would go down just as easy.

Mis' TROT: And her husband on thirty dollars a month. My good land, ain't folks the funniest things?

(*They all shake heads and compress lips, and* Mis' TROT *goes "T-t-t-t-t."*)

GRANDMA: Ah—ain't you got used to that about folks yet, Mis' Trot? I want to know—I want to know. It don't hurt folks none to be funny, does it?

INEZ (*who is entering from the shed*): Grandma, look. Here was one of your balls of carpet rags rolled way out there. Would you think it could?

GRANDMA (*peering at it*): That's the very one I been lookin' for. I want it for the head.

INEZ: The head of *what*, Grandma?

GRANDMA: Never you mind. I got my own occupations. You ain't the only busy folks in the world, if you do act so cocky about it. I need something to do for as well as you.

INEZ (*who has been looking out the window*): Mother, Mis' Ellsworth is coming.

Mis' ABEL: Mis' Ellsworth! (*The women scurry around but they are too late.* Mis' ELLSWORTH *enters. She is a slight, pretty woman in a light-blue gingham gown and wide straw hat. She is much agitated, and sinks in a chair by the door. She has a letter and a little parcel in her hand.* Mis' ABEL *is with the other two women, trying to hide the piles of garments.*) Why, Carry Ellsworth! You did give me a start. I'm—we've—we're—don't this look like carpet rags, though?

Mis' ELLSWORTH (*hardly hears*): Oh, ladies. I've just got a letter—I've had another letter. Seems my little boy ain't comin' at all.

ALL (*save* GRANDMA): Not comin'?

Mis' ELLSWORTH (*slowly*): No. A sister of his pa's decided

last minute she'd take him in. She's got five of her own, but she writes she dunno's one more'll make any difference.

Mis' ABEL (*sitting limply back in the clothes*): Well, ain't that just the end of everything!

Mis' MORAN: Well, Carry—you can't help it, but be glad the little fellow ain't had all the way to come alone.

Mis' TROT: An' I ain't a doubt in the world he's got a better home than you could give him—anybody that can afford to have five children is rich enough to have six.

Mis' ABEL: And it *was* going to be awful hard on you to have him to do for.

Mis' ELLSWORTH: I know, I know. But it's goin' to be awful hard for me not to have him to do for. Last night—when I begun to plan—it come over me like it never done before what I'd missed in *not* bein' left with one. I was goin' to make him a bed on the lounge—I'd got it planned what clothes I could spare for the bed, and what I could make more of. I never got meals for a child—and I'd begun thinkin' what he could eat and what little things I could fix up for him. I was plannin' to keep chickens and to fix a sand pile in the back yard and a swing under the maple out in front—and I was thinkin' about his school and who'd be his teacher and what desk he'd have. I just see this little cap in the post-office store and I bought it for him. (*Unwraps a cap from a little package.*) I thought the feather'd look kind o' cute, stickin' up in front. And now here comes this —and it's all for nothin'—it's all for nothin'.

Mis' ABEL: But, Mis' Ellsworth, it *would* be hard for you. It would now!

Mis' ELLSWORTH: I'd like that kind o' hard.

Mis' TROT: And s'pose you'd of took down sick?

Mis' ELLSWORTH: Better body sick than heart sick.

Mis' MORAN: And s'pose you'd of *died,* Mis' Ellsworth?

Mis' ELLSWORTH: I'd of lived first now, anyway. And now I ain't. I never knew it—but I ain't.

Mis' ABEL: Oh, but, Mis' Ellsworth, you've got your health and you're gettin' along economical to brood over as it is.

Mis' ELLSWORTH: This would of kept me from broodin'.

(INEZ *goes softly, and mutely slips her arm about* MIS'
ELLSWORTH.)

MIS' ABEL (*openly breaks down and wipes her eyes on the
garment she is holding*): Oh, ladies! What's the use? We all
know. I ain't had but one, but I know.

MIS' TROT: Yes. I've got seven an' sometimes I'm drove 'most
to death with 'em—but I know.

MIS' MORAN: Well, I never had none—but I know.

GRANDMA: Eh, mine's dead—all dead. But I know.

INEZ: Oh, Mis' Ellsworth. An' I know, too.

(*In a moment at the door appears* PETER, *his arms
ludicrously full of clothes and parcels.*)

PETER: Look, Inez, look-a-here. See all I got a holt of—for the
little chap. (*He sees their mood and pauses, crestfallen.*)

INEZ (*goes to him swiftly*): Peter! What a lot you got. Dear
Peter.

(*The door is pushed open by* EZRA WILLIAMS. *He has
a small, closely wrapped bundle under an arm, and he
is carrying a little chair.*)

EZRA (*handing bundle to* MIS' ABEL): There's a few little
things my wife just sent over. This here little chair—I made
it myself for our little boy before he was hardly out o' long
dresses. I done the whole thing—pegged it myself, so's he
could throw it around and it wouldn't get broke. He—he
never grew up enough to use it. . . . It's been settin' around
my workroom—kind of in the way. It ought to be doin'
somebody some good.

MIS' ABEL: That's certainly good of you, Ezra.

EZRA: Say, you'd ought to see Mis' Ellsworth's wood, piled by
her back door neat as a kitten's foot. She ain't to home—
(*Sees for the first time that* MIS' ELLSWORTH *is there, over
near* GRANDMA.) Good souls! Have I let the cat out of the
bag?

MIS' ABEL: No, Ezra—no, no. I was tryin' to tell you. He ain't
comin'. The little boy ain't comin' after all.

EZRA: He ain't comin'?

MIS' ELLSWORTH (*coming forward*): No, Ezra. They ain't
goin' to give him to me. Somebody else has took him.

EZRA: Well, ain't that a shame! (*Bristling.*) Who's got him? Want I should get him for you?

MIS' ELLSWORTH (*shaking her head*): No—you can't, Ezra. But you don't know—you'll never know how I feel about what you've done a'ready—you and the ladies and Peter and Grandma. . . . Would—you mind if we looked at the little clothes?

EZRA: No—why, look at 'em. They ain't much, I guess, for nowadays. But his ma says she'd like you to have 'em. They was real good cloth in the beginnin'.

MIS' ELLSWORTH (*fingering the garments, turns quickly to the women*): Ain't that what it is to have neighbors? Ain't it, though? Look at the bother you've been to. . . . An' now I won't need 'em.

MIS' ABEL: Don't you think a thing about us. We was glad to do it. I was feelin' cross as a wolf with all I had to do when Inez come in with the news. (*She is taking off her hat as she speaks.*) And now I feel—I feel like folks. An' Mis' Moran's leg and her back and Mis' Trot's buffalo bug—I guess they feel just the same about it.

GRANDMA: And me. So do I. I was just hatin' the sight o' my carpet rags. But look at what I stodged up for the little chap. (*She holds up an absurd black doll with a white head.*)

MIS' ELLSWORTH: Oh, Grandma!

GRANDMA: Don't you thank me. I liked doin' it. It was somethin' for somebody. It was real human to do.

MIS' ABEL: Well, we might as well pick 'em up.

INEZ (*turning to* PETER, *who stands apart*): Peter, how dear of you to get all these things for him.

>   (MIS' ABEL *unwraps them, and they draw about her to look, all save* PETER, *who is standing a little apart.* INEZ *turns to him.*)

PETER: I didn't get 'em *all* for him. I got 'em part for you.

INEZ: Well, it was dear of you anyway. What—what's that in your pocket, Peter?

PETER (*brings shyly from his pocket a little clown on a stick*):

I saw it in the store. I didn't know but what he might like it. If he ain't a-comin' we might as well throw it away.

INEZ: No! Give it to me.

PETER (*still holding toy and looking down at it*): Why, it's nothin' but a clown. Like me, I guess. . . .

INEZ: Well, I want it all the same. . . . Oh, Peter, Peter, what a dear you are when you forget yourself!

    (*He looks at her breathlessly, then suddenly takes her in his arms . . . and as he does so, tosses the clown-on-a-stick into the little vacant chair.*)

PETER: Inez—Inez! Do you *mean* that! Oh, Inez, I tell you I'm forgettin' now. I'll never remember any more. (*He kisses her.*)

    (*As they stand so, MIS' ABEL turns and sees them. The others follow her look, GRANDMA, too, and they all turn and look at each other, silent and smiling. And then GRANDMA rises, and comes slowly down to them—bent and peering and kindly, and holding by one arm the doll she has made. As she passes the little vacant chair, near which INEZ and PETER stand, she drops the doll over the chair's back in order to take their hands. She stands between and a little back of them, facing the audience. She looks up at them and tries to speak to each in turn, and gives it up with a little helpless gesture and a smile and a hand patting the shoulder of each. They are all gathered near the two, the little garments EZRA has brought still in the women's hands and MIS' ELLSWORTH still holding the cap with the feather.*)

MIS' ABEL (*wiping her eyes swiftly*): Strikes me the little chap is accountable for a whole heap he never even heard of.

GRANDMA: Eh—most folks always is.

IMPROMPTU

TAD MOSEL was born in Steubenville, Ohio, in 1922, and studied at Amherst College, the Yale Drama School, and Columbia University. He started writing plays when he was eighteen and has become one of the best-known writers of original television dramas in this country. He is a slow and careful writer, sometimes spending four months on one hour-long show. His plays have been performed by such stars as Eileen Heckart, Kim Stanley, Lili Darvas, Mildred Dunnock, Barbara Bel Geddes, Claire Trevor, Jessica Tandy, Patricia Neal, Nina Foch, Tony Randall, Buster Keaton, Gary Merrill, Rod Steiger, Ed Begley, Dennis King, E. G. Marshall, and Hume Cronyn; directed by Arthur Penn or Delbert Mann; and produced by Fred Coe, David Susskind, and others. Mr. Mosel's plays have been televised in England, Denmark, Belgium, Holland, Czechoslovakia, Germany, Australia, and Canada. Mr. Mosel has found the television screen an ideal medium for his special abilities. He understands many kinds of people and he gradually reveals their dreams and frustrations through small but significant intimate glimpses that make us more understanding of ourselves.

Impromptu was written for the living theatre while Mr. Mosel was studying at Yale. He calls it a product of his "Pirandello Period," but the play is not a copy of Pirandello. It is a provocative treatment of the popular theme: How much truth and how much illusion does a person need to live a balanced life?

IMPROMPTU

Tad Mosel

The scene is a nondescript room, the walls of which are not very high. They are set at peculiar angles to one another. There is a distorted doorway rear center. The furniture consists of a sofa, a chair, and perhaps a small table. Beyond the entrance and surrounding the room there is nothing but blackness.

The stage is dark. Nothing is visible but the glow of WINIFRED's *cigarette. There is a pause, and then the actors speak out of the darkness.*

WINIFRED: Well, we're here. Somebody say something.

TONY: Is the curtain up?

WINIFRED: Yes.

TONY: But we can't see anything. It's like the end instead of the beginning. What's wrong?

ERNEST: That fool stage manager has forgotten to bring up the lights.

WINIFRED: Oh, no, Ernest, he didn't forget. There's something deliberate about this. I don't trust him.

LORA: You've got him wrong, Winifred. He was very nice. He wouldn't play tricks on us. Not him.

ERNEST: Just leave everything to me. I'll go out and talk to him.

TONY: But you can't!

ERNEST: Why not?

TONY: Don't you remember what he said? We're not to leave the stage until we have acted out the play.

ERNEST: He was just trying to be impressive. I've met his kind before. It's time he learned that actors are more important than stage managers.

TONY: He said it as if it were a law.

ERNEST: Well, I won't stand here in the dark. (*Shouting.*) Lights! Hey, you, out there—lights! (*There is a pause.*)

LORA: Maybe we're not as important as you think, Ernest. Let's just be quiet and wait.

TONY: Is there an audience out there?

WINIFRED: Yes, I can hear them soughing.

ERNEST: You can hear them what?

WINIFRED: Soughing, dear. Breathing heavily, as in sleep.

TONY: I feel as if I'm asleep, too.

WINIFRED: If everybody's going to feel things, we won't get anywhere at all. (*Pause.*)

TONY: Yes. Asleep and dreaming. I'm a child again. I can see myself being led into a room full of people. They laugh and tell me to dance. I don't know what to do. I can't dance. So I hop up and down on one foot. Up and down, up and down. Now they're applauding. I'm a great success. Why do I want to cry? (*There is a pause. The lights come on.*)

ERNEST: That's more like it!

LORA: I knew he'd take care of us! I knew it!

WINIFRED: The stage manager said, "Let there be light," and there was light.

TONY: But the lights won't stand still. They seem to be changing! It's worse than it was before.

WINIFRED: Why don't you go off in a corner and have that cry? (TONY *looks at her.*)

ERNEST: And look, Winifred, you were right. There is an audience!

WINIFRED: So there is!

LORA: Isn't it wonderful? Do you see them, Tony?

TONY: Yes, I see them.

ERNEST: They're waiting for us to begin.

TONY: Do they know what we're going to do? Has it been explained to them?

WINIFRED: I defy you to explain anything that is happening on this stage.

TONY: I was just asking a question.

LORA: Don't ask questions, Tony. You'll only make yourself unhappy. Ernest says they're waiting for us to begin. Well, let's begin!

ERNEST: Wait a minute, Lora. Tony may have a point there. I wonder if they do know what we're doing.

TONY: Maybe we ought to tell them.

WINIFRED: All right, then, tell them!

TONY: Me?

WINIFRED: Certainly. It's your bright idea.

ERNEST: I'm sure I could explain everything very lucidly.

WINIFRED: You probably could, Ernest. That's why I want him to do it.

TONY: I wouldn't know what to say.

WINIFRED: I know you wouldn't.

TONY (*naively, inquiringly*): Are you making fun of me, Winifred?

WINIFRED: Whatever gave you that idea? (*She laughs lightly.* TONY *looks at her a moment, then he steps down to the edge of the stage and addresses the audience.*)

TONY: Ladies and gentlemen, we are here to—they say that every actor has a dream—a recurring dream—and he's on a stage and there's an audience, and—he doesn't know what the play is or what his lines are. That's the way it is with us. This afternoon. Maybe we are dreaming—maybe we're not really here—I don't know—

WINIFRED: You can stop right there! I know that I'm here, thank you. Irrevocably, unwillingly, disgustingly here.

ERNEST (*with great tolerance*): You'd better let me do it, Tony. (*To the audience.*) Ladies and gentlemen, an hour ago each of us received a message to report to this theater; there were jobs waiting for us. When we arrived, the stage manager told us we were to go on stage immediatcly, before an audience, and improvise a play—which we are about to do. (*To* TONY.) You see how easy it is?

TONY: Yes, it's easy to say what happened. You didn't say what it means. Who are we? Why are we here? That's the important thing.

WINIFRED: That young man has rocks in his head.

LORA: Would it help if we told them our names, Tony?

ERNEST: An excellent suggestion, Lora. I was about to think of it myself. (*He turns to the audience.*)

WINIFRED: Here we go!

ERNEST (*to the audience*): You have no programs, so you know nothing about us. My name is Ernest. I am returning to the stage after several successful seasons on the West Coast, where I scored personal successes in more than two-score films. Born of a theatrical family, I was reared in stage dressing rooms. At the age of five, I scored a personal success in—

TONY: Ernest, you're not explaining anything!

ERNEST: I'm telling them who I am!

TONY: But it's more than that!

LORA: Be quiet, Tony. This is very interesting. I love hearing about other people.

TONY: All right. I'll be quiet.

LORA: Go on, Ernest.

(ERNEST *begins to speak.*)

WINIFRED (*quickly*): Why don't you be quiet, too, Ernest?

ERNEST: I haven't finished.

WINIFRED: Surely they know all about you—an actor of your standing. You don't want to bore them by telling them things they know, do you?

ERNEST: Well—no.

WINIFRED: Then sit down. (*He does so.*)

LORA: It's your turn, Winifred.

WINIFRED (*shrugs her shoulders, moves down to the edge of the stage, and addresses the audience*): I'm Winifred. I have had rather a cloudy career as an actress. You may have seen me, but you won't remember. I usually play the leading lady's best friend. I don't like the theater because you can't trust it. This is an example of what I mean. Next. (*Indicating* LORA.)

LORA (*after thinking a moment*): My name used to be Lora-lee, but somebody said a long stage name is bad luck, so I shortened it to Lora. It hasn't helped me much, but I don't really mind. Perhaps I wasn't meant to be an actress. I think that's all. (*She steps back.*)

WINIFRED: Hold tight, everybody. (*With mock seriousness.*) Your turn, Tony.

TONY: I have nothing to say.

LORA: But, Tony, you've got to tell them something about yourself.

TONY: Why? None of you did. It's all so unreal. (*To the audience.*) Who are you? Why are you here? Did you come for escape, for enlightenment, for curiosity? Or were you, too, commanded?

ERNEST: We weren't any of us commanded!

TONY: Then what are we doing here? It's the only explanation! You're a celebrity—surely this is beneath you. Lora wasn't meant to be an actress. Winifred hates the stage.

WINIFRED (*cuttingly*): And you're afraid, aren't you?

TONY: Yes, I'm afraid! There—I've told them something about myself!

WINIFRED: If that's all you've got to say, sit down. You were amusing for a while, but no longer. Soul-searching is the lowest form of entertainment.

ERNEST: I don't see why you're afraid, Tony. You ask what we're doing here, and the answer is simple. We are here to please the audience, and they are here to be pleased.

WINIFRED: Why can't you be like Ernest, Tony? He knows everything.

LORA: The stage manager's not going to like it if we don't do something soon.

ERNEST: Of course, Lora. (*To the audience.*) I hope you will be patient with outbursts of this sort, ladies and gentlemen. Naturally, some of us are a little confused. But don't worry, we're going to begin our play as soon as we've made a few preparations. You see, the stage manager gave us instructions—

WINIFRED: He wrote upon the tables the words of the Covenant—

ERNEST: Shut up, Winifred. (*To the audience.*) And I think it only fair to let you know what they are. First of all, our play will not end until he is completely satisfied with our performance.

WINIFRED: That's a cheerful thing to tell them. (*To the audience.*) He's one of those sour little men who never like anything.

LORA: You'd better stop talking that way about him, Winifred. He's right over there behind that wall; he can hear you. You might offend him.

WINIFRED: That's nothing compared to what he's done to me.

LORA: But he's so important, and—good. I think he's been very kind to us. I have great faith in him.

ERNEST: I thought you wanted to begin, Lora.

LORA: Oh—I'm sorry, Ernest.

ERNEST (*to the audience*): Secondly, we are not permitted to leave the stage until the play has ended. And last of all, our play is to be an imitation of life.

TONY: No, that's wrong! (ERNEST *looks at him, annoyed.*) Well, it is. He didn't say that.

LORA: Are you sure, Tony?

TONY: I listened very carefully. He didn't say it was to be an imitation of life. It's supposed to *be* life.

LORA: Oh. I think maybe you're right.

TONY: That's one thing I know.

ERNEST: Ridiculous. Plays can be about life, like life, for life, or against it.

WINIFRED: The best ones are against it.

ERNEST: But they can't be life.

TONY: That's what he said.

LORA: Yes. Those were his very words.

WINIFRED (*with a laugh*): Well, Ernest, for once you're wrong. This is an unexpected pleasure.

ERNEST: I'm not wrong! I know that's what he said. I just wanted to see if you remembered.

WINIFRED (*enjoying herself*): We did!

ERNEST: All right, all right. Let's go.

LORA: What do we do?

WINIFRED: We smile and say brilliant things. (*To* ERNEST.) How do you do, Lord Fiddle?

ERNEST (*catching on*): How do you do, Lady Faddle?

WINIFRED: How nice of you to come.

ERNEST: How nice of you to let me.

WINIFRED: How nice of you to say so.

ERNEST: How nice!

WINIFRED: How charming!

ERNEST: How delightful!

WINIFRED: Curtain! (*She looks at the curtain, which does not move.*) Guess that wasn't enough.

ERNEST: Of course not, Winifred. I didn't even have a characterization yet.

TONY: We won't get anywhere that way. We can't jump into the middle of it—we've got to know what we're doing.

ERNEST: I beg your pardon. I know what I am doing.

TONY: We've got to have someplace to start.

ERNEST: You're so sure of yourself—find it!

TONY: There must be something here that will help us. (*He looks around.*) Maybe if we looked at the set.

WINIFRED (*with a shudder*): I've already looked.

LORA: What's wrong with it?

WINIFRED: Nothing. It's served its purpose admirably for generations.

TONY: It's new to me. Look at the distortions.

LORA: Where?

TONY: The doorframe's crooked—the walls are uneven.

LORA: Oh, yes!

ERNEST: There are no distortions. The set is perfectly all right!

LORA: What could it be?

ERNEST: It's obviously a room, and you only find rooms in houses. It must be somebody's home.

LORA (*brightly*): What is home without a mother?

ERNEST: There, Tony, I've got you one character already.

TONY: But who will play it?

ERNEST: Well—there's Winifred.

WINIFRED: Oh, no, there isn't Winifred!

ERNEST: Why not? You're perfect.

WINIFRED: I won't do it!

ERNEST: Yes, you will. You have just the right quality. I have decided.

WINIFRED: Then you can turn around and undecide. When I was in high school I played a reindeer in a Christmas pageant. My first professional role was a maid—the kind who gives exposition. Since then I have played nothing but wisecracking cynics of unmistakably easy virtue. I had the right quality for them, too.

LORA: I should think a mother would be a nice change for you.

WINIFRED: Me!

ERNEST: What do you want to do?

WINIFRED (*looking from one to the other, wondering if she ought to say it*): Well, I'm sticking my neck out, but once—just once, mind you—I would like to play the sweet young thing everybody falls in love with. Don't laugh! Don't laugh any of you or I'll leave the theater this minute—I don't care what God Almighty out there says. I'm serious.

ERNEST: But that's Lora's part.

WINIFRED: It's always Lora's part. I want to do it once.

LORA: I'm sure I don't know why. Ingénues are such sticky, spineless things.

WINIFRED: I want to be sticky!

LORA: But there's so much more to a good character role.

WINIFRED: Then you play the mother!

LORA (*really wishing she could*): I'd like to, but I don't think Ernest would let me. (*She looks at* ERNEST *hopefully.*)

ERNEST: I certainly wouldn't. That's Winifred's part.

WINIFRED: All right. I just thought I'd have my say.

ERNEST: And Tony will play your son.

WINIFRED: Is that the best I could do?

TONY: Don't worry, Winifred; I don't like it any more than you do.

ERNEST: And what's the matter with you?

TONY: Me play her son? I wouldn't know the first thing to do.

WINIFRED: Try hopping up and down on one foot.

TONY: Another joke! Good for you, Winifred!

WINIFRED: Stop feeling sorry for yourself.

TONY: The reason I can't play the part is because I've never been a son. Oh, I had parents—wonderful parents—so wonderful that when I was six they told me I'd been a mistake, they hadn't wanted me, and would I please not get in their way. I was keeping them from having a good time. They wanted to laugh. That was what they did best. They laughed at anything—especially things they didn't want to understand. The way Winifred does. (*There is a pause.*)

WINIFRED (*quietly, but with bite*): They were probably very cruel. Am I?

TONY: If I say yes, you'll think I'm feeling sorry for myself. If I say no, I won't be telling the truth.

WINIFRED: I never intend to be cruel. I feel very kindly about most things. But I'm ashamed of it, so it doesn't come out that way. There's something humiliating about letting yourself go. (*Directly, sincerely.*) I think you can play my son, Tony.

TONY: All right. I will.

ERNEST: And Lora will be your sweetheart. You've just become engaged and you've brought her home to meet your mother.

LORA: What will you play, Ernest?

ERNEST: I'm a friend of the family. Wealthy, handsome, dashing, influential, wise. The backbone of the play. The one who resolves the conflict in the end.

LORA (*rather alarmed*): Does there have to be a conflict?

ERNEST: Of course. Whoever heard of a play without a conflict?

LORA: What will it be? Am I in it?

ERNEST: Yes. Winifred doesn't like you because you're stealing her son. And she's a fighter. She's determined to break up the engagement. But it so happens you're a fighter, too. Neither of you will give in. Conflict.

WINIFRED: How do you propose to resolve that?

ERNEST (*to* WINIFRED): You're only jealous of Lora because you're lonely and you have no one but Tony to love. So I'll marry you and that will settle everything.

WINIFRED: Won't Tony's father object?

ERNEST (*after a moment's thought*): He's dead.

WINIFRED: That's the part I want to play.

LORA: And Tony and I get married?

ERNEST: Yes.

LORA: I'm so glad it has a happy ending. That's perfect, Ernest. I don't know how you thought it up. Go ahead and say the first line.

ERNEST: Give me a minute. (*He puts his hand to his brow and moves slowly around the stage. He ends up by* TONY, *removes his hand from his brow, and speaks very dramatically.*) My boy. This is a very serious step you are about to take. Marriage is the most important event in a man's life. (*Turning majestically to* LORA.) In a woman's, too. (*Spreading his arms to include them both.*) Be sure, my children, be terribly sure that you love each other. (*Long pause.*) Enough.

WINIFRED (*drawing herself up into a caricature of an old, grand lady*): Of course she loves my son. Women have always been attracted to him. When he was three, his governess cut her throat for unrequited love.

LORA (*with stars in her eyes*): Oh, I do love him! I do, I do, I do! Just the sight of him—the sound of his voice, the touch of his hand—the way his eyes crinkle up at the corners when he smiles!

WINIFRED: How sticky can you get?

LORA: Wasn't that line all right? It's a sentimental comedy.

WINIFRED: It's a farce.

ERNEST: You're both wrong. It's a drama.

TONY: What difference does it make? The important thing is that you don't mean what you're saying—it doesn't make sense.

ERNEST (*icily*): You don't like it.

TONY: It's not a question of liking.

ERNEST: Now, listen, Tony, I have been in the theater a great deal longer than you have, and I'm tired of your telling me how to do things.

TONY: But it's pointless if we don't believe in ourselves. Isn't it? (*He looks imploringly at the three of them.* WINIFRED *has been listening to what he said.* ERNEST *turns away impatiently.*)

ERNEST: You were right, Winifred. (*Pointing to his head.*) Rocks. Big ones! (*He sulks with his back to them.*)

WINIFRED (*almost ashamed of being reminded of her flippancy*): Yes.

LORA: Please let's keep going. It spoils it if we stop after every line.

WINIFRED (*to* TONY): Come here—son. (*He moves to the sofa.*) Sit down. (*He sits at the far end. She pats the cushion next to her.*) Here. (*He moves in.* ERNEST *turns to watch. Impatiently.*) For heaven's sake give me your hand.

TONY (*giving her his hand*): I'm sorry—Mother.

WINIFRED: Now. Tell me all about it. (*She waits for him to speak. He does not.*) How did you meet?

TONY: We—met.

ERNEST: Where, my boy? That's the important thing. I've always felt that one should be very careful where one falls in love. Now, in my case—

WINIFRED: Ernest!

ERNEST: What's the matter? I was going to get in a nice bit of character exposition.

WINIFRED: It's not your scene. (*To* TONY.) Tell me how you met.

TONY: I don't know.

WINIFRED: Try. (TONY *looks imploringly at* LORA, *who can't think of a thing.*)

LORA (*whispering to* ERNEST): Ernest, where did we meet?

ERNEST (*out of the corner of his mouth*): On a bus.

LORA (*to* TONY): On a bus.

TONY (*to* WINIFRED): On a bus.

LORA: We were sitting together.

TONY: In the same seat. (*Slight pause.*)

LORA: I'd lost my purse.

TONY: She didn't have any money.

LORA: He paid my fare!

TONY: It was only ten cents!

LORA: The conductor was about to throw me off. It was awfully funny!

TONY (desperately): I almost died laughing! (WINIFRED has observed TONY's desperation. Suddenly she realizes there is a silence, but she can't think of anything to say.)

WINIFRED: Say something, Ernest.

ERNEST: Well— (He starts to speak, but gives it up.) Oh, what's the use. The audience will be walking out in a minute.

WINIFRED (sincerely): I wish we could.

LORA: We've got to go on.

WINIFRED (after a pause, to TONY, half in the play, half out): Are you happy?

TONY: I—I don't know.

ERNEST: You don't know?

LORA: Darling—

ERNEST: You're supposed to be very happy in this scene. Happy and self-assured. You're a fighter!

WINIFRED (rising and moving away, her back to TONY): Oh my God, Ernest. We can't all be fighters.

TONY (after a pause, looking at WINIFRED): Once I was walking down a crowded street. My mother and father were in front of me, arm in arm. I was very small. Suddenly, I stopped walking. They kept on, not noticing. I remember watching people fill in the gap between us. Finally I couldn't see them at all. I was alone. I think I was happy then. But that's the only time. (WINIFRED is moved by this speech. She suddenly laughs lightly, turns, and begins to speak flippantly.)

WINIFRED: Well, you should have— (Her eyes meet TONY's and she stops.)

TONY: Go on, Winifred. Say something brittle and smart.

WINIFRED: I was going to. (Suddenly, impulsively, she moves to the sofa and sits facing him.) Tony, I want to be kind—

LORA: You weren't acting, Tony. That really happened.

TONY (looking at WINIFRED): I know.

LORA: But don't you see, you're happy in this scene.

ERNEST: Never mind, Lora. He's hopeless. (LORA and ERNEST

are almost in shadow at the edge of the set, and at times their voices seem to come from a great distance.)

WINIFRED (*still staring at* TONY): There's plenty of time, Ernest.

ERNEST: Is there? That stage manager isn't going to put up with this forever. We've been out here a lifetime already.

WINIFRED: You're always so impatient.

ERNEST: We've completely lost the thread of the play. We're not doing anything the way we planned it.

WINIFRED: Maybe it's better this way.

ERNEST: It would be so simple if he would only act!

WINIFRED: He hasn't had as much experience as you've had.

ERNEST: Then why does he have to be the center of attention? Let me take the stage for a while!

WINIFRED (*turning her head away from* TONY, *but not looking at* ERNEST, *tossing her lines out over the auditorium*): You always blunder in and take charge of everything! You cast him in the part. Now give him a chance!

ERNEST: How much of a chance does he need!

WINIFRED (*with great conviction*): Leave him alone, Ernest! He's trying as hard as he knows how! And I think he's doing very well! He's giving a fine performance! (*Turning back to* TONY. *Quietly.*) Did you hear me, Tony? I was defending you.

TONY: I know. Even though I'm not doing very well.

WINIFRED: I have never defended anyone before in my life.

TONY: You thought it was humiliating to let yourself go.

LORA (*her voice coming from very far away*): He said we should improvise. We're not improvising. We're being ourselves.

WINIFRED (*to* TONY, *as if in a dream*): Shall we go on with the play?

TONY: If you want to.

WINIFRED: Where were we?

TONY: You were asking me—

WINIFRED: I remember, now. Are you happy?

TONY: Nothing is any clearer. Lights and colors are still diffused and whirling like a pinwheel. The world is inside out as it has always been. But something has happened. It's easier.

WINIFRED: What has happened?

TONY: You were kind. (*There is a pause. Then he leans forward and gently kisses* WINIFRED. ERNEST *and* LORA *suddenly move into the picture.*)

ERNEST: Winifred, if you won't think of us, you might at least think of the audience—

LORA (*almost simultaneously*): Tony, you're supposed to be in love with me!

TONY (*rising and moving away*): I'm not in love with you! I won't pretend that I am!

LORA: But that's all you can do! That's all any of us can do! Pretend! That's all there is!

TONY (*turning to her*): Yes. That's all there is. But that's not all there might be. For just a second there was something more—the only right thing that's happened to me since I came out here. If that was wrong because it wasn't part of the play, then I don't want to be part of the play either!

LORA: What are you going to do?

TONY: There's only one thing I can do!

ERNEST: You wouldn't dare leave!

TONY: Why not? Because of them? (*Indicating the audience.*) I have nothing to give them, Ernest, except myself. And that doesn't seem to be enough.

LORA: But, Tony—the stage manager—what will he do to you?

TONY: I don't care any more! He tells us the play is the most important thing we do. He's convinced you of it! Well, I can neither fear nor respect anyone who puts such high value on hypocrisy! He can damn me if he wants to! (*He moves to the door.* WINIFRED *stops him.*)

WINIFRED: Tony—don't you wonder about me?

TONY: Will you come with me, Winifred? I'd like that.

WINIFRED: I want to. But there's a difference between us, Tony. You've tried here. I haven't. Your conscience is free. Mine is laden with all the things I have not done and said. So I can't go—just yet. (*He hesitates a moment, then strides through the door. There is a pause.*)

LORA: Will he come back?

ERNEST: Not after this. He'll never see the inside of a theater again.

LORA: Then our play is ruined. (*She looks at the others helplessly, then sits in the chair. Almost to herself.*) Disappointment is not new to me. Things are always going to be so wonderful, and they never are. I keep saying to myself, "Never mind—that's how it must be—there's nothing you can do about it." But this time—there was something I should have done. And I don't know what it was.

ERNEST (*sitting on the table, musingly*): Poor Tony. The kid was no actor. Anyone could tell that. I don't see how he got the job. (WINIFRED *looks at him, and her anger increases as he goes on.*) He didn't have anything—no experience, no imagination—none of the things you've got to have to be a success on the stage. Thank God I've never been worried that way. If I had, I wouldn't be what I am today.

WINIFRED (*vehemently*): And what are you today, Ernest?

ERNEST (*looking at her, surprised*): What?

WINIFRED: I said, what are you today?

ERNEST: What a ridiculous question, Winifred. You know perfectly well that I—

WINIFRED: Yes, I know! But do *you*? Sitting smugly back and shaking your head over "poor Tony." He's the only one of us who's made a go of it!

ERNEST: What do you mean? I was doing an excellent job until this happened!

WINIFRED (*scornfully*): Oh, Ernest!

ERNEST: Wasn't I?

WINIFRED: Do you really want me to tell you? Shall I say it? Shall I put into words just what you are today?

ERNEST (*she holds his eye for a moment; then he slowly turns away from her*): I have always believed strongly in my own abilities and the chance they gave me for success. They placed me just a notch above other people. I have always been sure that I could cope with any situation, any circumstances, and act with precision and wisdom. This is what my life has been built upon. If I lose it, I lose myself.

(*Turning to her, with faltering dignity.*) No, Winifred. I don't want you to say it. I have no need of your opinion. It is unimportant. It means nothing to me. (*He moves unsteadily away from her, gesturing vaguely toward the audience.*) As long as the audience likes me— (*But he cannot face them, either, and his voice trails away as he turns upstage.* WINIFRED *watches him a moment, her expression softening into pity.*)

WINIFRED (*gently*): That's all that matters, isn't it? Their approval. (*He says nothing. She turns her head and looks at* LORA. *Then, slowly.*) And this is our play. An improvisation. Acting parts so different from ourselves, and trying to keep ourselves from showing through. Why do we do it? (*Looking at* LORA.) Because the stage manager said so. That's the way it must be. (*Looking at* ERNEST.) A pathetic yearning for applause. (*Then.*) By the way, whatever became of that play?

LORA: I don't understand you, Winifred.

WINIFRED: Never mind, Lora. What do you say, let's pick it up where we left off.

LORA: I know we should. But I can't be disappointed again.

WINIFRED: Come on, Ernest and I will help you. Won't we, Ernest?

ERNEST (*still confused*): Why—of course, Winifred—

WINIFRED: What we've got to do is think up some way to go on with the scene without Tony. How about it, Ernest? (*And she adds a gentle dig.*) You always have good ideas.

ERNEST: Give me a minute—I'll think of something.

WINIFRED: Lora? Any suggestions?

LORA: You do it, Winifred. You do it.

WINIFRED: Well, could he have taken sick, or gone to the kitchen for something—

ERNEST: Perhaps he had a telephone call—that's always good—

LORA: Yes! An important message—about a job he's been offered—he had to go right away—

WINIFRED: That's it! We'll make something of it after all! (*The lights begin to dim.*)

LORA: Oh! The lights!

ERNEST: What about the lights? (LORA *is watching the lights dim.* WINIFRED *looks at* ERNEST *but says nothing.*) They're still the same! (*Uncertainly, to* WINIFRED.) Aren't they?

WINIFRED: The play is ended.

LORA: And we haven't done anything.

WINIFRED: Yes, we have. We have done everything that was expected of us. (*The lights go out completely, leaving them in darkness once more.*)

ERNEST: What happened? It's dark again! I don't understand!

WINIFRED: Poor Ernest. At last you don't understand.

ERNEST: But the audience. What about them?

WINIFRED: Still worrying about them, Ernest? Don't you see, they're no different from us. Except that when the curtain falls and the house lights come up, they'll have to go on—improvising.

(*There is silence for a moment.*)

THE DEVIL AND
DANIEL WEBSTER

STEPHEN VINCENT BENÉT (1898–1943) was born in Bethlehem, Pennsylvania, and grew up in a family of writers. He studied at Yale University and at the Sorbonne, in Paris. At the age of seventeen he published his first book, a group of six dramatic monologues in verse, entitled *Five Men and Pompey*. Twice his poems were awarded Pulitzer prizes, once for *John Brown's Body* and again for his unfinished epic *Western Star*.

The Devil and Daniel Webster appeared originally as a short story, then as an opera with music by Douglas Moore. The play is an excellent example of Benét's deep interest in American history and of his poetic genius as he weaves a fascinating tale around two great powers, both equally real. At least they seem real to the reader and that, of course, is the mark of a superb storyteller.

THE DEVIL AND DANIEL WEBSTER

Stephen Vincent Benét

The scene is the main room of JABEZ STONE's New Hampshire farmhouse in 1841, a big, comfortable room that hasn't yet developed the stuffiness of a front parlor. A door leads to the kitchen, another door to the outside. Windows, in center, show a glimpse of summer landscape. Most of the furniture has been cleared away for the dance which follows the wedding of JABEZ and MARY STONE, but there is a settle or bench by the fireplace, a table with some wedding presents upon it, at least three chairs by the table, and a cider barrel on which the FIDDLER sits, in front of the table. Near the table there is a cupboard where there are glasses and a jug. There is a clock.

A country wedding has been in progress—the wedding of JABEZ and MARY STONE. He is a husky young farmer, around twenty-eight or thirty. The bride is in her early twenties. He is dressed in stiff store clothes but not ridiculously—they are of good quality and he looks important. The bride is in a simple white or cream wedding dress and may carry a small, stiff bouquet of country flowers.

Now the wedding is over and the guests are dancing.

Copyright, 1938, 1939, by Stephen Vincent Benét. *The Devil and Daniel Webster* is reprinted by permission of Dramatists Play Service, Inc. The use of the play in present form must be confined to study and reference. Attention in particular is called to the fact that this play, being duly copyrighted, may not be publicly read or performed or otherwise used without permission from the author's representative. All inquiries should be addressed to Dramatists Play Service, 440 Park Avenue South, New York, N.Y. 10016.

- important details. year - what do you expect?
- names
- what's going on?

The FIDDLER is perched on the cider barrel. He plays and calls square-dance figures. The guests include the recognizable types of a small New England town— doctor, lawyer, storekeeper, old maid, schoolteacher, farmer, etc. There is an air of prosperity and hearty country mirth about the whole affair.

At rise, JABEZ and MARY are up left center, receiving the congratulations of a few last guests, who talk to them and pass on to the dance. The others are dancing. There is a buzz of conversation that follows the tune of the dance music.

FIRST WOMAN: Right nice wedding.

FIRST MAN: Handsome couple.

SECOND WOMAN (*passing through crowd with dish of oyster stew*): Oysters for supper!

SECOND MAN (*passing cake*): And layer cake—layer cake—

AN OLD MAN (*hobbling toward cider barrel*): Makes me feel young again! Oh, by jingo!

AN OLD WOMAN (*pursuing him*): Henry, Henry, you've been drinking cider!

FIDDLER: Set to your partners! Dosy-do!

WOMEN: Mary and Jabez.

MEN: Jabez and Mary.

A WOMAN: Where's the State Senator?

A MAN: Where's the lucky bride?

(*With cries of "Mary—Jabez—strike it up, fiddler—make room for the bride and groom," the* CROWD *drags* MARY *and* JABEZ, *pleased but embarrassed, into the center of the room, and* MARY *and* JABEZ *do a little solo dance, while the* CROWD *claps, applauds, and makes various remarks.*)

A MAN: Handsome steppers!

A WOMAN: She's pretty as a picture.

A SECOND MAN: Cut your pigeon wing, Jabez!

THE OLD MAN: Young again, young again, that's the way I feel! (*He tries to cut a pigeon wing himself.*)

THE OLD WOMAN: Henry, Henry, careful of your rheumatiz!

Poverty?

A THIRD WOMAN: Makes me feel all teary, seeing them so happy.

(*The solo dance ends, the music stops for a moment.*)

THE OLD MAN (*gossiping to a neighbor*): Wonder where he got it all. Stones was always poor.

HIS NEIGHBOR: Ain't poor now. Makes you wonder just a mite.

A THIRD MAN: Don't begrudge it to him—but I wonder where he got it.

THE OLD MAN (*starting to whisper*): Let me tell you something—

THE OLD WOMAN (*quickly*): Henry, Henry, don't you start to gossip. (*She drags him away.*)

FIDDLER (*cutting in*): Set to your partners! Scratch for corn!

(*The dance resumes, but as it does so, the* CROWD *chants back and forth.*)

WOMEN: Gossip's got a sharp tooth.

MEN: Gossip's got a mean tooth.

WOMEN: She's a lucky woman. They're a lucky pair.

MEN: That's true as gospel. But I wonder where he got it.

WOMEN: Money, land, and riches.

MEN: Just came out of nowhere.

WOMEN AND MEN (*together*): Wonder where he got it all. But that's his business.

FIDDLER: Left and right—grand chain!

(*The dance rises to a pitch of ecstasy with the final figure. The fiddle squeaks and stops. The dancers mop their brows.*)

FIRST MAN: Whew! Ain't danced like that since I was knee-high to a grasshopper!

SECOND MAN: Play us "The Portland Fancy," fiddler!

THIRD MAN: No, wait a minute, neighbor. Let's hear from the happy pair! Hey, Jabez!

FOURTH MAN: Let's hear from the State Senator!

(*They crowd around* JABEZ *and push him up on the settle.*)

OLD MAN: Might as well. It's the last time he'll have the last word!

- state Senator?

OLD WOMAN: Now, Henry Banks, you ought to be ashamed of yourself!

OLD MAN: Told you so, Jabez!

THE CROWD: Speech!

JABEZ (embarrassed): Neighbors, friends—I'm not much of a speaker, spite of your 'lecting me to State Senate—

THE CROWD: That's the ticket, Jabez. Smart man, Jabez. I voted for ye. Go ahead, Senator, you're doing fine.

JABEZ: But we're certainly glad to have you here—me and Mary. And we want to thank you for coming and—

A VOICE: Vote the Whig ticket!

ANOTHER VOICE: Hurray for Daniel Webster!

JABEZ: And I'm glad Hi Foster said that, for those are my sentiments, too. Mr. Webster has promised to honor us with his presence here tonight.

THE CROWD: Hurray for Dan'l! Hurray for the greatest man in the U.S.!

JABEZ: And when he comes, I know we'll give him a real New Hampshire welcome.

THE CROWD: Sure we will—Webster forever—and to hell with Henry Clay!

JABEZ: And meanwhile—well, there's Mary and me (takes her hand) and, if you folks don't have a good time, well, we won't feel right about getting married at all. Because I know I've been lucky—and I hope she feels that way, too. And, well, we're going to be happy or bust a trace! (He wipes his brow to terrific applause. He and MARY look at each other.)

A WOMAN (in kitchen doorway): Come and get the cider, folks!

> (The CROWD begins to drift away—a few to the kitchen, a few toward the door that leads to the outside. They furnish a shifting background to the next little scene, where MARY and JABEZ are left alone by the fireplace.)

NATURAL STOP

JABEZ: Mary.

MARY: Mr. Stone.

JABEZ: Mary.

MARY: My husband.

JABEZ: That's a big word, husband.

MARY: It's a good word.

JABEZ: Are you happy, Mary?

MARY: Yes. So happy I'm afraid.

JABEZ: Afraid?

MARY: I suppose it happens to every girl—just for a minute. It's like spring turning into summer. You want it to be summer. But the spring was sweet. (*Dismissing the mood.*) I'm sorry. Forgive me. It just came and went, like something cold. As if we'd been too lucky.

JABEZ: We can't be too lucky, Mary. Not you and me.

MARY (*rather mischievously*): If you say so, Mr. Stone. But you don't even know what sort of housekeeper I am. And Aunt Hepsy says—

JABEZ: Bother your Aunt Hepsy! There's just you and me and that's all that matters in the world.

MARY: And you don't know something else—

JABEZ: What's that?

MARY: How proud I am of you. Ever since I was a little girl. Ever since you carried my books. Oh, I'm sorry for women who can't be proud of their men. It must be a lonely feeling.

JABEZ (*uncomfortably*): A man can't always be proud of everything, Mary. There's some things a man does, or might do, when he has to make his way.

MARY (*laughing*): I know—terrible things—like being the best farmer in the county and the best State Senator—

JABEZ (*quietly*): And a few things besides. But you remember one thing, Mary, whatever happens. It was all for you. And nothing's going to happen. Because he hasn't come yet —and he would have come if it was wrong.

MARY: But it's wonderful to have Mr. Webster come to us.

JABEZ: I wasn't thinking about Mr. Webster. (*He takes both her hands.*) Mary, I've got something to tell you. I should have told you before, but I couldn't seem to bear it. Only, now that it's all right, I can. Ten years ago—

A VOICE (*from off stage*): Dan'l! Dan'l Webster!

(JABEZ *drops* MARY's *hands and looks around. The*

CROWD *begins to mill and gather toward the door. Others rush in from the kitchen.*)

ANOTHER VOICE: Black Dan'l! He's come!

ANOTHER VOICE: Three cheers for the greatest man in the U.S.!

ANOTHER VOICE: Three cheers for Daniel Webster!

(*And, to the cheering and applause of the* CROWD, DANIEL WEBSTER *enters and stands for a moment upstage, in the familiar pose, his head thrown back, his attitude leonine. He stops the cheering of the* CROWD *with a gesture.*)

WEBSTER: Neighbors, old friends—it does me good to hear you. But don't cheer me—I'm not running for President this summer. (*A laugh from the* CROWD.) I'm here on a better errand—to pay my humble respects to a most charming lady and her very fortunate spouse.

(*There is the twang of a fiddle string breaking.*)

FIDDLER: 'Tarnation! Busted a string!

A VOICE: He's always bustin' strings.

(WEBSTER *blinks at the interruption but goes on.*)

WEBSTER: We're proud of State Senator Stone in these parts —we know what he's done. Ten years ago he started out with a patch of land that was mostly rocks and mortgages and now—well, you've only to look around you. I don't know that I've ever seen a likelier farm, not even at Marshfield, and I hope, before I die, I'll have the privilege of shaking his hand as Governor of this state. I don't know how he's done it—I couldn't have done it myself. But I know this—Jabez Stone wears no man's collar. (*At this statement there is a discordant squeak from the fiddle and* JABEZ *looks embarrassed.* WEBSTER *knits his brows.*) And what's more, if I know Jabez, he never will. But I didn't come here to talk politics—I came to kiss the bride. (*He does so amid great applause. He shakes hands with* JABEZ.) Congratulations, Stone—you're a lucky man. And now, if our friend in the corner will give us a tune on his fiddle—

(*The* CROWD *presses forward to meet the great man. He shakes hands with several.*)

Scratch ... the bell tolling.

A MAN: Remember me, Mr. Webster? Saw ye up at the State House at Concord.

ANOTHER MAN: Glad to see ye, Mr. Webster. I voted for ye ten times.

(WEBSTER *receives their homage politely, but his mind is still on music.*)

WEBSTER (*a trifle irritated*): I said, if our friend in the corner would give us a tune on his fiddle—

FIDDLER (*passionately, flinging the fiddle down*): Hell's delight—excuse me, Mr. Webster. But the very devil's got into that fiddle of mine. She was doing all right up to just a minute ago. But now I've tuned her and tuned her and she won't play a note I want.

(*And, at this point,* MR. SCRATCH *makes his appearance. He has entered, unobserved, and mixed with the* CROWD *while all eyes were upon* DANIEL WEBSTER. *He is, of course, the devil—a New England devil, dressed like a rather shabby attorney but with something just a little wrong in clothes and appearance. For one thing, he wears black gloves on his hands. He carries a large black tin box, like a botanist's collecting box, under one arm. Now he slips through the* CROWD *and taps the* FIDDLER *on the shoulder.*)

SCRATCH (*insinuatingly*): Maybe you need some rosin on your bow, fiddler?

FIDDLER: Maybe I do and maybe I don't. (*Turns and confronts the stranger.*) But who are you? I don't remember seeing you before.

SCRATCH: Oh, I'm just a friend—a humble friend of the bridegroom's. (*He walks toward* JABEZ. *Apologetically.*) I'm afraid I came in the wrong way, Mr. Stone. You've improved the place so much since I last saw it that I hardly knew the front door. But, I assure you, I came as fast as I could.

JABEZ (*obviously shocked*): It—it doesn't matter. (*With a great effort.*) Mary—Mr. Webster—this is a—a friend of mine from Boston—a legal friend. I didn't expect him today but—

SCRATCH: Oh, my dear Mr. Stone—an occasion like this—I

wouldn't miss it for the world. (*He bows.*) Charmed, Mrs. Stone. Delighted, Mr. Webster. But—don't let me break up the merriment of the meeting. (*He turns back toward the table and the* FIDDLER.)

FIDDLER (*with a grudge, to* SCRATCH): Boston lawyer, eh?

SCRATCH: You might call me that.

FIDDLER (*tapping the tin box with his bow*): And what have you got in that big tin box of yours? Law papers?

SCRATCH: Oh, curiosities for the most part. I'm a collector, too.

FIDDLER: Don't hold much with Boston curiosities, myself. And you know about fiddling, too, do you? Know all about it?

SCRATCH: Oh— (*A deprecatory shrug.*)

FIDDLER: Don't shrug your shoulders at me—I ain't no Frenchman. Telling me I needed more rosin!

MARY (*trying to stop the quarrel*): Isaac, please—

FIDDLER: Sorry, Mary—Mrs. Stone. But I been playing the fiddle at Cross Corners weddings for twenty-five years. And now here comes a stranger from Boston and tells me I need more rosin!

SCRATCH: But, my good friend—

FIDDLER: Rosin, indeed! Here—play it yourself then and see what you can make of it! (*He thrusts the fiddle at* SCRATCH. *The latter stiffens, slowly lays his black collecting box on the table, and takes the fiddle.*)

SCRATCH (*with feigned embarrassment*): But really, I— (*He bows toward* JABEZ.) Shall I, Mr. Senator?

(JABEZ *makes a helpless gesture of assent.*)

MARY (*to* JABEZ): Mr. Stone, Mr. Stone—are you ill?

JABEZ: No—no—but I feel—it's hot—

WEBSTER (*chuckling*): Don't you fret, Mrs. Stone. I've got the right medicine for him. (*He pulls a flask from his pocket.*) Ten-year-old Medford, Stone. I buy it by the keg down at Marshfield. Here— (*He tries to give some of the rum to* JABEZ.)

JABEZ: No— (*He turns.*) Mary—Mr. Webster— (*But he cannot explain. With a burst.*) Oh, let him play—let him play! Don't you see he's bound to? Don't you see there's nothing we can do?

> (*A rustle of discomfort among the guests.* SCRATCH *draws the bow across the fiddle in a horrible discord.*)

FIDDLER (*triumphantly*): I told you so, stranger. The devil's in that fiddle!

SCRATCH: I'm afraid it needs special tuning. (*Draws the bow in a second discord.*) There, that's better. (*Grinning.*) And now for this happy—this very happy occasion—in tribute to the bride and groom—I'll play something appropriate—a song of young love—

MARY: Oh, Jabez, Mr. Webster—stop him! Do you see his hands? He's playing with gloves on his hands.

> (WEBSTER *starts forward, but, even as he does so,* SCRATCH *begins to play and all freeze as* SCRATCH *goes on with the extremely inappropriate song that follows. At first his manner is oily and mocking. It is not till he reaches the line "The devil took the words away" that he really becomes terrifying and the* CROWD *starts to be afraid.*)

SCRATCH (*accompanying himself fantastically*):

> Young William was a thriving boy.
> (Listen to my doleful tale.)
> Young Mary Clark was all his joy.
> (Listen to my doleful tale.)
>
> He swore he'd love her all his life.
> She swore she'd be his loving wife.
>
> But William found a gambler's den
> And drank with livery-stable men.
>
> He played the cards, he played the dice.
> He would not listen to advice.
>
> And when in church he tried to pray,
> The devil took the words away.

(SCRATCH, *still playing, starts to march across the stage.*)

The devil got him by the toe,
And so, alas, he had to go.

"Young Mary Clark, young Mary Clark,
I now must go into the dark."

(*These last two verses have been directed at* JABEZ.
SCRATCH *continues, now turning on* MARY.)

Young Mary lay upon her bed.
"Alas, my Will-i-am is dead."

He came to her a bleeding ghost—

(*He rushes at* MARY *but* WEBSTER *stands between
them.*)

WEBSTER: Stop! Stop! You miserable wretch, can't you see
that you're frightening Mrs. Stone? (*He wrenches the fiddle
out of* SCRATCH's *hands and tosses it aside.*) And now, sir—
out of this house!

SCRATCH (*facing him*): You're a bold man, Mr. Webster. Too
bold for your own good, perhaps. And anyhow, it wasn't
my fiddle. It belonged to— (*He wheels and sees the* FIDDLER
*tampering with the collecting box that has been left on the
table.*) Idiot! What are you doing with my collecting box?
(*He rushes for the* FIDDLER *and chases him around the
table, but the* FIDDLER *is just one jump ahead.*)

FIDDLER: Boston lawyer, eh? Well, I don't think so. I think
you've got something in that box of yours you're afraid to
show. And, by jingo— (*He throws open the lid of the box.
The lights wink and there is a clap of thunder. All eyes
stare upward. Something has flown out of the box. But
what?* FIDDLER, *with relief.*) Why, 'tain't nothing but a
moth.

MARY: A white moth—a flying thing.

WEBSTER: A common moth—*Telea polyphemus*—

THE CROWD: A moth—just a moth—a moth—

FIDDLER (*terrified*): But it ain't. It ain't no common moth! I seen it! And it's got a death's head on it! (*He strikes at the invisible object with his bow to drive it away.*)

VOICE OF THE MOTH: Help me, neighbors! Help me!

WEBSTER: What's that? It wails like a lost soul.

MARY: A lost soul.

THE CROWD: A lost soul—lost—in darkness—in the darkness.

VOICE OF THE MOTH: Help me, neighbors!

FIDDLER: It sounds like Miser Stevens.

JABEZ: Miser Stevens!

THE CROWD: The miser—Miser Stevens—a lost soul—lost.

FIDDLER (*frantically*): It sounds like Miser Stevens—and you had him in your box. But it can't be. He ain't dead.

JABEZ: He ain't dead—I tell you he ain't dead! He was just as spry and mean as a woodchuck Tuesday.

THE CROWD: Miser Stevens—soul of Miser Stevens—but he ain't dead.

SCRATCH (*dominating them*): Listen!

(*A bell off stage begins to toll a knell, slowly, solemnly.*)

MARY: The bell—the church bell—the bell that rang at my wedding.

WEBSTER: The church bell—the passing bell.

JABEZ: The funeral bell.

THE CROWD: The bell—the passing bell—Miser Stevens—dead.

VOICE OF THE MOTH: Help me, neighbors, help me! I sold my soul to the devil. But I'm not the first or the last. Help me. Help Jabez Stone!

SCRATCH: Ah, would you! (*He catches the moth in his red bandanna, stuffs it back into his collecting box, and shuts the lid with a snap.*)

VOICE OF THE MOTH (*fading*): Lost—lost forever, forever. Lost, like Jabez Stone.

(*The* CROWD *turns on* JABEZ. *They read his secret in his face.*)

THE CROWD: Jabez Stone—Jabez Stone—answer us—answer us.

MARY: Tell them, dear—answer them—you are good—you are brave—you are innocent.

(*But the* CROWD *is all pointing hands and horrified eyes.*)

THE CROWD: Jabez Stone—Jabez Stone. Who's your friend in black, Jabez Stone? (*They point to* SCRATCH.)

WEBSTER: Answer them, Mr. State Senator.

THE CROWD: Jabez Stone—Jabez Stone. Where did you get your money, Jabez Stone?

(SCRATCH *grins and taps his collecting box.* JABEZ *cannot speak.*)

JABEZ: I—I— (*He stops.*)

THE CROWD: Jabez Stone—Jabez Stone. What was the price you paid for it, Jabez Stone?

JABEZ (*looking around wildly*): Help me, neighbors! Help me!

(*This cracks the built-up tension and sends the* CROWD *over the edge into fanaticism.*)

A WOMAN'S VOICE (*high and hysterical*): He's sold his soul to the devil! (*She points to* JABEZ.)

OTHER VOICES: To the devil!

THE CROWD: He's sold his soul to the devil! The devil himself! The devil's playing the fiddle! The devil's come for his own!

JABEZ (*appealing*): But, neighbors—I didn't know—I didn't mean—oh, help me!

THE CROWD (*inexorably*): He's sold his soul to the devil!

SCRATCH (*grinning*): To the devil!

THE CROWD: He's sold his soul to the devil! There's no help left for him, neighbors! Run, hide, hurry, before we're caught! He's a lost soul—Jabez Stone—he's the devil's own! Run, hide, hasten! (*They stream across the stage like a flurry of bats, the cannier picking up the wedding presents they have given to take along with them.*)

(MR. SCRATCH *drives them out into the night, fiddle in hand, and follows them.* JABEZ *and* MARY *are left with* WEBSTER. JABEZ *has sunk into a chair, beaten, with his head in his hands.* MARY *is trying to comfort him.* WEBSTER *looks at them for a moment and shakes his predictive questions* ...

head sadly. As he crosses to exit to the porch, his hand drops for a moment on JABEZ' *shoulder, but* JABEZ *makes no sign.* WEBSTER *exits.* JABEZ *lifts his head.*)

MARY (*comforting him*): My dear—my dear—

JABEZ: I—it's all true, Mary. All true. You must hurry.

MARY: Hurry?

JABEZ: Hurry after them—back to the village—back to your folks. Mr. Webster will take you—you'll be safe with Mr. Webster. You see, it's all true and he'll be back in a minute. (*With a shudder.*) The other one. (*He groans.*) I've got until twelve o'clock. That's the contract. But there isn't much time.

MARY: Are you telling me to run away from you, Mr. Stone?

JABEZ: You don't understand, Mary. It's true.

MARY: We made some promises to each other. Maybe you've forgotten them. But I haven't. I said, it's for better or worse. It's for better or worse. I said, in sickness or in health. Well, that covers the ground, Mr. Stone.

JABEZ: But, Mary, you must. I command you.

MARY: "For thy people shall be my people and thy God my God." (*Quietly*) That was Ruth, in the Book. I always liked the name of Ruth—always liked the thought of her. I always thought—I'll call a child Ruth, sometime. I guess that was just a girl's notion. (*She breaks.*) But, oh, Jabez—why?

JABEZ: It started years ago, Mary. I guess I was a youngster then—guess I must have been. A youngster with a lot of ambitions and no way in the world to get there. I wanted city clothes and a big white house. I wanted to be State Senator and have people look up to me. But all I got on the farm was a crop of stones. You could work all day and all night but that was all you got.

MARY (*softly*): It was pretty, that hill farm, Jabez. You could look all the way across the valley.

JABEZ: Pretty? It was fever and ague—it was stones and blight. If I had a horse, he got colic. If I planted garden truck, the woodchucks ate it. I'd lie awake nights and try to figure out a way to get somewhere—but there wasn't any way.

And all the time you were growing up, in the town. I couldn't ask you to marry me and take you to a place like that.

MARY: Do you think it's the place makes the difference to a woman? I'd—I'd have kept your house. I'd have stroked the cat and fed the chickens and seen you wiped your shoes on the mat. I wouldn't have asked for more. Oh, Jabez—why didn't you tell me?

JABEZ: It happened before I could. Just an average day—you know—just an average day. But there was a mean east wind and a mean small rain. Well, I was plowing, and the share broke clean off on a rock where there hadn't been any rock the day before. I didn't have money for a new one—I didn't have money to get it mended. So I said it and I said loud, "I'll sell my soul for about two cents," I said. (*He stops.* MARY *stares at him.*) Well, that's all there is to it, I guess. He came along that afternoon—that fellow from Boston—and the dog looked at him and ran away. Well, I had to make it more than two cents, but he was agreeable to that. So I pricked my thumb with a pin and signed the paper. It felt hot when you touched it, that paper. I keep remembering that. (*He pauses.*) And it's all come true and he's kept his part of the bargain. I got the riches and I've married you. And, oh, God almighty, what shall I do?

MARY: Let us run away! Let us creep and hide!

JABEZ: You can't run away from the devil—I've seen his horses. Miser Stevens tried to run away.

MARY: Let us pray—let us pray to the God of Mercy that He redeem us.

JABEZ: I can't pray, Mary. The words just burn in my heart.

MARY: I won't let you go! I won't! There must be someone who could help us. I'll get the judge and the squire—

JABEZ: Who'll take a case against old Scratch? Who'll face the devil himself and do him brown? There isn't a lawyer in the world who'd dare do that.

(WEBSTER *appears in the doorway.*)

WEBSTER: Good evening, neighbors. Did you say something about lawyers—

MARY: Mr. Webster!

JABEZ: Dan'l Webster! But I thought—

WEBSTER: You'll excuse me for leaving you for a moment. I was just taking a stroll on the porch, in the cool of the evening. Fine summer evening, too.

JABEZ: Well, it might be, I guess, but that kind of depends on the circumstances.

WEBSTER: Hm. Yes. I happened to overhear a little of your conversation. I gather you're in trouble, neighbor Stone.

JABEZ: Sore trouble.

WEBSTER (*delicately*): Sort of law case, I understand.

JABEZ: You might call it that, Mr. Webster. Kind of a mortgage case, in a way.

MARY: Oh, Jabez!

WEBSTER: Mortgage case. Well, I don't generally plead now, except before the Supreme Court, but this case of yours presents some very unusual features and I never deserted a neighbor in trouble yet. So, if I can be of any assistance—

MARY: Oh, Mr. Webster, will you help him?

JABEZ: It's a terrible lot to ask you. But—well, you see, there's Mary. And, if you could see your way to it—

WEBSTER: I will.

MARY (*weeping with relief*): Oh, Mr. Webster!

WEBSTER: There, there, Mrs. Stone. After all, if two New Hampshire men aren't a match for the devil, we might as well give the country back to the Indians. When is he coming, Jabez?

JABEZ: Twelve o'clock. The time's getting late.

WEBSTER: Then I'd better refresh my memory. The—er—mortgage was for a definite term of years?

JABEZ: Ten years.

WEBSTER: And it falls due—?

JABEZ: Tonight. Oh, I can't see how I came to be such a fool!

WEBSTER: No use crying over spilt milk, Stone. We've got to get you out of it now. But tell me one thing. Did you sign this precious document of your own free will?

JABEZ: Yes, it was my own free will. I can't deny that.

WEBSTER: Hm, that's a trifle unfortunate. But we'll see.

What are they going to do?

MARY: Oh, Mr. Webster, can you save him? Can you?

WEBSTER: I shall do my best, madam. That's all you can ever say till you see what the jury looks like.

MARY: But even you, Mr. Webster— Oh, I know you're Secretary of State. I know you're a great man. I know you've done wonderful things. But it's different—fighting the devil!

WEBSTER (*towering*): I've fought John C. Calhoun, madam. And I've fought Henry Clay. And, by the great shade of Andrew Jackson, I'd fight ten thousand devils to save a New Hampshire man!

JABEZ: You hear, Mary?

MARY: Yes. And I trust Mr. Webster. But—oh, there must be some way that I can help!

WEBSTER: There is one, madam, and a hard one. As Mr. Stone's counsel, I must formally request your withdrawal.

MARY: No.

WEBSTER: Madam, think for a moment. You cannot help Mr. Stone. Since you are his wife, your testimony would be prejudiced. And frankly, madam, in a very few moments this is going to be no place for a lady.

MARY: But I can't—I can't leave him. I can't bear it!

JABEZ: You must go, Mary. You must.

WEBSTER: Pray, madam—you can help us with your prayers. Are the prayers of the innocent unavailing?

MARY: Oh, I'll pray—I'll pray. But a woman's more than a praying machine, whatever men think. And how do I know?

WEBSTER: Trust me, Mrs. Stone.

MARY (*turns to go, and, with one hand on* JABEZ' *shoulder, as she moves to the door, says the following prayer*):

Now may there be a blessing and a light betwixt thee and me forever.

For, as Ruth unto Naomi, so do I cleave unto thee.

Set me as a seal upon thy heart, as a seal upon thine arm, for love is strong as death.

Many waters cannot quench love, neither can the floods drown it.

As Ruth unto Naomi, so do I cleave unto thee.

The Lord watch between thee and me when we are absent, one from the other.

Amen. Amen. (*She goes out.*)

WEBSTER: Amen.

JABEZ: Thank you, Mr. Webster. She ought to go. But I couldn't have made her do it.

WEBSTER: Well, Stone, I know ladies—and I wouldn't be surprised if she's still got her ear to the keyhole. But she's best out of this night's business. How long have we got to wait?

JABEZ (*beginning to be terrified again*): Not long—not long.

WEBSTER: Then I'll just get out the jug, with your permission, Stone. Somehow or other, waiting's wonderfully shorter with a jug. (*He crosses to the cupboard, gets out jug and glasses, pours himself a drink.*) Ten-year-old Medford. There's nothing like it. I saw an inchworm take a drop of it once, and he stood right up on his hind legs and bit a bee. Come, try a nip.

JABEZ: There's no joy in it for me.

WEBSTER: Oh, come, man, come! Just because you've sold your soul to the devil, that needn't make you a teetotaler. (*He laughs and passes the jug to* JABEZ, *who tries to pour from it. But at the moment the clock whirs and begins to strike the three-quarters, and* JABEZ *spills the liquor.*)

JABEZ: Oh, God!

WEBSTER: Never mind. It's a nervous feeling, waiting for a trial to begin. I remember my first case—

JABEZ: 'Tain't that. (*He turns to* WEBSTER.) Mr. Webster—Mr. Webster—for God's sake harness your horses and get away from this place as fast as you can!

WEBSTER (*placidly*): You've brought me a long way, neighbor, to tell me you don't like my company.

JABEZ: I've brought you the devil's own way. I can see it all now. He's after both of us—him and his damn collecting box! Well, he can have me if he likes. I don't say I relish it, but I made the bargain. But you're the whole United States! He can't get you, Mr. Webster—he mustn't get you!

WEBSTER: I'm obliged to you, neighbor Stone. It's kindly thought of. But there's a jug on the table and a case in *how have things changed?*

hand. And I never left a jug or a case half finished in my life. (*There is a knock at the door.* JABEZ *gives a cry.*) Ah, I thought your clock was a trifle slow, neighbor Stone. Come in!

(SCRATCH *enters from the night.*)

SCRATCH: Mr. Webster! This *is* a pleasure!

WEBSTER: Attorney of record for Jabez Stone. Might I ask your name?

SCRATCH: I've gone by a good many. Perhaps Scratch will do for the evening. I'm often called that in these regions. May I? (*He sits at the table and pours a drink from the jug. The liquor steams as it pours into the glass while* JABEZ *watches, terrified.* SCRATCH *grins, toasting* WEBSTER *and* JABEZ *silently in the liquor. Then he becomes businesslike. To* WEBSTER.) And now I call upon you, as a law-abiding citizen, to assist me in taking possession of my property.

WEBSTER: Not so fast, Mr. Scratch. Produce your evidence, if you have it.

SCRATCH (*takes out a black pocketbook and examines papers*): Slattery—Stanley—Stone. (*Takes out a deed.*) There, Mr. Webster. All open and aboveboard and in due and legal form. Our firm has its reputation to consider—we deal only in the one way.

WEBSTER (*taking deed and looking it over*): Hm. This appears—I say it appears—to be properly drawn. But, of course, we contest the signature. (*Tosses it back, contemptuously.*)

SCRATCH (*suddenly turning on* JABEZ *and shooting a finger at him*): Is that your signature?

JABEZ (*wearily*): You know damn well it is.

WEBSTER (*angrily*): Keep quiet, Stone. (*To* SCRATCH.) But that is a minor matter. This precious document isn't worth the paper it's written on. The law permits no traffic in human flesh.

SCRATCH: Oh, my dear Mr. Webster! Courts in every state in the Union have held that human flesh is property and recoverable. Read your Fugitive Slave Act. Or shall I cite Brander versus McRae?

read to the end? . . .

WEBSTER: But, in the case of the State of Maryland versus Four Barrels of Bourbon—

SCRATCH: That was overruled, as you know, sir. North Carolina versus Jenkins and Co.

WEBSTER (*unwillingly*): You seem to have an excellent acquaintance with the law, sir.

SCRATCH: Sir, that is no fault of mine. Where I come from, we have always gotten the pick of the bar.

WEBSTER (*changing his note, heartily*): Well, come now, sir. There's no need to make hay and oats of a trifling matter when we're both sensible men. Surely we can settle this little difficulty out of court. My client is quite prepared to offer a compromise. (SCRATCH *smiles.*) A very substantial compromise. (SCRATCH *smiles more broadly, slowly shaking his head.*) Hang it, man, we offer ten thousand dollars! (SCRATCH *signs No.*) Twenty thousand—thirty—name your figure! I'll raise it if I have to mortgage Marshfield!

SCRATCH: Quite useless, Mr. Webster. There is only one thing I want from you—the execution of my contract.

WEBSTER: But this is absurd. Mr. Stone is now a State Senator. The property has greatly increased in value!

SCRATCH: The principle of *caveat emptor* still holds, Mr. Webster. (*He yawns and looks at the clock.*) And now, if you have no further arguments to adduce, I'm rather pressed for time— (*He rises briskly as if to take* JABEZ *into custody.*)

WEBSTER (*thundering*): Pressed or not, you shall not have this man. Mr. Stone is an American citizen and no American citizen may be forced into the service of a foreign prince. We fought England for that, in 'twelve, and we'll fight all hell for it again!

SCRATCH: Foreign? And who calls me a foreigner?

WEBSTER: Well, I never yet heard of the dev—of your claiming American citizenship.

SCRATCH: And who with better right? When the first wrong was done to the first Indian, I was there. When the first slaver put out for the Congo, I stood on her deck. Am I not in your books and stories and beliefs, from the first settle-

- how does this contest of wills end?
refer to Mary, Jabez, Daniel and Mr. Scratch?

ments on? Am I not spoken of still in every church in New England? 'Tis true the North claims me for a Southerner and the South for a Northerner, but I am neither. I am merely an honest American like yourself—and of the best descent—for, to tell the truth, Mr. Webster, though I don't like to boast of it, my name is older in the country than yours.

WEBSTER: Aha! Then I stand on the Constitution! I demand a trial for my client!

SCRATCH: The case is hardly one for an ordinary jury—and indeed, the lateness of the hour—

WEBSTER: Let it be any court you choose, so it is an American judge and an American jury. Let it be the quick or the dead, I'll abide the issue.

SCRATCH: The quick or the dead! You have said it. (*He points his finger at the place where the* JURY *is to appear. There is a clap of thunder and a flash of light. The stage blacks out completely. All that can be seen is the face of* SCRATCH, *lit with a ghastly green light, as he recites the invocation that summons the* JURY. *As, one by one, the important* JURYMEN *are mentioned, they appear.*)

> I summon the jury Mr. Webster demands.
> From churchyard mold and gallows grave,
> Brimstone pit and burning gulf,
> I summon them!
> Dastard, liar, scoundrel, knave,
> I summon them! Appear!
> There's Simon Girty, the renegade,
> The haunter of the forest glade,
> Who joined with Indian and wolf
> To hunt the pioneer.
> The stains upon his hunting shirt
> Are not the blood of the deer.
> There's Walter Butler, the loyalist,
> Who carried a firebrand in his fist
> Of massacre and shame.
> King Philip's eye is wild and bright.
> They slew him in the great Swamp Fight,

But still, with terror and affright,
The land recalls his name.
Blackbeard Teach, the pirate fell,
Smeet the strangler, hot from hell,
Dale, who broke men on the wheel,
Morton, of the tarnished steel—
I summon them, I summon them
From their tormented flame!
Quick or dead, quick or dead,
Broken heart and bitter head,
True Americans, each one,
Traitor and disloyal son,
Cankered earth and twisted tree,
Outcasts of eternity,
Twelve great sinners, tried and true,
For the work they are to do!
I summon them, I summon them!
Appear, appear, appear!

(*The* JURY *has now taken its place in the box,* WALTER BUTLER *in the place of foreman. They are eerily lit and so made up as to suggest the unearthly. They sit stiffly in their box. At first, when one moves, all move, in stylized gestures. It is not till the end of* WEBSTER'S *speech that they begin to show any trace of humanity. They speak rhythmically, and, at first, in low, eerie voices.*)

JABEZ (*seeing them, horrified*): A jury of the dead!

JURY: Of the dead!

JABEZ: A jury of the damned!

JURY: Of the damned!

SCRATCH: Are you content with the jury, Mr. Webster?

WEBSTER: Quite content. Though I miss General Arnold from the company.

SCRATCH: Benedict Arnold is engaged upon other business. Ah, you asked for a justice, I believe. (*He points his finger and* JUSTICE HATHORNE, *a tall, lean, terrifying Puritan, appears, followed by his* CLERK.) Justice Hathorne is a jurist of experience. He presided at the Salem witch trials. There

Trial -- who was Judge ? -- types of jury
-- how was he biased ? characters ?

were others who repented of the business later. But not he, not he!

HATHORNE: Repent of such notable wonders and undertakings? Nay, hang them, hang them all! (*He takes his place on the bench.*)

  (*The CLERK, an ominous little man with clawlike hands, takes his place. The room has now been transformed into a courtroom.*)

CLERK (*in a gabble of ritual*): Oyes, oyes, oyes. All ye who have business with this honorable court of special session this night, step forward!

HATHORNE (*with gavel*): Call the first case.

CLERK: The World, the Flesh, and the Devil versus Jabez Stone.

HATHORNE: Who appears for the plaintiff?

SCRATCH: I, Your Honor.

HATHORNE: And for the defendant?

WEBSTER: I.

JURY: The case—the case—he'll have little luck with this case.

HATHORNE: The case will proceed.

WEBSTER: Your Honor, I move to dismiss this case on the grounds of improper jurisdiction.

HATHORNE: Motion denied.

WEBSTER: On the grounds of insufficient evidence.

HATHORNE: Motion denied.

JURY: Motion denied—denied. Motion denied.

WEBSTER: I will take an exception.

HATHORNE: There are no exceptions in this court.

JURY: No exceptions—no exceptions in this court. It's a bad case, Daniel Webster—a losing case.

WEBSTER: Your Honor—

HATHORNE: The prosecution will proceed—

SCRATCH: Your Honor—gentlemen of the jury. This is a plain, straightforward case. It need not detain us long.

JURY: Detain us long—it will not detain us long.

SCRATCH: It concerns one thing alone—the transference, barter, and sale of a certain piece of property, to wit, his soul, by Jabez Stone, farmer, of Cross Corners, New Hampshire.

That transference, barter, or sale is attested by a deed. I offer that deed in evidence and mark it Exhibit A.

WEBSTER: I object.

HATHORNE: Objection denied. Mark it Exhibit A.

(SCRATCH *hands the deed—an ominous and impressive document—to the* CLERK, *who hands it to* HATHORNE. HATHORNE *hands it back to the* CLERK, *who stamps it. All very fast and with mechanical gestures.*)

JURY: Exhibit A—mark it Exhibit A. (SCRATCH *takes the deed from the* CLERK *and offers it to the* JURY, *who pass it rapidly among them, hardly looking at it, and hand it back to* SCRATCH.) We know the deed—the deed—it burns in our fingers—we do not have to see the deed. It's a losing case.

SCRATCH: It offers incontestable evidence of the truth of the prosecution's claim. I shall now call Jabez Stone to the witness stand.

JURY (*hungrily*): Jabez Stone to the witness stand—Jabez Stone. He's a fine, fat fellow, Jabez Stone. He'll fry like a batter cake, once we get him where we want him.

WEBSTER: Your Honor, I move that this jury be discharged for flagrant and open bias!

HATHORNE: Motion denied.

WEBSTER: Exception.

HATHORNE: Exception denied.

JURY: His motion's always denied. He thinks himself smart and clever—lawyer Webster. But his motion's always denied.

WEBSTER: Your Honor! (*He chokes with anger.*)

CLERK (*advancing*): Jabez Stone to the witness stand!

JURY: Jabez Stone—Jabez Stone.

(WEBSTER *gives* JABEZ *an encouraging pat on the back, and* JABEZ *takes his place on the witness stand, very scared.*)

CLERK (*offering a black book*): Do you solemnly swear—testify—so help you—and it's no good, for we don't care what you testify?

JABEZ: I do.

SCRATCH: What's your name?

JABEZ: Jabez Stone.

what emotions does he tap to get them to change their minds?

SCRATCH: Occupation?

JABEZ: Farmer.

SCRATCH: Residence?

JABEZ: Cross Corners, New Hampshire.

> (*These three questions are very fast and mechanical on the part of* SCRATCH. *He is absolutely sure of victory and just going through a form.*)

JURY: A farmer—he'll farm in hell—we'll see that he farms in hell.

SCRATCH: Now, Jabez Stone, answer me. You'd better, you know. You haven't got a chance, and there'll be a cooler place by the fire for you.

WEBSTER: I protest! This is intimidation! This mocks all justice!

HATHORNE: The protest is irrelevant, incompetent, and immaterial. We have our own justice. The protest is denied.

JURY: Irrelevant, incompetent, and immaterial—we have our own justice—oho, Daniel Webster! (*The* JURY'S *eyes fix upon* WEBSTER *for an instant, hungrily.*)

SCRATCH: Did you or did you not sign this document?

JABEZ: Oh, I signed it! You know I signed it. And if I have to go to hell for it, I'll go!

> (*A sigh sweeps over the* JURY.)

JURY: One of us—one of us now—we'll save a place by the fire for you, Jabez Stone.

SCRATCH: The prosecution rests.

HATHORNE: Remove the prisoner.

WEBSTER: But I wish to cross-examine—I wish to prove—

HATHORNE: There will be no cross-examination. We have our own justice. You may speak, if you like. But be brief.

JURY: Brief—be very brief—we're weary of earth—incompetent, irrelevant, and immaterial—they say he's a smart man, Webster, but he's lost his case tonight—be very brief—we have our own justice here.

> (WEBSTER *stares around him like a baited bull. He can't find words.*)

MARY'S VOICE (*from off stage*): Set me as a seal upon thy heart, as a seal upon thine arm, for love is strong as death—

JURY (*loudly*): A seal!—ha, ha—a burning seal!

MARY'S VOICE: Love is strong—

JURY (*drowning her out*): Death is stronger than love. Set the seal upon Daniel Webster—the burning seal of the lost. Make him one of us—one of the damned—one with Jabez Stone!

> (*The* JURY's *eyes all fix upon* WEBSTER. *The* CLERK *advances as if to take him into custody. But* WEBSTER *silences them all with a great gesture.*)

WEBSTER: Be still!

I was going to thunder and roar. I shall not do that.

I was going to denounce and defy. I shall not do that.

You have judged this man already with your abominable justice. See that you defend it. For I shall not speak of this man.

You are demons now, but once you were men. I shall speak to every one of you.

Of common things I speak, of small things and common.

The freshness of morning to the young, the taste of food to the hungry, the day's toil, the rest by the fire, the quiet sleep.

These are good things.

But without freedom they sicken, without freedom they are nothing.

Freedom is the bread and the morning and the risen sun.

It was for freedom we came in the boats and the ships. It was for freedom we came.

It has been a long journey, a hard one, a bitter one.

But, out of the wrong and the right, the sufferings and the starvations, there is a new thing, a free thing.

The traitors in their treachery, the wise in their wisdom, the valiant in their courage—all, all have played a part.

It may not be denied in hell nor shall hell prevail against it.

Have you forgotten this? (*He turns to the* JURY.) Have you forgotten the forest?

GIRTY (*as in a dream*): The forest, the rustle of the forest, the free forest.

what qualities do Americans pride themselves in?

WEBSTER (*to* KING PHILIP): Have you forgotten your lost nation?

KING PHILIP: My lost nation—my fires in the wood—my warriors.

WEBSTER (*to* TEACH): Have you forgotten the sea and the way of ships?

TEACH: The sea—and the swift ships sailing—the blue sea.

JURY: Forgotten—remembered—forgotten yet remembered.

WEBSTER: You were men once. Have you forgotten?

JURY: We were men once. We have not thought of it nor remembered. But we were men.

WEBSTER: Now here is this man with good and evil in his heart.

Do you know him? He is your brother. Will you take the law of the oppressor and bind him down?

It is not for him that I speak. It is for all of you.

There is sadness in being a man but it is a proud thing, too.

There is failure and despair on the journey—the endless journey of mankind.

We are tricked and trapped—we stumble into the pit—but, out of the pit, we rise again.

No demon that was ever foaled can know the inwardness of that—only men—bewildered men.

They have broken freedom with their hands and cast her out from the nations—yet shall she live while man lives.

She shall live in the blood and the heart—she shall live in the earth of this country—she shall not be broken.

When the whips of the oppressors are broken and their names forgotten and destroyed,

I see you, mighty, shining, liberty, liberty! I see free men walking and talking under a free star.

God save the United States and the men who have made her free.

The defense rests.

JURY (*exultantly*): We were men—we were free—we were men—we have not forgotten—our children—our children shall follow and be free.

HATHORNE (*rapping with gavel*): The jury will retire to consider its verdict.

BUTLER (*rising*): There is no need. The jury has heard Mr. Webster. We find for the defendant, Jabez Stone!

JURY: Not guilty!

SCRATCH (*in a screech, rushing forward*): But, Your Honor—
(*But even as he does so, there is a flash and a thunderclap, the stage blacks out again, and when the lights come on, JUDGE and JURY are gone. The yellow light of dawn lights the windows.*)

JABEZ: They're gone and it's morning—Mary, Mary!

MARY (*in doorway*): My love—my dear. (*She rushes to him.*)
(*Meanwhile SCRATCH has been collecting his papers and is trying to sneak out. But WEBSTER catches him.*)

WEBSTER: Just a minute, Mr. Scratch. I'll have that paper first, if you please. (*He takes the deed and tears it.*) And now, sir, I'll have *you!*

SCRATCH: Come, come, Mr. Webster. This sort of thing is ridic—ouch—is ridiculous. If you're worried about the costs of the case, naturally I'd be glad to pay.

WEBSTER: And so you shall! First of all, you'll promise and covenant never to bother Jabez Stone or any other New Hampshire man from now till doomsday. For any hell we want to raise in this state we can raise ourselves, without any help from you.

SCRATCH: Ouch! Well, they never did run very big to the barrel but—ouch—I agree!

WEBSTER: See you keep to the bargain! And then—well, I've got a ram named Goliath. He can butt through an iron door. I'd like to turn you loose in his field and see what he could do to you. (SCRATCH *trembles.*) But that would be hard on the ram. So we'll just call in the neighbors and give you a shivaree.

SCRATCH: Mr. Webster, please—oh—

WEBSTER: Neighbors! Neighbors! Come in and see what a long-barreled, slab-sided, lantern-jawed, fortunetelling noteshaver I've got by the scruff of the neck! Bring on your

kettles and your pans! (*A noise and murmur outside.*)
Bring on your muskets and your flails!

JABEZ: We'll drive him out of New Hampshire!

MARY: We'll drive old Scratch away!

>   (*The* CROWD *rushes in, with muskets, flails, brooms, etc.*
>   *They pursue* SCRATCH *around the stage, chanting.*)

THE CROWD: We'll drive him out of New Hampshire!
>   We'll drive old Scratch away!
>   Forever and a day, boys,
>   Forever and a day!

>   (*They finally catch* SCRATCH *between two of them and*
>   *fling him out of the door bodily.*)

A MAN: Three cheers for Dan'l Webster!

ANOTHER MAN: Three cheers for Daniel Webster! He's licked
the devil!

WEBSTER (*moving to center stage, and joining* JABEZ' *hands
and* MARY's): And whom God hath joined let no man put
asunder. (*He kisses* MARY *and turns, dusting his hands.*)
Well, that job's done. I hope there's pie for breakfast, neighbor Stone.

>   (*Some of the women, dancing, bring in pies from the*
>   *kitchen.*)

PRODUCTION NOTES

This anthology of *15 American One-Act Plays* is designed for your reading pleasure. In most instances a performance fee is required from any group desiring to produce a play. Usually the organization that handles such performance rights also publishes individual production copies of the plays. Any amateur group interested in additional information concerning performance fees or production copies of the plays included in this anthology should apply to the following companies:

Baker's Plays 100 Summer Street Boston 10, Mass.	*Aria da Capo* *The Neighbors* *Trifles* *The Trysting Place*
Dramatic Publishing Co. 86 East Randolph Street Chicago, Ill. 60601	*The Lottery*
Dramatists Play Service, Inc. 440 Park Avenue South New York, N.Y. 10016	*The Devil and* * Daniel Webster* *Sorry, Wrong Number*
Samuel French, Inc. 25 West 45th Street New York, N.Y. 10036	*Dust of the Road* *The Man Who Died* * at Twelve O'Clock* *Red Carnations* *The Still Alarm* *The Undercurrent*

307

David McKay Company, Inc.   *Thursday Evening*
750 Third Avenue
New York, N.Y. 10017

Tad Mosel   *Impromptu*
c/o William Morris Agency
1350 Avenue of the Americas
New York, N.Y. 10019

Maurice Valency   *Feathertop*
c/o Washington Square
    Press
630 Fifth Avenue
New York, N.Y. 10020